The Organization of African Unity after Thirty Years

Edited by YASSIN EL-AYOUTY

PRAEGER

Westport, Connecticut
London

Library of Congress Cataloging-in-Publication Data

The Organization of African Unity after thirty years / edited by
Yassin El-Ayouty.
        p.   cm.
    Includes bibliographical references and index.
    ISBN 0–275–94439–5 (alk. paper)
    1. Organization of African Unity.   I. El-Ayouty, Yassin.
DT30.5.O77   1994
341.24′9—dc20   93–24830

British Library Cataloguing in Publication Data is available.

Library of Congress Catalog Card Number: 93–24830
ISBN: 0–275–94439–5

First published in 1994

Praeger Publishers, 88 Post Road West, Westport, CT 06881
An imprint of Greenwood Publishing Group, Inc.

Printed in the United States of America

The paper used in this book complies with the
Permanent Paper Standard issued by the National
Information Standards Organization (Z39.48–1984).

10 9 8 7 6 5 4 3 2 1

To my wife, Grace Lasser, and our son, Joseph, and from the three of us,
to my mentor at New York University and friend,
the late Professor Thomas Hovet, Jr.,
and to all the institutions of higher learning that
shaped my intellectual and professional careers:
The Teachers Institute, Zeitoun, Cairo, Egypt (1945–1948),
State Teachers College, Trenton, New Jersey (1952–1953),
Rutgers University, New Brunswick, New Jersey (1953–1957),
New York University, New York, New York (1958–1966), and
Benjamin N. Cardozo School of Law, New York, New York (1991–1994),
with the later institution, which is a school of
Yeshiva University, having the special distinction of
transforming me from a Professor of Politics to a student
of law.

Contents

Preface and Acknowledgments

This is the third, and most probably the last, of my three edited volumes on the Organization of African Unity (OAU). The series has spanned twenty years (1973–1993) and has served to heighten scholarly and policy-maker interest in the African continental organization.

The contributors to this volume, a galaxy of distinguished authors (see About the Editor and Contributors), have, in their collectivity, shed a great deal of light on various facets of the OAU after thirty years of existence. Each one of them has sacrificed time and effort taken away from busy agendas to help create this volume. I am indebted to all and each one of them. Without such collaboration, it would have been impossible to produce this book. All of us wish the OAU through its distinguished Secretary-General, H.E. Mr. Salim Ahmed Salim, a very happy and productive thirtieth birthday for this historic continental organization.

By way of gratitude, I should like to acknowledge the tremendous help and encouragement given to me by our late brother, Mr. Gebre E. Dawit, Assistant Executive Secretary of the OAU's office to UN Headquarters, New York City. His untimely passing was a great loss to African world diplomacy and to all those who came to know and appreciate him.

I am also indebted to my friends and colleagues, Dr. Berhanykun Andemicael (Eritrea), Director of the Liaison Office of the International Atomic Energy Agency to the UN, New York City, Dr. Ivor Richard Fung (Cameroon), of the UN Disarmament Department, and Dr. Azzedine Layachi (Algeria). In addition to their contributions to this book, they have constantly offered me valuable criticism, advice, and above all, encouragement to produce this volume. It is also with gratitude that I acknowledge the helpful material supplied to me by *Gemini News Service* through Mr. Derek Ingram, including the map of Africa that appears as Appendix I to this volume.

My special thanks to the entire staff of the UN Dag Hammarskjold Library, at UN Headquarters, New York City, for their invaluable assistance.

Needless to say, the views and conclusions of each contributor are to be attributed to that contributor.

Abbreviations

ACP	African, Caribbean, and Pacific
ADB	African Development Bank
AEC	African Economic Community
ANC	African National Congress
APPER	African Priority Program for Economic Recovery
ASEAN	Association of South East Asian States
CELHTO	Center for Linguistic and Historical Studies by Oral Tradition
CERDOTOLA	Regional Center for Research and Documentation on Oral Traditions for the Development of African Languages
CSCE	Conference for Security and Cooperation in Europe
EAC	East African Community
ECA	Economic Commission for Africa
ECOMOG	ECOWAS Cease-Fire Monitoring Group
ECOSOC	Economic and Social Council
ECOWAS	Economic Community of West African States
EEC	European Economic Community
EPLF	Eritrean Peoples Liberation Front
EPRDF	Ethiopian People's Revolutionary Democratic Front
FAO	Food and Agricultural Organization
FAR	Royal Armed Forces (Morocco)
G-5	Group of Five
G-15	Group of Fifteen

GDP	Gross Domestic Product
IAEA	International Atomic Energy Agency
ICARA	International Conference on Assistance to Refugees in Africa
ICJ	International Court of Justice
ILO	International Labor Organization
IMF	International Monetary Fund
LDC	Least Developed Country
MINURSO	United Nations Mission for the Referendum in Western Sahara
MPLA	Popular Movement for the Liberation of Angola
NAFTA	North American Free Trade Association
NGO	Nongovernmental Organization
NIEO	New International Economic Order
OAS	Organization of American States
OAU	Organization of African Unity
ODA	Official Development Assistance
OECD	Organization for Economic Cooperation and Development
ONUC	United Nations Organization in the Congo
OPEC	Organization of Petroleum Exporting Countries
PAC	Pan-African Congress
PNUD	United Nations Development Programme
POLISARIO	Popular Front for the Liberation of Saguia El-Hamra and Rio de Oro
RENAMO	Revolutionary National Movement for Mozambique
SAARC	South Asian Association for Regional Cooperation
SADCC	Southern African Development Coordination Conference
SADR	Saharan Democratic Republic
SEA	Single European Area
SPLA	Sudanese People's Liberation Army
SPLM	Sudanese People's Liberation Movement
SWAPO	South West Africa People's Organization
TPLF	Tigraelan People's Liberation Front
UDHR	Universal Declaration of Human Rights
UDI	Unilateral Declaration of Independence
UNDP	United Nations Development Program
UNEF	United Nations Emergency Force
UNEP	United Nations Environment Programme
UNHCR	United Nations High Commission for Refugees
UNICEF	United Nations Children's Fund

UNITA	National Union for the Total Independence of Angola
UNITAR	United Nations Institute for Training and Research
UNPAAERD	United Nations Program of Action for African Economic Recovery and Development
UNPROFOR	United Nations Protection Force

_____ *Part I*

Peace, Security, and International Law

The OAU: Peace Keeping and Conflict Resolution

JAMES O. C. JONAH

INTRODUCTION

Thirty years ago, when African leaders met in Addis Ababa to establish the Organization of African Unity, their primary focus was the creation of a continental organization that would foster African unity. The Organization of African Unity, as its name implies, represents a remarkable achievement of the African leaders, who fought and attained the independence of their countries, and overcame the undesirable division between the so-called moderate African States and the so-called radical African States. It is also true that the achievement in Addis Ababa at that time fell short of the vision of a number of African leaders, who had hoped and worked for a continental African government as part of a grand design to achieve economic and political development of the African continent.

In addition to these central objectives of the Organization of African Unity, there was also a deep concern among African leaders that Africa should learn from the experience of other regions, especially Europe, in creating a mechanism to resolve disputes among African States. There were two major concerns at that time. African leaders were keenly aware that colonial boundaries, which had been drawn up in Europe without the consent of the African people and their authorities, were flawed in that many of them generated ethnic and tribal strife. In fact, many—rightly at that period—envisaged a whole array of boundary disputes among African countries that would result in innumerable wars and conflicts among African States as they emerged from colonialism. In order to avert such a bleak outcome, African leaders recognized that they should undertake steps to resolve boundary disputes peacefully. In fact, even while they were contemplating the formation of the OAU, there were boundary disputes in north and central Africa.

Another major concern of African leaders, thirty years ago, was the danger of ethnic and tribal conflicts in Africa. This issue was closely linked to the boundary disputes. Tribal groups were on both sides of national boundaries, and such a situation presented grave danger for irredentist forces. It was believed that a strong tendency toward African unity, in the form of the OAU, could ease the temptation to highlight ethnic and tribal cleavages. The notion of pan-Africanism was promoted to emphasize the commonality among the African peoples.

PEACE KEEPING AND PEACE MAKING IN THE OAU CONTEXT

As is the case with the Charter of the United Nations, there are no special references to peace keeping in the OAU Charter. In fact, one can argue that thirty years ago the concept of "peace keeping" was an anathema to a large number of African States. The United Nations' peace-keeping experience in the Congo, in the form of the United Nations Organization in the Congo (ONUC) had left a bitter taste in the mouths of the Africans. Even though they had welcomed the peace-keeping emplacement of the United Nations in the then Republic of the Congo, they came to see ONUC, particularly following the death of Premier Lubumba, as an imperialistic instrument to subvert African independence. This peace-keeping "allergy," in fact, was a strong motivation for the African States to devise a system by which African problems would be solved by African methods, without the intervention of extra-African powers. This posture did not represent an isolationist penchant of African States; rather, it was a carefully crafted arrangement by which a regional organization was shaped to resolve disputes among African States, while willing and ready, in disputes of African States with extra-African States, to resort to global organizations such as the United Nations, and, more specifically, the General Assembly or the Security Council. It is thus significant that the OAU Charter went to great lengths to prepare frameworks for conciliation and arbitration in tackling disputes among African States. Regretably, these procedures have not yet been fully elaborated in concrete provisions that could enable the African States to have a standing machinery for conflict resolution.

Perhaps one should not be surprised by such a development. It has been demonstrated, in other contexts, that member States of regional groupings have a tendency to avoid resorting to formalized structures for conflict resolution, preferring to utilize more informal arrangements. Such an approach has been widely utilized in the OAU context in tackling a number of African disputes. The OAU has resorted to the establishment of ad hoc commissions for various disputes, ignoring the outline of specific commissions that were provided for in the Charter of the OAU. In the past few years, this practice has evolved into a situation where the current Chairman of the OAU has been utilized as the focal point for the resolution of a number of African disputes. While this is a welcome development, the arrangements remain inchoate; that is to say, there is no precise idea as to what are the responsibilities of the Chairman of the Assembly of Heads of State and Government of the OAU.

This OAU practice, that of making use of the current Chairman of the Assembly of Heads of State and Government of the OAU, has been complicated by a lack of clarity in the respective roles of the Chairman and the Secretary-General of the organization. It is readily accepted that the Chairman, who is formally a head of government of one member State of the OAU, is a political figure with accepted political responsibilities. There is no equally ready acceptance of the political role of the Secretary-General of the OAU. Thirty years ago, the general perception of the role of the Secretary-General of the OAU was of a strictly administrative character. The Secretary-General of the OAU did not benefit from legal provisions similar to Articles 98 and 99 of the United Nations Charter, which have been used to argue that the Secretary-General of the UN has specific political functions. Even with these provisions, the Secretary-General of the UN was beset by controversies over whether he could exercise political functions or not. At one point, some members argued that his functions were strictly administrative, going more toward Article 97 of the Charter.

Similar arguments surrounded the first Secretary-General of the OAU, who was constantly reminded that his role should be essentially administrative. It would appear, at this juncture, that there has been a change in attitude in the OAU. A large number of member States gradually now accept that the Secretary-General can perform political functions to promote conflict resolution. What is required is to define more clearly the links between the role of the Chairman with the role of the Secretary-General, particularly in the areas of conflict resolution and peace keeping.

One can deduce a working definition from the experience that has evolved over the past thirty years. It is now customary that, when the Chairman of the OAU is assigned functions relating to conflict resolution, he relies on the support provided by the Secretary-General, through the secretariat. When they are working in tandem, they present a smooth machinery that can have a positive impact on the OAU capacity for conflict resolution. But these arrangements are left to the Secretary-General and Current Chairman of the OAU. Specific guidelines for conflict resolution have not yet evolved. We have witnessed situations when the Secretary-General of the OAU alone has been called upon to exercise his good offices in tackling conflicts, without any reference to the current Chairman of the OAU. Prudence may argue that the Secretary-General should liaise closely with the Chairman of the OAU before undertaking such good offices efforts, but this is again not a requirement. On the other side, however, it has been clearly established that when the current Chairman undertakes missions to solve conflicts, he is invariably accompanied by the Secretary-General or his representative.

The confusion that could arise in the absence of a definition of the role of the Secretary-General and the current Chairman could be seen in situations where invitations are extended to the current Chairman in respect to peace-making efforts, and it is not clear whether the input of the Secretary-General is required. In one or two instances, the Secretary-General has argued that unless he is explicitly invited also, he could not be involved, merely on the basis of an invitation to the current Chairman. It is then essential that the OAU, after deliberating on the issue, formulate appropriate arrangements encompassing the role of the Chairman and the Secretary-General in the peace-keeping efforts by the OAU.

Apart from the absence of precision in the roles of the Secretary-General and the Chairman in peace making, there is no certainty of the political impact on the role of either the Secretary-General or Chairman in carrying out peace-making functions. It is true that these officials of the OAU can indeed convene meetings of parties to a conflict, make proposals, merge proposals between parties, and even report their findings or impressions to the annual meeting of Heads of State and Government. But it is not clear whether one is acting as an honest broker, or a mediator, or merely acting as a cooling element. Little has yet been clarified to encourage resort to the OAU.

Perhaps it is appropriate to allude to another lacuna in the OAU arrangements for conflict resolution insofar as the Secretary-General is concerned. What is the authority of the Secretary-General in determining whether a party, or parties, to a conflict has or have failed to exhaust all procedures of conflict resolution within the OAU? This became an issue in the case of former Secretary-General Kodjo, in the Western Sahara case. As may be recalled, there was a great deal of controversy, when in the absence of progress in peace-making efforts between Morocco and the Polisario, Secretary-General Kodjo determined that the conditions had been fulfilled for the admission of the Polisario front as a member of the OAU. This incident provoked the withdrawal of Morocco from the OAU, and other African States could have followed Morocco's example.

OAU AND PEACE KEEPING

In the area of the OAU's experience in peace-keeping efforts, one can also observe great difficulties in the roles of the Secretary-General and the current Chairman. The OAU experience in Chad is a classic example. The intention here is to highlight the difficulties that arose in the relations of the Secretary-General and the current Chairman. When the OAU established its peace-keeping forces in Chad, there were no adequate arrangements for reporting.

Anyone experienced in peace keeping realizes that a report is vital. Yet, in the OAU, in contrast with the well-tried and tested experience of the United Nations, there is no clear-cut procedure for the commander of the forces to make regular reports to the Secretary-General of the OAU. Even when reports are filed with the Secretary-General of the OAU, he does not know what he should do with the reports. Here, he may be advised to refer to the UN experience. As it is known, UN peace-keeping operations, whether in the form of unarmed military observers or organized military troops, are under the overall authority of the Security Council. The Secretary-General exercises the day-to-day supervision in the field and is required to report regularly, as appropriate, to the Security Council. The Secretary-General of the UN, who appoints the commander of the forces with the concurrence of the Security Council, receives reports regularly from the commander, which form the basis for his report to the Security Council. The Security Council makes political decisions on the basis of such reports by the Secretary-General, or in the light of statements in formal or informal sessions of the Security Council.

In the OAU, as hinted above, there are no such arrangements. It is not clear if the Secretary-General passes reports from the commander to the current Chairman, who may be hundreds of miles away from the headquarters of the OAU. It is also not clear what political decisions can be made even if he were in the vicinity of the headquarters. This existing situation is a serious impediment to the OAU's peace-keeping role. In the past, various suggestions have been made to ensure that appropriate arrangements are devised to provide for a greater political role by the current Chairman, or by the Secretary-General, in conducting the OAU's peace keeping in the field. One such proposal is for the Secretary-General of the OAU, when given the responsibility to supervise peace-keeping operations in the field, to set up an advisory group, at OAU headquarters, to lend him political support for his instructions to the commander in the field.

Such an arrangement would be similar to an early experiment in UN peace-keeping operations. When the General Assembly, in 1957, established the first UN emergency force outside the framework of the Security Council, the Secretary-General devised a system of establishing an advisory body composed of member States to lend political support. This arrangement was followed in 1960 when the Security Council established a peace-keeping force in the Congo. It has been argued that such experimentation may strengthen the hand of the Secretary-General of the OAU in dealing with the commander in the field, in the absence of more precise arrangements. This procedure is highly recommended.

A more elaborate proposal that may have relevance, not only in peace keeping but also in conflict resolution, was first proposed by the delegate of Sierra Leone who suggested that the OAU give serious consideration to the establishment of a standing Security Council. In essence, such a council of the OAU would function as the Security Council of the organization with specific peace-keeping, conflict resolution, and perhaps enforcement functions. As can be seen from a perusal of the OAU Charter, there are provisions for military actions, although it is not clear what these provisions mean. Some have argued that the military aspect was meant to provide for an African army that would have fought against South Africa. Others have argued that all such a defense force could do was to provide support to liberation movements engaged in wars of liberation. One cannot exclude the possibility that the provisions regarding the defense commissions could be incorporated in a larger Security Council arrangement of the OAU. Even though it is not clear why such proposals have not been adopted, there is still considerable interest in the OAU in moving toward adopting such proposals.

OAU COOPERATION WITH UNITED NATIONS PEACE KEEPING

Apart from the lack of clarity on the question of reports in OAU peace-keeping arrangements, there is also widespread recognition that lack of adequate financing, and inadequacy of logistical support, have bedeviled OAU peace-keeping functions. Here again the experience in Chad is significant. It was not possible for the OAU to allocate sufficient financing for the operation in Chad. It was left to the individual troop contributor countries to make provisions for payment and upkeep of their troops. Such an arrangement cannot enhance the functioning of any peace-keeping operation as a unit. It is, therefore, not surprising that under such an arrangement there was an absence of uniform command control in Chad. Inadequacy of logistical arrangements also adversely affected the functions of the organization's peace keeping in Chad. In tackling the logistical inadequacy, the OAU turned to the UN. Some technical advice was provided by the UN, but in terms of financing, the results were negative. As may be recalled, the OAU sought the assistance of the UN Security Council in its operation in Chad. The Security Council was lukewarm in its response, and the operation was thereby doomed to failure. The OAU appeal was honored in the breach rather than in the observance. It is now clear that the OAU cannot rely on external support for its peace-keeping operations, and it should provide for its own operations.

What is more and more likely is that the UN would be called upon to provide peace-keeping operations in close cooperation with the OAU, as is being done in the case of the Western Sahara. Even in such circumstances, though, there have been problems. It is widely known that Morocco was reluctant to allow the OAU, because of its admission of the Polisario, to participate in peace-keeping functions in the Western Sahara. Nevertheless, the Secretary-General, in formulating plans for a proposed solution in the Western Sahara, collaborated with the current Chairman of the OAU and the proposal offered was a joint UN–OAU proposal. The Secretary-General of the OAU has been called upon to send an observer to observe the implementation of the plan.

THE OAU AND INTERNAL CONFLICTS

Over the years the OAU has come under severe criticism for its reluctance to tackle internal conflicts. Since Africa is beset by a number of serious internal conflicts, it has been argued that the OAU cannot afford to stand aside when millions of lives are being lost. It is, consequently, understandable why the OAU did not want to rush into the fray as far as internal conflicts were concerned. In the first place, the OAU, like the UN itself, has been bedeviled by the requirement in its Charter that the organization must refrain from interfering in the internal affairs of member States. Prior to the establishment of the OAU in 1963, there were a number of allegations by the African States that the neighbors of African States were involved in the sponsorship of various coups d'etat. Furthermore, many African States were equally threatened by internal conflicts and were, therefore, reluctant to see the organization involved in their internal disputes. These factors, among many others, may have been responsible for the OAU shying away from dealing with internal conflicts.

However, as has been hinted above, the OAU was involved in an internal conflict in Chad. Chad, however, presented a different kind of internal conflict. The evidence was clear that some African States were involved in support of the civil strife. In addition, the Chad conflict took on an international dimension in view of the antipathy that existed between Libya and a number of other countries. Perhaps it was the fact of the deep involvement of extra-African powers that made it possible for the OAU to overcome its reluctance to intervene and give considerable attention to the problem of Chad. But even in this case, as we have already seen, the OAU involvement was not a happy one. The OAU maintained its traditional policies of not involving itself in internal conflicts in the attempted invasions in Zaire—now popularly known as the Shaba I and Shaba II, despite the deep extra-African involvement—France and the United States—in efforts to repair the incursion. The OAU was not directly involved. It should, nevertheless, be noted that the government of Zaire itself did not actively seek direct OAU involvement, but rather, relied on the United States and France to assist it in coping with problems in the Shaba province.

It is in the Horn of Africa that the OAU has most exemplified its hesitation in getting involved in internal conflicts. For over thirty years, which paralleled the life of the organization, the OAU stood by as internal conflicts raged in Ethiopia, the Sudan, and to some extent Somalia. The impact of this reluctance to involve itself in conflict resolution in the Horn may precisely explain why, in the recent events, the OAU had taken the back seat in picking up the pieces following the overthrow of former President Mengistu of Ethiopia and former President Siad Barre of Somalia. It may also present the OAU with a ticklish problem about how to deal with the outcome of those events.

It has been comparatively easier for the OAU to respond to developments in Somalia. While not making any active efforts to promote reconciliation among various factions in Somalia engaged in internecine war, the Assembly of Heads of State and Government of the OAU, when they met in Abuja, adopted a traditional OAU stand in vigorously opposing the declaration of independence by the break-away province of Northern Somaliland. The efforts of the government of Djibouti to promote agreements among the various factions, as represented in "Djibouti 1" and "Djibouti 2," have won OAU support but not active participation.

The recent developments in Ethiopia may present a different situation for the OAU, which has its headquarters in Addis Ababa, the seat of the former Mengistu government. It was understandable that the OAU had to forge a delicate relationship with that government in its conflict with the Eritrean and other liberation movements opposed to the military regime. With the overthrow of the Mengistu government, the OAU saw no difficulty in accepting the interim government that has now established itself in Addis Ababa. In fact, the Assembly of Heads of State and Government of the OAU in Abuja, in June 1991, gradually recognized the EPRDF (Ethiopian People's Revolutionary Democratic Front) government, which is the core of the interim government. The dilemma that the OAU now faces is how to deal with the the fact that Eritrea was declared independent on May 24, 1993, and admitted to UN membership on May 28, 1993. On the basis of its traditional approach, the OAU has always looked with disfavor at all secessionist movements in Africa, given the fact that a number of African States could easily become affected by such movements. It is, therefore, not surprising that the OAU has shown no readiness to accept the breakup of Ethiopia.

It may turn out, nevertheless, that the OAU's traditional approach in dealing with such issues should be reevaluated. The case of Eritrea presents a particular aspect. The manner in which the EPLF (Eritrean Peoples Liberation Front) has approached the issue has made it more difficult for the OAU. In the latter phase of its dealing with the government in Ethiopia, the EPLF forged a judicious alliance with a number of liberation movements engaged in the conflict. In fact, the final onslaught on the regime of Mengistu was coordinated with the EPLF, TPLF (Tigraelan People's Liberation Front), and EPRDF. Consequently, with the overthrow of the Mengistu administration, there is a cordial relationship between the interim government of Ethiopia in Addis Ababa and the provisional government of Eritrea in Asmara.

What, then, should be the posture of the OAU in a situation where the interim government that is recognized in Addis Ababa has already accepted, formally, a separate administration in Asmara—in the form of a provisional government, and has formally supported the notion of a referendum to enable the people of Eritrea to determine their destiny? In addition, both governments have signed bilateral agreements that leave two administrations, as opposed to one, in what was known as Ethiopia during the past thirty years of the OAU's existence.

The challenge for the OAU, as for many governments, will be how to deal with such governments during the coming two years before the referendum in Eritrea is conducted. This alone is enough evidence to show that some confusion prevails as to how the OAU should best deal with such situations. Happily, though, the government of Eritrea has shown flexibility in not demanding that third parties, including the OAU, should recognize its sovereignty. The major concern now is that the old-style OAU, as an exemplification of its traditional approach, may show coolness toward Eritrea and its cause for a referendum. If the OAU is to become a credible machinery of peace keeping and conflict resolution, it will be necessary for it to formulate a carefully balanced approach in tackling the issue of Eritrea in the coming months.

The OAU's unwillingness to involve itself in the long-standing conflict in Sudan presents, perhaps, a special factor. African leaders are conscious that most of the southern part of Sudan is populated by black Africans, who are at war with the northern part, which is mainly Arab. (Incidentally, the Sudanese People's Liberation Army/Sudanese People's Liberation Movement [SPLA/SPLM] believes, in fact, that in the North there are a considerable number of black Africans.) But, in the OAU, the majority of its members, who are from south of the Sahara, are mostly reluctant to get involved in situations where their objectivity may be questioned. Consequently, as the civil war has continued with a great loss of life and attendant difficulties in providing humanitarian assistance, private groups outside the OAU, such as the Carter Center, have felt obliged to lend their efforts to find solutions to the civil strife. It is, thus, only recently that the Chairman of the OAU has shown interest in exercising his good offices in bringing about a solution to the dispute.

The task of the OAU has been facilitated by the ready willingness of both the government in Khartoum and the SPLA/SPLM to accept the mediation of the OAU Chairman. The former OAU Chairman, President Museveni of Uganda, began this process of mediation and has now turned the files over to the current Chairman of the OAU, President Babangida of Nigeria. It now seems that the Nigerian initiative is picking up momentum. Useful exchanges have already taken place, involving the government in Khartoum and the leader of SPLA, Dr. Garang. Hopefully, this new process may help the OAU to move away from its reluctance to get involved in internal conflicts.

In the international context, the OAU's reluctance to intervene in internal affairs has had its consequences. More often than not, outside powers gauge their attitude toward African problems based on the posture of the OAU. Whenever the OAU has shown unwillingness to get involved in internal conflicts, the UN and other powers have followed the approach of the OAU. This is why scholars and statesmen have been critical of the OAU and have often argued that the OAU should be ready to lend its good offices in internal African conflicts. This may also explain why the current Chairman of OAU is receiving warm support from major powers in his efforts to tackle conflicts within the African continent.

EFFORTS FOR THE FURTHER DEVELOPMENT OF THE OAU'S PEACE-MAKING AND PEACE-KEEPING MACHINERY

The current Secretary-General of the OAU, Salim Ahmed Salim, the former Chairman of the OAU, President Yoweri Museveni of Uganda, and the current Chairman, President Ibrahim Babangida of Nigeria, have recently suggested various ways and means whereby the OAU could assist further in the resolution of internal African conflicts as well as in the establishment of an OAU peace-keeping capacity. The recent efforts have already led to interesting developments. Thus, in the attempt to resolve the Rwanda conflict, an agreement was reached on 29 March 1991 in N'sele, Zaire, between the Rwandese parties to the conflict to establish a formal cease-fire that would be supervised by the OAU. The agreement provided for the creation of a group of neutral military observers, composed of fifty officers, under the supervision of the OAU Secretary-General, whose responsibility is to observe the cease-fire and to report on instances of its violation by the parties. As has already been seen, one of the hindrances of successful peace-keeping missions under the OAU has been the lack of financial support. This led to great impediments in the Chad exercise, as well as in the ECOMOG (ECO-WAS Cease-Fire Monitoring Group) experience. Insofar as the Rwanda experience is concerned, it was fortunate that many non-African governments decided to support the OAU efforts financially. Such support came from the governments of France and Belgium.

The Secretary-General of the OAU, in his report to the Fifty-fourth Session of the Council of Ministers in Abuja, Nigeria, at the end of May 1991, cited this agreement as a major breakthrough upon which the OAU could build, both politically and institutionally, to sustain political initiatives to deal with conflicts in Africa. He further stated that there was need to elaborate political frameworks and mechanisms within which internal conflicts could be considered, contained, and resolved. The Secretary-General indicated that this new approach to conflict resolution in Africa, as well as the establishment of the African Economic Community (AEC), will call for a fundamental review of the secretariat in terms of its agenda, mandate, and structure. In order to achieve this, the Secretary-General has set up a task force to study and advise on how the secretariat "sees and situates itself within the new imperatives."

Interesting suggestions have also been forthcoming from African experts in peace keeping and peace making. Thus, General E.A. Erskine, who was the commander of the UNEF (United Nations Emergency Force) troops in the Middle East, has put forward some ideas to assist the OAU in further developing its peace-keeping mission. Noting that there was an absence, within the OAU, of a body such as the Security Council in the United Nations, whose mandate is to establish peace-keeping missions, he points out that this has led to a number of difficulties in setting up the Economic Community of West African States (ECOWAS) Cease-Fire Monitoring Group (ECOMOG). He, therefore, suggests that the OAU should consider the possibility of having the Bureau of the OAU Summit become the sponsoring authority for such missions. He points out the necessity for the conclusion of agreements on the operations of peace-keeping missions and warns about the dangers of such missions beginning their operations before the cessation of hostilities between the parties to the conflict, as ECOMOG had done. If a cease-fire agreement is reached before the intervention of a peace-keeping mission, this could, in his view, force the parties to commit themselves to giving the mission full political support and, thereby, possibly lessen the casualty rate, both among the peace-keepers and the parties to the conflict.

He further emphasizes the need to have a peace-keeping mission operating under a unified command structure. In the UN system, the Security Council is the highest authority in establishing peace-keeping missions, which are then directed by the Secretary-General. General Erskine states that the absence of a clearly defined command structure was one of the principal handicaps of the Chad operations and ECOMOG. He indicates that a unified command structure tends to lessen political interventions from governments contributing troops to the mission and also ensures political objectivity and impartiality.

There is also, in his view, need for broad political consensus and support from the contributing member States. He indicates that such a political consensus had been lacking in ECOMOG, which led to competing sides within the ECOMOG Standing Mediation Committee. He further states that the OAU needs to develop clear guidelines insofar as the use of force by a peace-keeping mission is concerned. He points out that in the Chad experience, force was not allowed even in self-defense, whereas, in the ECOMOG experience, force has been used excessively, leading to high casualty rates.

The OAU and International Law

MICHEL-CYR DJIENA WEMBOU

The Organization of African Unity performs a legislative function based on the objectives and principles of its Charter. Thus, since 1963, it has adopted many conventions, declarations, and resolutions involving the norms of international law.

It is no longer necessary to establish the existence of an African political system. I.W. Zartman has done so in his work published in 1966, *International Relations in the New Africa*. Indeed, as Professor Borella has rightly pointed out in the journal *Annuaire Français de droit international* (Paris, 1971) three types of phenomena that constitute a legal order can readily be identified in this system: first of all, the presence of a set of organs and procedures responsible for formulating and enacting individual rules or decisions; then the existence of a body of rules enacted and decisions taken; and finally, a set of organs and procedures responsible for enforcing the body of rules.

Examining the set of substantive rules established by the OAU will constitute the core of this study.

Indeed, the legal work of the OAU is difficult to interpret. The OAU has formulated and adopted texts whose legal validity is often challenged, given the problem of the legal validity of standards derived from the resolutions and recommendations of international organizations. Moreover, the codification and gradual development of international law is not mentioned *expressis verbis* in the OAU Charter, as is the case, for example, with Article 13 of the UN Charter.

Still, it is appropriate to note that the many texts of a legal nature adopted by the OAU that we will be commenting upon are undeniably important. They constitute, indeed, both an increasingly coherent set of rules and principles created by the construction of States seeking an order that corresponds to the realities of Africa,[1] what many authors have described as "African international law,"[2] as well as universal rules affecting the entire body of contemporary international law.

INTERNATIONAL LAW FORMULATED BY THE OAU

A close study of the norms of international law formulated and adopted by the OAU shows that they seek to strengthen the African States in their various constituent elements, to struggle against colonialism, to further inter-African cooperation, and to promote human rights.

The Strengthening of the African States

As Professor Borella emphasizes, the role played in this area by the OAU is explained by the special situation of the African States:

Created only a few years after the independence of many African States, it was normal that the continental Organization should devote itself to the objective (Art. 2.1.c. of the Charter) of defending their sovereignty, their territorial integrity and their independence.

Many resolutions adopted by the OAU continually strengthen the territorial foundation of the African States and their respective frontiers. Resolution A.G.H./16.1 of July 21, 1964, to cite just one, incorporates the rule of uti possidetis: "All the member States are committed to respect the frontiers existing at the time of their independence."[3]

With respect to the domestic conflicts that have troubled the OAU (the Togo situation in 1963, Congo Kinshasa in 1964, Ghana in 1966, Mali in 1968, and Uganda in 1972, to cite just these few), as well as various border disputes that have created hostility between African States (Morocco-Algeria, Ethiopia-Somalia, Kenya-Ethiopia, Burkina Faso-Mali, Chad-Libya), the OAU has adopted, summit after summit, resolutions clearly reaffirming that the territorial base of an African State can only be modified by bilateral or multilateral convention.

Another rule that appears constantly in the OAU texts has to do with noninterference in the domestic affairs of a State. This principle, which is stated in Article 3 of the OAU Charter, was restated by the organization in February 1965, in July 1969, and in June 1970, by resolutions adopted in the Council of Ministers. Moreover, the African States insisted especially upon codification of this principle and its reinforcement by the UN General Assembly, in connection with the adoption of the declaration on friendly relations in 1970, and the resolution of 1987 on strengthening the efficacy of the principle of nonrecourse to force in international relations.

In addition, the OAU texts associate noninterference in domestic affairs of a State with the notion of subversion. Indeed, they specifically call for prohibiting indirect interventions in the form of attempted "subversion" of political regimes.

From the very first years of its existence, one of the major concerns of the OAU has been the strengthening of the governments of the African States. As early as 1963, the Charter had laid down the principle of condemning political assassination. Indeed, paragraph 5 of Article 3 of the Charter states: "condemnation without reservation of political assassination as well as of subversive activities engaged in by neighboring States or by any other States."

Subsequently, on 24 October 1965, the Assembly of Heads of State and Government of the OAU adopted a declaration on the issue of the struggle against internal subversion and noninterference. On 23 June 1972, the OAU adopted a convention concerning mercenaries, which seeks to strengthen the governments in power by facilitating the extradition of any individual considered to be a mercenary.

More recently, in 1980, President Leopold Sedar Senghor was named by his peers to preside over the work of the conference at the special summit in Lagos (April 1980) because Master Sergeant Samuel Doe, the new President of Liberia, could not be accepted by the other Heads of State present, since he had acceded to power following the assassination of then President of the OAU, W. Tolbert.

It is important to point out that one of the principles reaffirmed by the OAU in the area of strengthening of the African State is the principle of the condemnation of "foreign" interference. This seeks to defend Africa against the interference and policies followed by powers outside the continent. The OAU has not been satisfied with merely establishing this rule of law, which is aimed precisely at ensuring the security of the African States; it has also studied and adopted practical procedures for its application.

At the Cairo Summit in 1964, the OAU adopted a declaration on the denuclearization of Africa, with the goal of guaranteeing the security of the continent and transforming it into a nuclear-free zone.

The Assembly of Heads of State and Government of the Organization of African Unity, meeting in its Fourteenth Regular Session in Libreville, Gabon on 25 July 1977, focused specifically on the question of the security of African States.

It was at this point that it recommended that "in accordance with the OAU Charter, the member States take every step possible in order to protect their identity and remain outside conflicts, especially ideological conflicts, originating outside the African continent." It asked the non-African powers, especially the major powers, to refrain from interfering in the domestic affairs of the African States. It asked member States to prohibit "the use of their territory as a base for subversive political activities against another African State, as well as the maintenance or installation of foreign military bases."

Finally, it recalled, "that in this context, intervention in domestic affairs of the States may cause serious risk to international peace and security, since it creates favorable conditions for renewed challenge of the personality and values of the African States."

Two years later, the Council of Ministers of the OAU, meeting in Monrovia 6–20 July 1979, asked "the Western powers to refrain from furnishing South Africa with nuclear materiel and technology and condemned Israel and all other States for nuclear collaboration with South Africa." Since the adoption of the declaration on the denuclearization of Africa by the UN General Assembly,[4] the African States have continued to act within the universal organization and its various special committees[5] to obtain the reduction and destruction of South Africa's military nuclear capability.

The Promotion of Economic, Social, and Cultural Development

The principles of international law formulated in the OAU seek also to promote the economic, social, and cultural development of the African States.

The substantive law formulated by the OAU in the first years of its existence was dominated by political concerns, justified by the construction of the political bases of the newly independent States. But, faced with the constant deterioration of the living standards of their peoples, the African States mobilized within the OAU to "coordinate and intensify their cooperation and efforts in order to provide the best living conditions to the peoples of Africa," as paragraph B of Article 2 of the Charter stipulates.[6] The standards the OAU has formulated are concerned with cultural, economic, and social matters.

In the cultural sphere the OAU has established numerous norms of international law concerning cultural and informational matters. It adopted the African Cultural Charter at Port-Louis in 1976, and in 1979 it adopted a convention establishing a Pan-African Information Agency, which became operational in 1983.[7]

Owing to these two important legal instruments, which codify the right to culture and the right to information, the OAU has been able to support many cultural activities: the World Negro Arts Festival, the creation in 1980 of an international fund to "maintain and promote cultural studies and programs,"[8] the organization of the Colloquium of the Center for Linguistic and Historical Studies by Oral Tradition (CELHTO) in Niamey, the aid granted to the Regional Center for Research and Documentation on Oral Traditions for the Development of African Languages (CERDOTOLA) in Yaounde, and other activities.

In the sphere of social affairs, on the basis of recommendations of the Third Conference of African Ministers of Social Affairs (October 1980), the OAU formulated a set of standards relative to protection of rights of the handicapped in Africa. The creation of an African Institute for Readaptation was decided at the Thirty-sixth Regular Session of the Council of Ministers in February 1981, at the same time that regional projects to be carried out in cooperation with the PNUD were being defined.

At this same meeting of the Council of Ministers, the OAU adopted a resolution on African traditional medicines and medicinal plants, which includes principles for establishing cooperation among African States in this area. In addition to the basic principles of continental cooperation essentially aimed at the exchange of information and the harmonization and strengthening of regulations concerning the protection of forests and their application to medicinal plants classified as special products, this text asks the member States of the OAU to formulate plans for the utilization of medicinal plants and traditional medicine in each country and to implement legislation governing this utilization in their respective countries.

In the sphere of transportation and communications, inter-State relations concerning international air transport are, as we know, based essentially on the legal system established in Chicago in 1944. Nevertheless, the OAU established its own specific standards, which, without contravening the five freedoms of the air established by the Chicago Convention, strive to facilitate cooperation among African States in the matter of air transport, taking into account the difficulties of the African companies.

The first conference of African ministers in charge of transportation, communications, and planning, meeting in Addis Ababa on 9–12 May 1979, adopted a solemn declaration in which the African States undertook to facilitate the granting of traffic rights and, in particular, "fifth freedom" rights to airline companies of member States of the OAU. In this declaration, the African States have the right to decide whether they will resort to forms of cooperation, such as the purchase of reserved space or other arrangements, with a view to developing transportation networks among their countries.

During the meeting of its Council of Ministers held in Monrovia in 1979, the OAU adopted a resolution designed to establish an African Conference of Air Tariffs as an institution responsible for determining tariffs for passenger and freight transport that the African airline companies would be expected to implement. This resolution was finally adopted on 12 December 1980.[9] The far-reaching consequences of these texts adopted by the OAU can be precisely measured when one considers the increasing number of agreements entered into among African airlines.

The OAU has also made an effort to facilitate cooperation among the riparian States of major African rivers. The legal system governing African rivers had been established by the colonial powers; riparian rights for the Congo, for example, were provided by the General Act of Brussels, 2 July 1890, and the General Act of Berlin, 25 February 1885, both of which were rescinded at the end of World War I by the Convention of Saint-Germain en Laye, 10 September 1919.

The African States, on the initiative of the OAU, have adopted many Acts relating to navigation and cooperation among States occupying the basins of various rivers: Niger, Senegal, Nile, Zaire (Congo), as well as agreements on navigation, mineral exploitation, and fishing in the lakes (e.g., Lake Chad, the Great Lakes between Tanzania, Zaire, and Burundi, etc.).

The texts adopted by the OAU, while seeking to promote an inter-African inland waterways law, do not challenge the two main principles of international inland waterways law, freedom of navigation and equality of treatment. They provide, however, in accordance with the principles defined in the related Act, that the use of a river be open to each riparian State in that portion of the river basin found within its sovereign territory. Of much more importance, the rules formulated and adopted under the terms of these conventions concern the navigational, agricultural, and industrial use of the rivers and lakes as well as the gathering of the products of their fauna and flora.

Action on Behalf of Human and Peoples' Rights

We need not dwell upon the legal norms formulated by the OAU to ensure adequate protection of the rights of African peoples and of men and women living in the various States of Africa. Many very thoroughgoing studies have already been devoted to the subject.[10]

Nevertheless, it is necessary to point out that the OAU Charter does not solemnly consecrate African human rights. To be sure, several provisions of the Charter do refer to the United Nations Charter and to the Universal Declaration of the Rights of Man. But, as P. Daniel pointed out so well, the OAU Charter is first and foremost "an imperative safeguard for the States set up in a system, specifically according to paragraphs 2, 3, and 5 of Article 3. It did not provide for the possibility of control or intervention regarding the rights of man; it seems, on the contrary, to represent a clear setback in the process of internationalizing these rights."[11]

On the other hand, the OAU has not been totally inactive regarding human rights. Meeting for its Thirty-fifth Regular Session in Freetown on 18–28 May 1980, the OAU Council of Ministers, after having studied the temporary report of the Secretary-General on the formulation of a draft African Charter, adopted a resolution on human and peoples' rights. It was adopted at the meeting of the Council of Ministers held on 7–9 January 1981 before being amended and permanently adopted at the Eighteenth OAU Summit meeting in Nairobi, 24–27 June 1981.

This Charter, "which indissolubly binds human rights and peoples' rights," protects man's civil and political rights: equality before the law (Article 3), inviolability of the human person (Article 4), the right to liberty and to the security of persons (Article 6), and freedom of association (Article 10). It mentions also the duties of individuals and States, as well as the rights of peoples. Finally, it creates an African commission on human and peoples' rights responsible for ensuring the implementation of the Charter.

It is evident that the Organization of African Unity has formulated many rules of international law with the goal of strengthening the African States and facilitating economic, technical, and cultural cooperation among them. But the OAU has not been content to simply reaffirm the classical standards of international law and adapt them, if need be, to the realities of Africa. It also has contributed to the formulation by the international community of new norms of international law in spheres of common interest for the future of mankind, such as the environment and the law of the sea.

THE OAU AND THE NEW ASPECTS OF INTERNATIONAL LAW

The OAU has focused on three new spheres of activity that the international community has been attempting to codify since the seventies: the environment, the law of the sea, and human rights.

Environmental Protection

As Professor Edmond Jouve has noted, "the member countries of the OAU have not been indifferent to the damage done to the natural environment due to drought, desertification, and deforestation."[12]

Therefore, at its Ninth Regular Session held in Kinshasa, 4–10 September 1967, the OAU Council of Ministers approved an African plant health convention, with a view to protecting plant life. This convention establishes a set of controls that the organization deems necessary for the importing of plants; it facilitates cooperation between the African States in the sphere of plant health. Moreover, the member States are proposing, inside their own territories, appropriate legislative or regulatory measures.

On 12 September 1968, the Fifth Summit of the Heads of State and Government in Algiers adopted an African convention on the conservation of nature and natural resources. This text includes a set of rules that the States are committed to obeying to ensure the conservation, use, and development of soils, caves, flora, and fauna. It prohibits the hunting, on the territory of signatory States, of species of animals classified in category A (banbini macaque, chimpanzee, gorilla, ibis, sea turtle, etc.). It establishes specific protection for species in category B, which can only be classified, killed, or captured pursuant to a special authorization issued by the responsible national authority.

As is well known, the UN General Assembly has made a unified effort, since its Forty-fourth Session in 1989, to organize the reaction of the international community to the continuing degradation of the environment that threatens even the survival of mankind. An international conference took place in June 1992 in order to adopt urgent proposals of a legal, institutional, and financial nature to ensure the protection of the ecosystem in all countries and to promote development.

The OAU participated actively in the preparation of this conference, which is expected to codify and harmonize environmental international law, through the African Group at the UN. This group was given the mandate, under the resolution adopted by the Council of Ministers in Nairobi, on 26 June 1981, to ensure the defense of African interests by the formulation of appropriate recommendations regarding the final adoption of the world charter on nature and conventions on the protection of forests and the climate, as well as all other appropriate institutional and financial arrangements.

The Law of the Sea

The OAU has played a decisive role in harmonizing the positions of African countries with respect to questions posed by the formulation of a new legal structure governing the sea. The principles upheld by OAU, such as adjusting the principle of sovereignty of the sea to benefit all coastal States within the framework of an economic zone that could extend out to 200 nautical miles, as well as the concept of common heritage of mankind, were able to be integrated into the United Nations Convention on the Law of the Sea of 1982.

The African countries, aware that at the time of the 1958 and 1960 conferences on the law of the sea, most of them had not achieved independence, decided to unify their views and present a common position at the Conference of Caracas in 1972. Meeting for the first time on questions concerning the law of the sea in Yaounde, 20–30 June 1972, under the auspices of the Institute of International Relations of Cameroon, eighteen African States[13] had unanimously adopted a set of recommendations concerning the right of noncoastal States to access to the sea, the territorial sea, straits, the contiguous zone, the exclusive economic zone, the continental shelf, the high seas, and the concept of the common heritage of mankind.

Subsequently, the OAU Council of Ministers, meeting in Addis Ababa on 17–20 May 1973 adopted a "Statement on Questions Relating to the Law of the Sea." This text, while reiterating the principle that noncoastal countries have a right of access to the sea, proclaims the faith of the African countries in the principle of the common heritage of mankind; it recognizes the right of all coastal States to establish, beyond their territorial sea, an exclusive economic zone not extending more than 200 nautical miles; with specific regard to the international zone of sea bottoms, it advocates the establishment of an international system and regime guaranteeing that the great ocean resources (oil, polymetallic nodules, fish stocks, etc.) will not be exploited for the sole benefit of the industrialized countries that are equipped with the financial and technical means to exploit the deep sea bottoms.

It must be noted that the legal norms established by the Convention of

Montego Bay have perfectly followed the wording proposed by the African States which, as Evelyn Peyroux notes,[14] were often incorporated into a larger document drawn up by the Group of 77.

As a matter of fact, the Convention of Montego Bay established riparian State sovereignty over inland waterways; it affirms the sovereignty of the archipelago State over its waters, soil and subsoil, and the archipelago airspace, without, however, conferring upon archipelago waters the status of inland waterways; it defines territorial sea, and extends the sovereignty of the riparian State to the airspace above this sea, to its sea bed, as well as its subsoil (Articles 1 and 2); it consecrates the notion of exclusive economic zones (in the fifth part of the Convention), as well as that of continental shelf (Article 76); finally, "it attempts to support the truly revolutionary idea (of mankind's common heritage) by defining the legal regime applicable to sea beds and to their subsoil beyond limits of national jurisdiction, which comprise the 'Zone' (Article 1) and 'their resources.' "[15]

By participating in this manner in the formulation of the new legal regime of the sea set forth in the Convention of Montego Bay, which has not yet taken effect, the OAU and the Group of 77 have contributed inestimably to the development and adaptation of classic international law, to the strengthening of international solidarity and, finally, to maintenance of international peace and security in the oceans.

Clearly, over the past thirty years, the Organization of African Unity has carried out intense legislative activity on the continental as well as on the international scene, and especially at the UN. It should be pointed out that some rules proposed by the OAU do not have binding validity, either because they are part of conventions that have not yet taken effect, or because they stem from resolutions of the organization. Without getting involved in the controversy on the question of the legal validity of international organization resolutions, one must take into account the fact that this criticism does not apply exclusively to the normative work of the OAU. It also applies to resolutions adopted by the UN General Assembly.

Besides, the problem of the application of a legal norm depends not only upon the technical quality or validity of the instrument in which it is contained. It depends upon the will of the States and, by virtue of this, it becomes a political problem, as Judge Bedjaqui has noted.[16] The issue does not lie in whether the norm is derived from a resolution or from a treaty, because the obligation exists from the time the instrument that contains it is adopted. But its application truly depends upon the force of relationships existing at any given time on the international scene.

It is not possible here to review the arguments developed by many authors[17] on the scope of the normative work of the OAU, on its utility, or on its contribution to the development of international law. However, taking everything into account, the improvement of this work necessarily entails improvement of the decision-making process within the OAU, revision of its work methods, and establishment of an appropriate body capable of helping the organization formulate and interpret the norms of international law.

NOTES

1. Joseph Maria Bipoum-Woum, *Le droit international Africain* (Paris: L.G.D.J., 1970), p. 6.

2. Ibid. See also J.C. Gautron, *Le régionalisme Africain et le modèle interaméricain* in *Annales Africaines* (1966), pp. 48–86.

3. Francois Borella, "Le systeme juridique de l'OUA," in *Annuaire Français de droit international* (Paris: C.N.R.S., 1971), p. 242.

4. Resolution 2033 (xx).

5. Specifically, the First Commission of the General Assembly, the Disarmament Commission, the Security Council, and the Special Committee Against Apartheid.

6. On this point, refer to the work by Jean-Emmanuel Pondi, "The OAU: From Political to Economic Pan-Africanism," *S.A.I.S. Review* 7(1) (Winter/Spring 1987), pp. 199–212.

7. See Edmond Jouve, *L'Organisation de l'Unité Africaine* (Paris: P.U.F., 1984), pp. 205–206.

8. Article 31, section B, of the African Cultural Charter adopted at Port-Louis, 5 July 1976.

9. Twenty-seven States had participated in the diplomatic conference that adopted the proposal to create the African Conference on Air Tariffs on 12 December 1980 in Addis Ababa: Algeria, Angola, Burundi, Cameroon, Comoros, Djibouti, Egypt, Ethiopia, Gabon, Gambia, Ghana, Guinea, Libya, Madagascar, Mali, Mauritania, Niger, Nigeria, Rwanda, Senegal, Sierra Leone, Sudan, Tanzania, Togo, Uganda, Zaire, and Zambia.

10. See on this point: H. Ait-Ahmed, *L'Afro-facisme: Les droits de l'homme dans la Charte et la pratique de l'OAU* (Paris: L'Harmattan, 1980); M. Glele, "Introduction à la Charte Africaine des droits de l'homme et des peuples," *Mélanges offerts à Claude Albert Colliard* (Paris: Editions A. Pèdone, 1984); P.F. Gonidec, *Un espoir pour l'homme et les peuples Africains? La Charte Africaine des droits de l'homme et des peuples*, in *Le Mois en Afrique*, June–July 1983, pp. 22 ff.; Emmanuel G. Bello, "The African Charter on Human and Peoples' Rights: A Legal Analysis," *Recueil des cours de l'Académie de droit international de La Haye* 194(5) (1985), pp. 9–268.

11. P. Daniel, cited by Jouve, *L'Organisation de l'Unité Africaine*, p. 221.

12. Jouve, ibid., p. 202.

13. The countries that participated in this seminar are: Algeria, Cameroon, Central African Republic, Dahomey, Egypt, Equatorial Guinea, Ethiopia, Ghana, Ivory Coast, Kenya, Mauritius, Nigeria, Senegal, Sierra Leone, Tanzania, Togo, Tunisia, and Zaire.

14. See Evelyn Peyroux, "Les Etats Africains face aux questions actuelles du droit de la mer," which appeared in *Revue générale de droit international public* (Paris: Éditions A. Pédone, 1974).

15. Dinh Nguyen Quoc, Patrick Daillier, and Alain Pellet, *Droit International Public* (Paris: L.G.D.J., 1987), p. 1026.

16. Mohamed Bedjaoui, *Pour un nouvel ordre économique international* (Paris: UNESCO, 1979).

17. See Boutros Boutros-Ghali, *L'Organisation de l'Unité Africaine* (Paris: A. Colin, Collection U, Series Institutions Internationales, 1969); Jouve, *L'Organisation de l'Unité Africaine*; Peyroux, "Les Etats Africains"; Borella, "Le systeme juridique."

The OAU and Western Sahara:
A Case Study

AZZEDINE LAYACHI

The question of Western Sahara proved to be the most difficult challenge ever faced by the OAU since 1963. While trying to deal with it, the organization's existence itself was dangerously threatened in the early 1980s by deep divisions among the membership. This case is the best illustration of the organization's attempt to move to a mature stage of its development: After having been mainly concerned with freeing African territories from Western domination, it started tackling disputes involving member States only (e.g., Chad and Western Sahara). When the issues at hand were clearcut cases of independence from Western colonialism, the organization was able to command a strong consensus among its members, but when the issues involved solely member States (intra-State disputes and self-determination), deep divisions appeared and curtailed the organization's ability to help solve the disputes. The Western Sahara case stimulated not only divisions and immobility, but also threatened the existence of the organization itself. Fortunately, the OAU survived this first major crisis, but the issue remains unresolved, and the OAU is no longer the international organization handling the Western Sahara case. The United Nations has in the last three years forcefully acted to make the parties in dispute—Morocco and the Polisario—work through the Secretary-General on a referendum plan that would dispose of this issue peacefully. Even though the case was transferred back to the UN, it is important to note that the OAU has greatly contributed to the current settlement framework. It was, in fact, the OAU resolutions that inspired and encouraged the resurgence of a UN role in the Morocco-Polisario dispute, and these same resolutions have inspired most UN actions with regard to this issue. If a deep division among African States inhibited the OAU's potential for resolving the dispute, at the United Nations, the relative unity of the African Group has encouraged and stimulated numerous Security Council resolutions and Secretary-General initiatives that, finally, seem to be leading toward the long-waited-for referendum in Western Sahara.[1]

One of the worse legacies of colonialism in Africa and the Middle East has been the artificial borders that it created in these areas for the metropole's strategic, economic, and military conveniences. States were created without regard to ethnic, cultural, and tribal distinctions; borders were established where none existed before; and many new States, at the time of their independence, were placed in the hands of a political elite that was friendly to the former colonizer. As local realities, history, and racial and ethnic configurations of indigenous populations were ignored or disregarded when borders and States were established by the Western powers, most countries in Africa inherited tremendous problems inside their borders and with neighboring States—mainly problems of legitimacy and national integration. These problems often led to bloody conflicts for secession, for the recovery of lost ancestral territories, or for the reunification of communities divided by artificial borders. The newly independent African States found themselves faced with three major tasks: the consolidation of their existence as individual entities with satisfactory and recognized borders, national integration, and economic development. Of course, all three tasks are interdependent since, in order to defend one's legitimate existence, a State has to realize some degree of national unity and cohesion, and to sustain that cohesion an evenly distributed economic development has to take place, among other requirements.

The African States tackled these issues individually, bilaterally, and multilaterally, through various regional organizations and one continental organization, the Organization of African Unity. The relatively young African organization was set up not only to encourage peaceful conflict resolution among its members but also to push for the total independence of Africa from colonialism—in 1963, many African States were still colonized. This chapter looks at this decolonization task through the case of Western Sahara (formerly known as Spanish Sahara), with its complex ramifications for the organization itself and for the parties involved. This case was one of many tests that challenged the OAU's ability to promote a peaceful resolution of African conflicts—while keeping non-African powers from negatively interfering with this process—to effectively help decolonize remaining colonies, and to guarantee the respect of internationally recognized borders.

Before going into the discussion of the role of the Organization of African Unity—and that of the UN as well—in this dispute, it is necessary to review the origin and the main characteristics of this case that tested the OAU's ability to survive differences among its membership and its capacity to transform itself from a decolonization tool to a mediation and conflict resolution forum when disputes arise among—and involve only—African States.

WESTERN SAHARA: IRREDENTISM VERSUS DECOLONIZATION

Since most African borders were inherited from the colonial era, they constituted time bombs that were going to go off all over the Continent as States started questioning their legitimacy or their definition. However, early enough, the OAU members foresaw these potential explosions and agreed to respect all colonially inherited boundaries as the best solution possible for a peaceful coexistence on the Continent.[2] Unfortunately, in many instances, this consensus was not respected. Morocco's territorial claims on Western Sahara constituted a good and difficult test case for the OAU. It was a case where a member State, Morocco, was claiming national integrity and recovery of a lost territory after Spain, the colonizing power, abandoned it, while an indigenous liberation movement, the Popular Front for the Liberation of Saguia El-Hamra and Rio de Oro (Polisario), claimed the same territory as a distinct entity in search of statehood and international recognition.

Not long ago a large wasteland inhabited by nomadic tribes, Western Sahara is located between the Atlantic Ocean on the west, Algeria on the east, Morocco on the north, and Mauritania on the south. Excellent fishing grounds and large phosphate deposits constitute its most important economic assets. Between 1884 and 1934, it fell under Spanish colonization, and with close cooperation with France—the dominant colonial power in North Africa then—the latter acquired territories in the south and north of Morocco (Ifni and Tarfaya), and in Saguia El-Hamra and Rio de Oro. In 1958, these areas were declared Spanish provinces with representation in the Spanish parliament.

Right after gaining independence from France in 1956, Morocco started claiming the "lost territories" for the purpose of reconstituting what it referred to as the "Old Sherifian Empire," or the "Great Morocco." In 1968 and 1969, Spain respectively relinquished its control over the Rif mountain region of Ifni and Tarfaya. The rest, known as Spanish Sahara, was retained as a Spanish province where Spain started developing the giant phosphate reserves of Bou-Craa and built the largest conveyor belt in the world for the evacuation of the mineral.

When the United Nations called for the decolonization of Western Sahara, its resolutions were at first very vague so as not to antagonize any of the "concerned" or interested parties (Morocco, Mauritania, Spain, and Algeria). It proposed a referendum among the indigenous population to determine whether the latter wanted to be an independent entity or join any of the neighboring states. Spain was then asked to prepare the referendum in consultation with all interested parties. Madrid ignored the UN calls, claiming that the territory was not subject to decolonization because it was Spanish. Morocco also began calling for its decolonization, but for its own irredentist ambitions. In fact, Morocco's irredentism went well beyond the Spanish Sahara. In 1956, the nationalist party, Istiqlal, under the leadership of Allal Al-Fassi, started calling for the reconstitution of a "Great Morocco," that would include not only Western Sahara, but also southwestern Algeria, northern Mali, all of Mauritania, parts of Senegal, and the Canary Islands.[3] Later, Morocco abandoned its claims over Mauritania, Senegal, and Mali, and has just recently given up its demands on the Algerian region of Tindouf. But its claims on Western Sahara were never given up.

At the time of the first UN calls for self-determination of Western Sahara, in the 1960s, a nationalist Saharan elite started developing in a few urban centers and began underground activities against the Spanish occupation. Spain showed no intentions of leaving this phosphate-rich area; its relations with Morocco became strained and escalated to a near military confrontation. Among the factors that helped avoid such a conflict and precipitated the withdrawal of Spain, was a sudden unity of Morocco, Mauritania, and Algeria—each having its own reason—for the implementation of the UN self-determination resolutions. The leaders of the three Maghrebi states met in Rabat, Tlemcen, and Nouadhibou, between 1969 and 1973, to take a common approach to the issue and settle their own border disputes. The three countries seemed then have settled their border disputes[4] and agreed to work together for the decolonization and self-determination of Western Sahara. However, this cooperation on the Spanish Sahara lasted for a short time only, for each party had a different view of its future. Morocco, which recognized Mauritania as a state only in 1969, did not give up its claim to the territory in question. Mauritania wanted a piece of it, and Algeria indicated that it only wanted the indigenous Saharan people (the Sahrawis) to exercise freely their self-determination.

In 1973, General Franco of Spain finally announced that Spain would withdraw from the region once the Sahrawis exercised their right. The administration of the territory would then be progressively handed over to the Sahrawis, under the protection of the Spanish military. Spain informed the United Nations that it had started preparing the referendum. Morocco protested Spain's decision, arguing that it was in fact a disguise for a permanent Spanish stay. The Moroccan king suggested that the referendum be structured in a way that would confirm his sovereignty over that land. The alternatives he would give the Sahrawis were either the status quo (accepting Spanish occupation) or joining Morocco. Of course, the other interested parties, Algeria, Mauritania, and Spain, opposed this proposition. The controversies that followed almost led to an open conflict in the region, notably because decolonization was not the only issue at stake. Mauritania still felt threatened by Morocco's territorial designs, as did Algeria. The overall North African power balance was at stake, as well as the legitimacy of the Moroccan king, which became directly bound to the conflict—especially since the monarch had substituted annexing Western Sahara for the "Great Morocco" ambition.

"Above all . . . the king fears that, to abandon the Moroccan Sahara, after years of gruelling war, would amount to admitting a failure of such proportions that his credibility as a ruler would be shattered."[5]

As Spain prepared to withdraw from the territory and was about to begin organizing the referendum, Morocco and Mauritania started in 1974 an intensive diplomatic campaign geared toward acquiring international recognition for their claims on the territory. Morocco decided to take the issue to the International Court of Justice (ICJ) and ask for an advisory opinion on its claim to a historical title to the territory on the basis of tribal allegiance to the monarch. As a result, the General Assembly recommended the postponement of any consultation until the Court handed down its opinion.[6] As the United Nations tried intensely to bring about a peaceful solution to the crisis, the OAU remained aloof until 1978. After a visit to Western Sahara in May 1975, a UN Visiting Mission reaffirmed that the only solution to the issue was a self-determination referendum.[7]

Because the question submitted by Morocco to the ICJ did not deal with the decolonization aspect of the issue, the International Court of Justice reworded it and, on 16 October 1975, handed down an opinion that refuted the Moroccan—and Mauritanian—claims. While it found *some* allegiance ties between the Moroccan monarchy and *some* Sahrawi tribes, it declared that these ties did not establish any rights of sovereignty over the disputed territory. Therefore, refuting the Moroccan and Mauritanian claims, the ICJ recognized the right of the indigenous population to self-determination according to the UN guidelines, and urged the organization of a plebiscite. Morocco's King Hassan interpreted the ICJ opinion as a confirmation of his claim and announced the preparation for the "Green March." After Morocco announced its march into the disputed territory, the Security Council met on 22 October and adopted a mildly worded resolution that reaffirmed Resolution 1514 (XV) on decolonization and self-determination[8] and called upon Secretary-General Kurt Waldheim "to enter into immediate consultations with the concerned parties . . . and to report to the Security Council."[9] A second resolution, following the Secretary-General's report of 1 November, attempted merely to discourage any "unilateral action or other action" without naming any State in particular.[10] On 6 November 1975, while General Franco was on his deathbed and the Spanish government was preoccupied with the succession issue, King Hassan organized a massive march of some 350,000 civilians and 20,000 troops into the Sahara. The marchers almost collided with the Spanish forces, which stepped back in order to avoid a military confrontation. Spain took the matter to the United Nations, but with no effect on the Moroccan resolve. The third Security Council resolution merely "deplored" Morocco's action and asked that it withdraw and engage in negotiations.[11]

In the midst of internal political disarray, the Spanish government signed, on 14 November, a Tripartite Agreement with Morocco and Mauritania, according to which Spain would withdraw and transfer its administrative rights to the two other countries. The precipitous decision of Spain to hand the territory over to Mauritania and Morocco complicated matters further. As Spain abandoned its mission of preparing a referendum, the international community was split almost equally at the United Nations between those favoring a UN referendum and those who wanted Mauritania and Morocco to take over the matter. This split was reflected in two contradictory resolutions adopted at the same time by the General Assembly, Resolution 34581 A and Resolution 34581 B (XXX), of 10 December 1975.[12]

Following the Madrid Accord, Morocco and Mauritania announced in April 1976 the partition of Western Sahara into two zones. Morocco officially annexed two-thirds of the territory—the most populous and phosphate-rich north—and Mauritania obtained a resourceless desert in the south. As a result of these developments, Algeria cooled its relations with Spain and reinforced its western border defenses. The nationalist Sahrawi guerrilla movement, led by the Polisario Front, began a number of hit-and-run attacks on the new occupant forces. Thousands of Sahrawi civilian refugees poured into Algeria as the Moroccan and Mauritanian forces advanced in the Sahara. The Polisario guerrillas, with the financial and military support of Algeria and Libya, quickly organized themselves into a liberation army. A Sahrawi Arab Democratic Republic (SADR) was proclaimed on 27 February 1976, and a Sahrawi government was set up. After Algeria recognized the new republic, Morocco broke off diplomatic ties with its neighbor.

Following these developments, the issue changed from one of decolonization to one of international recognition of the Moroccan and Mauritanian *fait accompli*, that is, sovereignty over Western Sahara. The two North African countries claimed that there was a challenge to their sovereignty in Western Sahara and that Algeria was behind it. This contention would be at the heart of the division within the OAU later.

In 1976, the Organization of African Unity, which inherited the case from the United Nations, tried to tackle the issue for the first time at a meeting of the Council of Ministers in Addis Ababa in February 1976. The starting issue was then the recognition of the Polisario as a legitimate liberation movement, but it was quickly changed by events—the Madrid Tripartite Accord and the birth of the SADR—into one of recognition of the Sahrawi State. The meeting ended with only a resolution affirming that the matter of recognition was a matter to be decided by each member State individually.

The issue came back at the July 1976 Mauritius summit, which affirmed the right of the Saharan people to self-determination and independence. From then until 1983, the Organization of African Unity worked intensively on fulfilling this decision, even at the risk of breaking down.

Between 1976 and 1978, some members of the OAU tried to set up an extraordinary summit of the organization, but were unable to get the required quorum. Finally, a summit was convened in Khartoum, Sudan, in July 1978.

At that meeting, an ad hoc committee of five heads of states (Mali, Guinea, Nigeria, Ivory Coast, and Tanzania), called "wise men," was set up to investigate the issue and suggest how a referendum should be organized. After studying the question, the "wise men" proposed guidelines for a referendum under OAU and UN supervision. In that same month and just before the OAU summit, Mauritania had withdrawn from the annexing campaign after the fall of its President, Mokhtar Ould Daddah, on 10 July. When a new military government took over, that country was on the verge of collapse: Its economy was severely affected by that year's Sahel drought, 60 percent of its budget was devoted to the war efforts, and 9,000 threatening Moroccan troops were stationed in its territory. After the military coup, Mauritania accepted a cease-fire proposed by the Polisario and signed a peace agreement with the Sahrawis on 19 July 1979, thereby abandoning its territorial claims. Morocco broke diplomatic relations with it, and its troops moved into the southern part of the desert. Faced with a single enemy, Polisario attacks became stronger and bolder, hitting targets even within Morocco itself. The Polisario's objective was to pressure the king into negotiating a settlement, not to win the war. However, despite many defeats of the Royal Armed Forces (FAR), and the increasing cost of the war, the monarch did not change his mind. The situation worsened for Morocco, especially after a deep economic crisis was exacerbated by a drought, a fall in phosphate prices, an increase in the oil import bill, protectionist measures of the European Economic Community (EEC), foreign exchange difficulties, and heavy military expenditures.

The international setting was not favorable to Morocco either. After the withdrawal of Mauritania and the occupation of the southern part of the Sahara by Moroccan troops, the Polisario Front increased its diplomatic successes in most international forums and on all continents. The 1979 Monrovia (Liberia) summit called for an immediate cease-fire and the organization of a "general and free" referendum in which the Sahrawi population would choose between total independence or the maintenance of the status quo. Fifty-four countries had recognized it. By the time the Freetown (Sierra Leone) summit took place in July 1980, twenty-six African countries (out of fifty) had recognized the SADR and accepted that it should be admitted to the OAU as a member. The decision by this narrow majority started a crisis in the African organization. In order to avoid the worst, the twenty-six states agreed to postpone such admission until the "wise men" committee had finished its study and handed down its recommendations. In the June 1981 summit of Nairobi, the ad hoc committee came up with a formula that was accepted by all, including Morocco and its opponent, the Polisario. The proposal called for direct negotiations between the disputing parties, the establishment of a multinational peace-keeping force along with an interim administration of the territory, and for a referendum organized by the OAU and the United Nations. However, the Implementation Committee, which succeeded the "wise men" committee, was unable to set things in motion as decided by the last summit, mostly because Morocco was reluctant to submit to the OAU referendum plan, using various tactics of delay and procrastination. The Implementation Committee did not succeed in bringing Morocco and the Polisario to the negotiation table at three successive meetings in Nairobi (II and III).

The OAU's handling of the issue ultimately became more complicated and even impossible when, in February 1982, the Secretary-General of the OAU, Edem Kodjo of Togo, decided at the Council of Minister's meeting to admit the SADR as the fifty-first member, pending confirmation by the following summit meeting that was to take place in Tripoli (Libya) in August 1982. This decision sent the African organization into its deepest political and constitutional crisis ever, culminating in the inability to hold a summit meeting. Declaring this admission illegal—since the SADR was not an independent state (Article 28 of OAU Charter)—nineteen State delegations[13] walked out of the Tripoli meeting and threatened not to attend any meeting if the decision was not reversed.

Among the causes associated with the inability to hold the Tripoli summit were Morocco's refusal to attend meetings alongside the Polisario, the Chad crisis—the question of Chad's representation by either Hissen Habré or Goukouni Oueddei—and the opposition of eighteen members to holding the meeting in Tripoli, Libya—which would have made Colonel El-Kaddafi the OAU chairman for a year.

After three trials and intense OAU diplomatic efforts, a change of location, and the voluntary abstention of the SADR from attending, the Nineteenth OAU Summit finally took place in Addis Ababa in June 1983, under the chairmanship of President Mengistu Haile Mariam. It adopted Resolution 104 by consensus, which named Morocco and the Polisario as the parties in conflict and urged them to begin direct negotiations, called for a cease-fire, recommended that a referendum be held in December 1983, and reaffirmed the need for the establishment of an OAU–UN peace-keeping force.[14]

However, by the end of 1984, and in spite of some diplomatic opening toward Algeria, Morocco remained opposed to having direct contacts with the Sahrawi representatives, even though its military position had changed after sand walls were built around what it calls the "useful triangle." King Hassan's intransigence and refusal to deal directly with the Polisario led to a devastating Polisario attack, called "The Great Maghreb Offensive," in October 1984. This major attack across the newly erected protective wall indicated that the "unwinnable war" was still going on.

By 1989 some important changes had taken place in the area, and the conflict remained alive. Algeria and Morocco reestablished diplomatic relations in 1988, their borders were reopened to the movement of goods and people, and the Sahrawis and Moroccans inched toward direct negotiations. These developments seem to have been precipitated by domestic urgencies in both Morocco and Algeria, where economic difficulties led to violent confrontations between the State and people. Resolving regional conflicts and slowing down the arms race in the area suddenly became major priorities. However, no side changed its position on the Western Sahara question. But the conflict seemed to have reached a condition of ripeness for a promising attempt at settlement. There was a stalemate situation between the disputing parties where Morocco's military control of the territory was matched by an extensive diplomatic success for the Polisario. All concerned parties wanted to see it solved without losing much or at least without losing face; each side had many reasons to be forthcoming and to show more flexibility than before. Among these reasons were the economic difficulties experienced by both Algeria and Morocco and their negative effect on internal stability and peace. There was also the establishment of the United Arab Maghreb, which required a political *rapprochement* between Algeria and Morocco, and the settlement of most outstanding issues between the two. The Polisario might have been concerned with the effectiveness of the sand wall in successfully curtailing its harassing hit-and-run activities; its diplomatic successes—more than seventy countries recognized the SADR—became more and more difficult to match on the battle ground. Outside of the region, an assertive UN role became possible as the issue was removed from the OAU arena and as the *rapprochement* between the superpowers helped create an atmosphere of international cooperation for resolving other pending disputes in the world (e.g., Angola, Namibia, the two Yemens, and Nicaragua).

Since its 1982–1983 crisis, the OAU had become a difficult arena for any potential solution. In the 1970s, the OAU was the forum favored by Morocco as a mediator, but by the early 1980s it was no longer for the Moroccans a credible, impartial, and honest broker for any role as a mediator. After Morocco decided not to attend any meeting, the OAU took a back seat while the United Nations led the process of inching toward the actual referendum. Besides the unanimous agreement of all Security Council members on pushing for a referendum, for many people,

[t]he United Nations has the attraction of certain universalist principles which may be less constraining than the specific OAU norms, commands greater resources and a wider range of secretarial skills, and has an experience in peacekeeping activities that OAU lacks. . . . It is remarkable, however, to what extent the OAU has been preferred to the United Nations for specific African problems, and to what degree African members of the United Nations have sought to coordinate their own demands and actions within the wider body.[15]

In conjunction with the Chairman and the Secretary-General of the OAU, the Secretary-General of the United Nations started a set of initiatives that culminated in a detailed UN plan for a referendum to be held toward the end of 1991 or early 1992. The plan was approved by the Security Council[16] on 29 April and by the General Assembly on 17 May 1991.[17] The conflicting parties announced their acceptance of the plan and their agreement for a cease-fire on 6 September 1991. The United Nations quickly moved multinational staff and military observers (MINURSO) to oversee the implementation of the referendum plan. Even though the UN seems to have gone further than any previous effort toward settling the dispute, it appears that some obstacles remain to be resolved before the referendum takes place. The main hurdle at the time of this writing is the lack of agreement on who is eligible to vote in the referendum. The Polisario presented a list of approximately 74,000 people based on a 1974 Spanish census, whereas Morocco would like to include some 200,000 more people it claims to be Sahrawis also. When this issue and other minor details are finally resolved, the road to the referendum might finally become open. What is worth noting here is that Morocco made sure that the OAU plays almost no role in this process.

It is worth noting that the OAU and UN roles were reversed twice in the course of this dispute. In the 1960s, the United Nations called repeatedly for the decolonization of Spanish Sahara, while the OAU—born in 1963—was on the sidelines for various reasons; between 1976 and 1983, the OAU took the leading role as an international organization in trying to bring the parties to agree on a settlement; finally, from 1984 to date, the OAU has taken a back seat while the UN initiative returned with more force than would have been possible earlier.

In the international context of the 1970s, the OAU appeared as the natural forum for resolving the dispute, since "[i]ntrasystem solutions to African problems are preferred over extrasystem solutions, whenever possible."[18] As an organization, the OAU had a sense of mission but its members were often entangled in ideological rivalries and security conflicts that evolved in the form of alliances and counteralliances and cut across many issues and different regions of the continent. The Western Sahara question is one of the best examples of how these rivalries developed into a formidable obstacle to an OAU role in settling a dispute that involved not only issues of decolonization and self-determination but also claims of national integrity raised by Morocco. The two main camps were respectively led by Algeria and Morocco. Since the first debate that created the OAU, the two groups existed and represented two main tendencies, the "moderates" and the "progressives."

Moreover, the gathering within the OAU of these young countries that are underdeveloped and more or less economically dependent (if they are not just simply submitted to political pressures) on powers foreign to the African continent, seems to constitute a rather fragile unity and latent divergences [between members] pop up at one time or another when an African problem is debated within the Organization.[19]

In 1982, the split was so serious that the OAU was twice unable to hold its Nineteenth Summit meeting. Thus, since the OAU has been open to ideological splits, it was "left with no role it *can play*, whatever one may think that it *should* do. For after all, there is no OAU; there are only members, and their interests come first."[20] Also, because of the relative youth of independent Africa, various difficulties and problems faced the individual members of the system, from economic development, to national integration, to national security.

Because of the diversity of the issues it addressed and the limited means it had, the Organization of African Unity was suddenly overwhelmed by these problems, one of which almost jeopardized its own existence in 1982. However, the OAU managed to offer a substantial contribution—short of solving—to ending many African disputes and problems, thanks to a great flexibility and a conscious effort to avoid constitutional rigidity. This helped the organization survive one of its worst crises in the context of the Western Sahara dispute. As said earlier, it was the OAU that kept the Saharan issue alive and formulated the first referendum plan in 1981, after King Hassan acquiesced to its recommendations. The current UN activities related to organizing a referendum were in fact inspired by previous OAU actions and resolutions. The OAU was the natural framework for a solution to the dispute, but ideological splits, constitutional crises, and Morocco's decision to stop attending its meetings made it difficult for the OAU to pursue its original mission. However, the deadlock in the African organization was quickly overcome by a revival of the issue at the United Nations. Given the time period during which the issue was revived—notably after the beginning of a series of international events since 1985—the UN became a suitable tool for bringing about an end to the dispute. Just as in the case of many other issues that could not previously be resolved with UN help because of superpower rivalry and Cold War effects, the Western Sahara question had, up to the late 1980s, the same fate at the UN as it had in other international organizations; that is, it had no prospect of resolution. However, the multiplicity of organizations that attempted to deal with it was, in the words of Yassin El-Ayouty, a positive thing in itself since it "provided a platform and credibility for various parties to the dispute. SADR has its OAU representation; its liberation movement, Polisario, is a petitioner at the United Nations; Morocco and Algeria have their representatives at the United Nations, in the League of Arab States, the Conference of the Islamic Organization and the Non-Aligned Movement. No party was left out in the cold."[21] But since none of the other international organizations has the means or capacity to implement—or enforce, as in the 1990–1991 Gulf conflict—collective decisions, the United Nations appears to be the only hopeful forum left for a solution via a referendum. In this process, and according to the Secretary-General's referendum plan, the OAU is given a very minimal role. It barely mentions the Organization of African Unity. Many observers credit that to a desire not to antagonize Morocco, which still does not think of the OAU as an objective and impartial organization. If the referendum takes place and the issue is finally resolved without any active participation of the OAU, the African organization might see its credibility diminished in the area of re-solving conflicts of this sort among its members.

As long as the OAU does not have a way of enforcing its decisions and is not endowed with the means to do so, its role might remain inhibited to a point of immobilization in the face of intra-African disputes. The organization needs to learn from the lesson of its atrophy in 1982 because of the Western Sahara question. Constitutional reforms might be needed to inject more flexibility in the organization and to give it more muscle. As long as most States in Africa still have unsettled business with their neighbors and with important minorities claiming autonomy or independence, the Organization of African Unity is likely to be challenged by problems similar to the one of Western Sahara. It will have to devise some official and powerful instruments of conflict resolution and mediation with an authority similar to that of the Security Council of the United Nations. But, before this is achieved, there has to be a strong will among its members to transcend ideological differences and individual ambitions and to move the organization toward a powerful role in promoting economic development and in peacefully settling disputes among Africans.

The benefits of a strengthened OAU are numerous. The Africans will avoid the internationalization of their disputes, which might bring in foreign pow-ers, raise the costs, and maybe impose undesirable solutions or conditions, as the aftermath of the Gulf War suggests. A strengthened OAU is likely to contribute to the overall economic and social development of the Continent, notably by persuading disputing parties not to engage in costly hostilities and expensive arms races. A strengthened OAU will also advance African interests in other international forums, such as the UN. Finally, a strengthened OAU might encourage regional or subregional economic integration as a response to Africa's perennial economic plight and to the current international trend of formation of regional economic blocs such as the current one in Europe and the ones developing in Asia, North America, and North Africa.

NOTES

1. Report by the Secretary-General, UN document S/22464, 19 April 1991; Security Council Resolution 690, UN document S/Res/690, 29 April 1991.

2. Resolution 16 of the Assembly of Heads of State and Government, OAU document AHG/Res. 16, July 1964.

3. Azzedine Layachi, *The United States and North Africa: A Cognitive Approach to Foreign Policy* (New York: Praeger, 1990), p. 21.

4. Morocco did not ratify its agreement with Algeria, which was signed by King Hassan and President Boumediene in Ifrane on 15 January 1969, until spring 1989.

5. Tony Hodges, "The Western Sahara File," *Third World Quarterly* 6(1) (1984), p. 105.

6. UN General Assembly Resolution 3292, 29 GAOR Supp. 31, pp. 103–104, UN document A/9631 (1974).

7. Report of the United Nations Visiting Mission to Spanish Sahara, in *The Report of the Special Committee on the Situation with Regard to the Implementation of the Declaration on the Granting of Independence to Colonial Countries and Peoples,* UN document A/10023/Add. 5 (1975).

8. UN General Assembly Resolution 1541 (XI), 15 GAOR Supp. 16, UN document A/4684 (1960), pp. 29–30.

9. UN Security Council Resolution 377, 22 October 1975.

10. UN Security Council Resolution 379, 2 November 1975.

11. UN Security Council Resolution 380, 6 November 1975.

12. UN General Assembly Resolutions 3458 (A) and 3458 (B), UN document GA/5438 (1975), pp. 254–256.

13. Cameroon, Central African Republic, Comoros, Djibouti, Equatorial Guinea, Gabon, Gambia, Guinea, Ivory Coast, Liberia, Mauritius, Morocco, Niger, Senegal, Somalia, Sudan, Tunisia, Upper Volta, and Zaire.

14. Resolution of the Assembly of Heads of State and Government of the Organization of African Unity, AHG/Res. 104 (XIX) of June 1983.

15. Michael Wolfers, "The Organization of African Unity as Mediator," in Saadia Touval and I. William Zartman, *International Mediation in Theory and Practice* (Boulder, Co.: Westview, 1985), p. 178.

16. Security Council Resolution 690 of 29 April 1990, UN Document S/Res/690.

17. UN General Assembly Resolution of 17 May 1991, UN Document A/Res/45/266.

18. I. William Zartman, "The OAU and the African State System: Interaction and Evaluation," in Yassin El-Ayouty and I. William Zartman, eds., *The OAU After Twenty Years* (New York: Praeger, 1984), p. 28.

19. Meriem Amimour-Benderra, *Le Peuple Sahraoui et l'Autodetermination* (Algiers, Algeria: Entreprise Algerienne de Press, 1988), p. 299.

20. Zartman, "The OAU and the African State System," p. 41.

21. Yassin El-Ayouty, "The Organization of African Unity and Conflict Resolution: Looking at the Past, Aiming at the Future," *Disarmament* (New York: United Nations, 1991), p. 54.

_____ *Part II*

Economic, Social, and
Humanitarian Development

4

Southern Africa and the Role of SADCC in Subregional Development

LEONARD T. KAPUNGU

The history of the Southern African Development Coordination Conference[1] (SADCC), since its formation in April 1980, has been written over and over again by scholars of renown. To repeat the analysis of the period would not add anything to knowledge or to scholarship. At the time of this writing, toward the end of 1991, momentous events were taking place in southern Africa, in countries of the SADCC as well as in South Africa, events that will change the nature of SADCC and determine a new course for this subregional organization and its relationship with the OAU and Africa in general. At the same time, Africa has taken a gigantic step toward the establishment of the African Economic Community, in which SADCC, among others, is expected to play a major role. It is to these new developments and the future that this observer of the African scene would like to turn.

But to put the analysis in its proper context, we must restate the reasons why SADCC was formed. Its objectives as set out in its founding declaration, *Southern Africa: Toward Economic Liberation*, were:

1. Reduction of external dependence and, in particular, dependence on the Republic of South Africa

2. Creation of operational and equitable regional integration

3. Mobilization of domestic and regional resources to carry out national, inter-State, and regional policies to reduce dependence and build genuine regional coordination

4. Joint action to secure international understanding of, and practical support for, the SADCC strategy

Between 1981 and 1991, the organization survived against all odds including a systematic destabilization of SADCC countries by apartheid South Africa that cost the region more than $30 million.

In the middle of 1991, the leaders of apartheid South Africa not only denounced apartheid, but also repealed the pillars of apartheid and have begun to take steps, though haltingly, toward finding a common ground with the black people who have been the victims of the system for about forty-three years.

SADCC IN THE CONTEXT OF POSTDESTABILIZING SOUTH AFRICA

What the future holds for South Africa is for all of us to guess, but one thing is certain: South Africa will no longer be the source of destabilization in SADCC countries. Whether the removal of apartheid will lead to the democratization of South Africa is now for the people of South Africa as a whole to decide. South Africa can now be a positive force of both political and economic development in Africa. South Africa, no longer an international pariah, will be a member of SADCC and of the OAU, and will be a source of strength to SADCC, Africa, and the OAU.

Destabilization having been forsaken in mid–1991, other positive developments have now been given time to bud in SADCC countries: The civil war in Angola has ended and peace has now been given a chance. Angola in peace is on its way to democratization and hopefully to the full development of its potential after fifteen years of war. The Angolan people, who had not known what life was like without war since the first shot in the war of liberation was fired in 1961 and lived through to see the results of the war of liberation collapse into civil war, can now look forward to a new life. Indeed, to a generation born and bred in war it will be a strange life, albeit a welcome one.

In Mozambique, where apartheid South Africa's techniques of destabilization were at their meanest, there now is hope, agreement having been reached between the Mozambican government and RENAMO (Revolutionary National Movement for Mozambique) to settle the war of terrorism and democratize the political processes. Energies hitherto expended in banditry and defense against it will now be mobilized hopefully for development.

Zimbabwe, which both for its own security to protect its economic lifeline through Mozambique and for friendship's sake to the Frelimo government had for eight years thrown its military might in support of the Frelimo government, in mid–1991 began to withdraw its armies. The resources spent on the war can now be hopefully redirected toward development.

Zambia and Tanzania, respectively the headquarters of the exiled African National Congress (ANC) and the Pan-Africanist Congress (PAC) and the adopted home of many of the South African liberation leaders and cadres, will receive relief of the responsibility that for years they have alone shouldered, as these leaders and cadres return home. History will record, indeed, that these two countries, while their people suffered depredation and their economies collapsed for one reason or another, never flinched in their direct support of the liberation movements they were host to.

Namibia became free from South Africa on 21 March 1990 and has begun to grapple with the problems of development. Botswana, just a stone's throw away from South Africa, can now rest from the cross-border raids from apartheid South Africa. It can now hopefully develop its vast diamond reserves and cattle ranches. Lesotho and Swaziland, both entirely encircled by South Africa and victims of the bullying tactics of apartheid South Africa, can now breathe freely and expect the normal and ordinary problems of being surrounded by a dominant neighbor like most small states in the world.

Even Malawi, which for so long had been the only country in Africa to have a formal diplomatic presence in South Africa, had felt the collateral effects of the destabilization of apartheid South Africa. As Mozambique collapsed under the destabilization of apartheid South Africa, refugees by the thousands flocked into Malawi, creating enormous political and economic problems. With peace coming to Mozambique, Malawi can hopefully have the refugee problem resolved. With apartheid eradicated, Malawi will no longer be seen as being lesser than others for only doing openly with apartheid South Africa what a host of other African countries did clandestinely.

With the eradication of apartheid and hopefully the establishment of democratic institutions in South Africa, an essential alibi for sheer political and economic mismanagement in some SADCC countries will have been removed. The "the devil made me do it" mentality that encouraged some leaders at times to blame everything that went wrong in their countries on the long hand—or call it a long shadow—of apartheid South Africa should now disappear. Responsibility for political and economic mismanagement will hopefully be accepted by those who had developed a habit of hiding in the shadow of apartheid South Africa. The beginning of leadership is the acceptance of responsibility.

It has always been emphasized that SADCC was not basically formed "in unity" against South Africa. It was formed as an instrument for development, for improving the standard of living and the quality of life of the people in its member States. It was formed to reduce economic dependence, not only on South Africa but also on others outside Africa. President Robert Mugabe of Zimbabwe stated that any excessive external dependence perpetuates exploitative relations at Africa's expense and fosters the conditions under which African countries can be subjected to the most pernicious forms of economic and political manipulations, thereby subverting whatever political freedom had been gained.

But because of the destabilization activities of South Africa against the countries whose economies had been, according to the late President Samora

Machel of Mozambique, "conceived and organized as functions of South Africa," the political dimension of SADCC became more pronounced. If one looks at the transportation network in Southern Africa, one is struck that, of the ten seaports[2] only Dar-es-Salaam was not either directly under South African control or within the reach of its destabilization activities. Thus, the political and economic emancipation that comes to SADCC countries by the rehabilitation of South Africa and the end of destabilization almost boggles the mind. Where eight States, the original founding members of SADCC, had no seaports operating without hindrance, as even Dar-es-Salaam could not function well because of congestion, now ten States, adding Namibia and South Africa, will have ten seaports at their disposal functioning without fear of sabotage. Such a situation can now lead the SADCC countries to boldly move toward the attainment of the other objectives.

At the launching of SADCC, President Julius Nyerere had stated:

But our purposes are not simply greater independence from South Africa. If South Africa's *apartheid* rule ended tomorrow, there would still be need for the States of southern Africa to co-operate, to co-ordinate their transport systems, to fight foot and mouth disease together, to nationalize their industrial development. . . . One day— we hope before too long—Namibia will be free and we shall welcome that country into membership of SADCC.[3]

These words were uttered in April 1980. Indeed, true as they were, in January 1991 independent Namibia was the host of a meeting of the Foreign Ministers of SADCC, having been admitted soon after its independence on 21 March 1990.

SADCC IN THE CONTEXT OF THE AFRICAN ECONOMIC COMMUNITY

Not only did the founding fathers of SADCC see their efforts as directed to integrating their economies, they also shared a vision that went beyond their borders. The then Prime Minister Mugabe stated:

Our efforts in regional co-operation should naturally be seen in their proper context. SADCC is a building block in the movement toward the continental economic co-operation envisaged in the OAU's Lagos Plan of Action and the proposals for an Eastern and Southern Africa Preferential Trade Area. Our progress in SADCC will, to an extent at least, determine the speed with which these continental goals are achieved. Moreover, the success we achieve in this regard will, to that extent, bring nearer the realization of the objectives of the new International Economic Order.[4]

Eleven years after the Prime Minister and now the President of Zimbabwe had so stated, his vision of continental economic cooperation moved one step toward realization when the OAU member States signed the Treaty

Establishing the African Economic Community at Abuja, Nigeria, on 3 June 1991.

The establishment of the African Economic Community has been the objective of African leaders since the adoption by the OAU of the Lagos Plan of Action in 1980. While no serious attempts were made to implement the plan, regional economic organizations such as SADCC were formed and proceeded to do extremely well under difficult conditions. When the African leaders in 1990 decided to form the AEC, they decided that in order to succeed, the AEC should be established step by step within a period of thirty-four years. They wisely determined that the first stage, which would last five years, should be dedicated to the "strengthening of existing regional economic communities and, within a period not exceeding five (5) years from the date of entry into force of this Treaty, establishing economic communities in regions where they do not exist."[5] SADCC, therefore, emerges as one of the major regional organizations on which the AEC is to be built. As pointed out earlier, this was the vision of its founders. What, then, should be the first contribution of SADCC to the AEC?

What is SADCC's role in the context of the OAU efforts to rescue Africa from economic collapse? Regional and international cooperation, as SADCC reports have stated, "is an integral part of the SADCC philosophy." SADCC countries, when South Africa is democratized, will have a total population of about 100 million, thus providing a fairly sophisticated market for the AEC. Furthermore, the AEC will benefit from the efforts that SADCC countries have been making to develop their transport network. With peace coming to Angola and Mozambique and democratization coming to South Africa, railway lines will connect the Cape, at the southermost tip of Africa, passing through Botswana, Zimbabwe, and Zambia, with the port of Dar-es-Salaam in East Africa, and through Zimbabwe and Zambia with Maputo, Mozambique in the southeast of Africa and through Zaire with Lobito, Angola in southwest Central Africa. This railway network will provide the transport infrastructure the AEC could use for further development. It is common knowledge that, regardless of the amount and value of commodities a country can produce, if they cannot be moved they are of little value.

With peace coming to southern Africa, the natural resources of the subregion can now be effectively developed. Southern Africa in general is very rich in these resources. It has rich soil and good rains, leading to high-level agricultural production. It is rich in mineral resources as well as fisheries. Much of this has been covered by other authors.

The SADCC leaders have determined that the theme of SADCC's operation is development coordination. This theme leads to the avoidance of duplication in projects and to the sharing of resources. Thus, as Africa moves toward the African Economic Community, it could learn from the experience of SADCC. This experience has led to a division of labor and the awarding of sectoral responsibilities to member countries. Responsibility for the execution of each of the SADCC projects has been given to the member States, thus leading to the decentralization of the operations. This decentralization has enabled SADCC to operate with a small secretariat (based in Gaborone, Botswana) with only about a dozen staff members. Thus, SADCC has been freed from bureaucratization. It is a lesson that Africa and international organizations could learn. There is a tendency that when a new organization is formed, a large bureaucracy is established to service it. It has now been proven that organizations with large bureaucracies tend to be inefficiently run. The efficiency of the SADCC operation has come about partly from the smallness of its bureaucracy.

The founders of SADCC were of the view that establishing a large central headquarters would create unnecessary costs and that policy makers would lose control of the organization to a bureaucracy that would be out of touch with the realities on the ground. The late President of Botswana, Seretse Khama, stated that "the basis for our co-operation, built on concrete projects and specific programmes rather than on grandiose schemes and massive bureaucratic institutions, must be the assured mutual advantage of the participating states."[6]

Another lesson that SADCC could bring to Africa is that success can only come from objectives that are well defined and limited. Thus, SADCC, while created within the political environment of southern Africa, has been made to function mainly as an economic institution. The political objective was to reduce dependency on apartheid South Africa, but the main objective has been to promote balanced economic development. Every member of SADCC is made to feel that it receives its fair share from the organization. The past experiences of the members have served them well. Tanzania had been a member of the East African Community (EAC) with Kenya and Uganda. That community broke when some members felt they were not receiving their fair share from the community. Northern Rhodesia (now Zambia), Nyasaland (now Malawi), and Southern Rhodesia (now Zimbabwe) had been members of the Federation of Rhodesia and Nyasaland. That federation broke when Northern Rhodesia and Nyasaland felt that the federation was a partnership of a "horse" and a "rider," they being the horse and Southern Rhodesia being the rider. Angola and Mozambique were in association with Portugal in the Lusophone Union, with Portugal being the dominant partner. Botswana, Lesotho, Swaziland, and now Namibia, together with apartheid South Africa, are members of the Southern African Customs Union, with apartheid South Africa being the dominant partner. In both the Lusophone Union and the Southern African Customs Union, the States that are being dominated are not happy with the relationship.

SADCC is built on the "priorities of its member States." Each member defines what its priorities are and seeks projects that satisfy those priorities. It was the objective of SADCC that no one member should be dominant in the organization. But in affairs of state just as in human affairs, equal partnership in practice is difficult to achieve. In SADCC, Zimbabwe, being the most industrialized member, has emerged as the most dominant, participating in 80 percent of all intra-SADCC trade. However, Zimbabwe has refrained from flexing its muscle and thus no member feels threatened. After the democratization of apartheid South Africa, that country will become the dominant member in SADCC.

As Africa moves into the AEC, this experience of SADCC should provide a guide, if one is needed. States do not want to be made to feel that they are being dominated by others. States who run away from dependence on one State, in the SADCC's case dependency on apartheid South Africa, will not run into dependency on any other State, be it African or non-African. Thus, while the AEC will acknowledge the independence of sovereign states in its Charter, it is the behavior of the States that will count—and the commitment of its members to it may just depend on whether each member feels that its priorities are being met. Greater responsibility will rest on those States that are more powerful. They must learn to refrain from flexing their muscles if the community is to survive.

Unfortunate as it is, Africa will for some time continue to depend on external assistance. This has been the weakness of SADCC. It depends for its projects on external donors. However, realizing that this weakness could doom the organization, the SADCC's founding fathers sought ways to reduce the extent to which that weakness could immobilize them. First, SADCC sought donors who could also economically benefit from the projects they supported. Thus, SADCC preferred to call them "cooperating partners" rather than donors. Second, they sought this "cooperating partnership" with small States like the Nordic countries and members of the OECD (Organization for Economic Cooperation and Development) and from international organizations such as the World Bank and the International Monetary Fund. Third, they insisted that there should be more use of SADCC experts and consultants.

However, this determination to minimize the effects of the major weakness of dependency on external aid has also led to tensions between SADCC and its cooperating partners. The partners have not been as cooperating as SADCC members would wish. It seems it has come down to "He who pays the piper calls the tune." Battles have been fought on this issue, especially as the need for funds made SADCC start to look for support from major donors like the United States, the United Kingdom, and the Federal Republic of Germany, who by nature felt that they should exert more influence in cases in which they provide the funds. They want to call the tune while SADCC members continue to resist.

SADCC leaders have rightly concluded that if economic integration has to be achieved, they must build a regional market. Six years after SADCC had been established, no regional market had been allowed to develop. The cooperating partners and the international organizations like the World Bank and the IMF have been insisting on establishing in SADCC the "global free market system." This system at times works against regional goals and does not allow local business to grow.

It would appear that the AEC is heading in the same direction, with the same tensions. The need for external aid, which is made so clear in the AEC founding documents, will be its major weakness. AEC must look for ways of limiting the debilitating effects of this weakness. It will not be easy, but all efforts must be made if the community is to survive. The Secretary-General of the OAU, Dr. Salim Ahmed Salim, put it well in his report to the Fifty-fourth Ordinary Session of the OAU Council of Ministers held in May 1991 before the AEC treaty was signed, when he stated, "We have come to Abuja for a rendez-vous with history." He stated that "our member states committed themselves, individually and collectively, to the principle of collective self-reliance," a self-reliance that is based on strengthening existing regional economic communities such as SADCC.

The Report of the United Nations Secretary-General on the Critical Economic Situation in Africa: Final Review and Appraisal of the Implementation of the United Nations Programme of Action for African Economic Recovery and Development 1986–1990 (A/46/324, dated 6 August 1991) clearly demonstrates that as long as Africa relies on external aid and as long as it looks outward, the economies of its members will not improve. Despite the African Priority Program for Economic Recovery (APPER) presented by the OAU and adopted by the United Nations General Assembly in June 1986, the economic and social conditions of African countries have worsened even after all attempts had been made to improve economic management. According to the report, when APPER was presented, it had been assumed that "the efforts of African countries must be supplemented by complementary action on the part of the international community and that solutions to exogenous problems over which Africa has no control, would have to be found." The assumption proved to be wrong, as Africa fell victim to negative terms of trade, diminished income from an increased volume of commodity exports, mounting debt problems, and general lack of external support. Indeed, the report of the Secretary-General shows that the net resource flows to Africa in real terms declined between 1986 and 1990. It also shows that development assistance in real terms stagnated "while private flows fell sharply."

It is estimated in the report that in order for the APPER to have succeeded, Africa needed between 1986 and 1990 financial resources of about $128.1 billion, of which Africa itself could provide $82 billion. And yet, as the report sadly concluded, "net resource flows, in real terms, hardly rose during 1986 to 1990" and the targets "remained unfulfilled."

It is in such an environment that the AEC has been established, an environment that is worse than that which existed in 1986 when APPER was launched, since attention of the donors has now turned to Eastern Europe and the newly born Baltic independent states, and perhaps the former Soviet

Union. Thus, Africa has but one choice, and that is to rely on itself as much as possible. To do this, it must rely on its subregional economic framework, such as SADCC and the Economic Community of West African States (ECO-WAS). At the same time, the OAU should negotiate for the forgiveness of the $270 billion debt the African countries are laboring under. If these two objectives are achieved together with sound economic management and a democratization process of the political systems that would release the energies of the African youth, a good foundation for the AEC will have been established.

The task of the OAU in the coming years is to work on preventing Africa from being marginalized, if not trivialized. The OAU, therefore, must seek to strengthen subregional organizations, such as SADCC, so that Africa may draw from its inner strength.

NOTES

1. SADCC was originally composed of Angola, Botswana, Malawi, Mozambique, Swaziland, Tanzania, Zambia, and Zimbabwe. Namibia became the ninth member in March 1990.

2. Cape, Durban, Port Elizabeth, Beira, Nancala, Mozambique, Maputo, Dar-es-Salaam, Walvis Bay, Lobito, and Luanda.

3. SADCC Proceedings 1981, Blantyre, Malawi, 1982, pp. 13–14.

4. Ibid., p. 14.

5. Treaty Establishing the African Economic Community, Article 6 (2a).

6. Ibid.

The OAU and Human Rights: Regional Promotion of Human Rights

CLAUDE E. WELCH, JR.

The establishment and functioning of the OAU's newest subsidiary organization, the African Commission on Human and Peoples' Rights, challenges a basic principle of positivist international law on which the OAU has long based its policies: the sovereign domestic control of member States.

Classic conceptions of international law postulate that States hold essentially unfettered powers within their frontiers. Save by prior agreement through formal acceptance (ratification or accession) of a binding commitment (such as a treaty, convention, or special protocol to an existing document), or through preemptory norms (e.g., against slavery, torture, or genocide) that form part of customary international law, sovereignty cannot otherwise be limited. This fact of international relations has long been recognized. For example, the United Nations Charter precludes the UN from intervening in matters "essentially within the domestic jurisdiction of any State" (Article 2.7), an article reflecting the centuries-old pattern of state-to-state relations. Hence, too, negotiators for international instruments seek to establish limits in advance on the extent to which their States' behavior can subsequently be circumscribed by the particular treaties. The name of the game, in short, is preservation of sovereign autonomy in domestic affairs.

These sentiments marked the Organization of African Unity at its inception. Having recently led their countries to self-government, and convinced of the value of and necessity for their leadership, the heads of state gathered at Addis Ababa included strong status quo norms in the OAU Charter. Among the OAU's guiding principles were noninterference in the domestic affairs of member States and strong respect for domestic sovereignty. Inherited boundaries were to be protected from alteration. Changes in leadership—even if by coup d'etat or other unconstitutional means—remained purely internal matters.[1] Gross violations of human rights by governments passed unnoticed, or at least unremarked upon, at the annual OAU summits until the late 1970s.

This chapter summarizes the major provisions of the African Charter on Human and Peoples' Rights, compares its provisions for protection as well as promotion of human rights with other regional documents, and assesses the impact of growing pressures from nongovernmental organizations (NGOs). While promotion involves steps to bolster awareness of human rights, protection involves acting directly on behalf of individuals whose rights have been abridged. Promotion *affects* rights; protection *effects* them. Neither can be effectively carried out without adequate resources and commitment.

As might be expected, it is far easier and less costly to talk in general terms about human rights than to correct abuses committed by persons, groups, or entities, often themselves linked to regimes in power. The armature of protection provided domestically in most African States is far weaker than in Western European states, and significantly weaker than in almost all Western Hemisphere countries. Similar contrasts exist in the treaties establishing the respective regional human rights regimes. Contrasts among the commissions (the African, European, and Inter-American) can be attributed to the regional contexts in which each is embedded. That Africa has a human rights commission may be somewhat surprising; that it confronts severe limitations on its effectiveness is less so. Considering the special conditions of Africa—its lengthy, searing acquaintance with colonialism; its weakly established, often insecure organs of state government; its parlous economic situation, particularly in the late 1980s; its severely limited government capabilities; the heavy burdens the OAU secretariat carries with very limited funding—the recently established African Commission on Human and Peoples' Rights started its activities with several strikes against it. However, recent steps, especially at the Eleventh Session of the OAU (March 1992) suggest it is achieving a higher profile.

THE AFRICAN CHARTER ON HUMAN AND PEOPLES' RIGHTS: AN INADEQUATE BASIS FOR ACTION?

Emphasis on domestic sovereignty remained unchanged in the first fifteen years of the OAU's history, despite growing evidence of the abuses that could be committed in its name. The January 1961 call by the International Commission of Jurists (in the so-called Lagos Plan) for adoption of an African Convention of Human Rights and a continent-wide court fell on deaf ears. Increased repression, denial of political choice, restrictions on the freedom of association, and like events occurred, with rare murmurs of dissent from within the OAU. The organization seemed to function as a club of Presidents, engaged in a tacit policy of not inquiring into each other's practices. There were, it should be noted, a few obvious exceptions to the *noli me tangere* attitude: Residual colonialism, apartheid, and (by the end of the period) armed conflicts led to a response by the OAU or by adjacent States with OAU approval. On the whole, however, as the second Chairman of the African Commission on Human and Peoples' Rights wrote in 1979, "With regard to breaches of human rights, even of a grave nature such as genocide, the OAU has been bogged down by the domestic jurisdiction clause. The notable exceptions are the questions of colonialism and apartheid."[2] The OAU, in short, historically considered human rights largely in the context of self-determination, through the ending of alien or settler rule.

Those African leaders who broke the conspiracy of silence about flagrant, widespread human rights abuses in member States had little positive impact— at least initially. "See no evil, hear no evil, speak no evil" typified the views of OAU summiteers to a point. Politically sanctioned repression and murders in Uganda, the Central African "Empire," and Equatorial Guinea, and the election of Idi Amin as Chair despite his horrendous record, besmirched the organization's reputation and the overall credibility of African States in criticizing human rights abuses in other countries. The break came in 1979. The dramatic ousters that year of the tyrants Idi Amin,[3] Jean-Bedel Bokassa[4] and Macias Nguema evoked strong statements by African leaders about the importance of protecting human rights within member States. OAU and United Nations initiatives led to the 1981 summit endorsement of the African Charter on Human and Peoples' Rights.[5] It entered into force in October 1986, following the requisite number of ratifications.

In content and organization, the African Charter owes much to prior international human rights documents, notably the Universal Declaration of Human Rights (UDHR) (1948) and the two International Covenants, on Civil and Political Rights and on Economic, Social, and Cultural Rights.[6] Twenty-nine of the Charter's sixty-eight articles specify rights and freedoms that apply to "every person and every people," although some are manifestly aimed at individuals, while others involve collective rights. Most of these are familiar, the language reflecting earlier international agreements. The African Charter begins with a statement of nondiscrimination (i.e., no differentiation on the basis of race, ethnic group, color, sex, language, religion, political or any other opinion, national and social origin, fortune, birth, or other status). It lists a variety of civil and political ("first generation") rights in Articles 3– 14, and of economic, social, and cultural ("second generation") rights in Articles 15–18. The Charter blazes some new ground through its inclusion of rights of peoples ("third generation"), in Articles 19–24, and duties, in Articles 25–29. Duties apply both to States (including the responsibility "to promote and ensure through teaching, education, and publication the respect of the rights and freedoms contained in the present Charter") and to individuals. As Robertson observes, "the States concerned wished to put forward a distinctive conception of human rights in which civil and political rights were seen to be counter-balanced by duties of social solidarity, just as they were complemented by economic and social rights and supplemented by peoples' rights."[7]

Commentators on the African Charter have tended to stress its shortcomings.[8] Perhaps the mildest criticism comes from Okere, who deems the document "modest in its objectives and flexible in its means."[9] One of the strongest comes from the respected weekly *West Africa*, noting that "congenital defects [in the African Charter] in no small way account for the near irrelevance of the Charter and its institutions to Africa's political life."[10] Criticism is leveled particularly at "clawback" clauses that essentially confine the Charter's protections to rights as they are defined in national law. Qualifications of rights make no reference to circumstances that may lead to their limitation.[11] For example, Article 6 provides, "every individual shall have the right to liberty and to the security of his person," with the proviso, "No one may be deprived of his freedom *except for reasons and conditions previously laid down by law*" (emphasis supplied). Nowhere does the Charter define these reasons and conditions, nor subject them to any test of conformity with standards such as those in the International Covenant on Civil and Political Rights. Gittleman concludes,

the African Charter is woefully deficient with regard to the right to liberty. As that right is subject to national law, the Charter is incapable of supplying even a scintilla of external restraint upon a government's power to create laws contrary to the spirit of the rights granted. Even the African Commission's ability to provide some external restraint in situations where a governmental activity contravenes a national law is highly questionable. Without precise legal guidelines, the Commission will be severely handicapped in dealing with such situations.[12]

The major OAU instrument for ensuring the observance of these various rights is the African Commission on Human and Peoples' Rights. As much text of the Charter is devoted to its organization, mandate, and procedure as to the rights and duties just mentioned. Politically, the African Commission is subordinated to the OAU Assembly of Heads of State and Government, to which it reports. The Commission's eleven members, "chosen from amongst African personalities of the highest reputation, known for their high morality, integrity, impartiality, and competence in matters of human and peoples' rights," are elected for six-year terms by the Assembly. Publication of its reports comes only after consideration by the Assembly. It depends on the OAU for financial and staff support. Of the three functioning regional systems for protection of human rights, the African system is the only one lacking a court to complement the commission.[13]

The drafting of the African Charter coincided in time with a substantial expansion of international supervision of human rights through the United Nations as a whole, and in Western Europe and the Americas. However,

OAU Heads of State were reluctant to grant the African Commission a significant role in protecting human rights; its activities were to be primarily promotional. The African Charter gave the Commission on Human and Peoples' Rights the right to receive and consider communications from individuals, as well as from States, but left obscure what it should do with periodic reports from States and with petitions, and left to the OAU Assembly of Heads of State any enforcement of its findings. An opportunity—as well as a severe constraint—was thus laid upon the Commission from its inception. As an Algerian commentator on the Charter commented, "The Commission does, to be sure, enjoy a significant freedom of maneuver in exercising its function of promotion of human rights in Africa but is far more limited in its function of protecting these rights."[14] We need to ask how its duties compare with those of the comparable commissions in the two other regional systems for protection of human rights, and whether the African Commission can go beyond its almost exclusive focus on promotion.

THE ROLES OF REGIONAL COMMISSIONS

Intergovernmental organizations have long been reluctant to consider petitions for redress submitted directly to them. The most striking evidence comes from the short shrift given individual complaints sent to the United Nations Commission on Human Rights. Established in 1946 by ECOSOC (the Economic and Social Council), the Commission immediately began to receive pleas for action. After all, hadn't UN members, in ratifying its Charter, pledged to "take joint and separate action" to promote "universal respect for, and observance of, human rights and fundamental freedoms" (Articles 55 and 56)?[15] The Commission voted in 1947, however, that it had "no power to take any action in regard to any complaints regarding human rights."[16] ECOSOC itself that year denied access to even the details of petitions. For more than twenty years, this ostrichlike attitude prevailed. This meant, for example, that petitions emanating from South Africa could not be considered by the Commission on Human Rights, despite growing international abhorrence about apartheid, increasing African membership in the United Nations as a whole, and discussion elsewhere within the UN system. Obviously the system smacked of inconsistency. Although new states in the UN may have been reluctant to permit external scrutiny of their internal policies on the one hand, they strongly favored examining the blatantly discriminatory policies of South Africa. Third World pressure thus joined with efforts from some Western States to transform the UN's standpat attitude. The UN's greater involvement in matters of colonialism and apartheid—both denials of fundamental human rights—led indirectly to justifying scrutiny of human rights practices within newly independent African states.

Two resolutions adopted by the parent Economic and Social Council broadened the Commission's mandate. Resolution 1235, passed in June

1967, declared the right of the Commission on Human Rights, and its subsidiary Sub-Commission on the Prevention of Discrimination and Protection of Minorities, "to examine information relevant to gross violations of fundamental rights and fundamental freedoms" contained in individual petitions. The Commission could carry out studies and report to ECOSOC. Three years later, through Resolution 1503, ECOSOC requested the Sub-Commission to consider, in private, petitions and governmental responses "with a view to determining whether to refer to the Commission on Human Rights particular situations which appear to reveal a consistent pattern of gross and reliably attested violations of human rights." The Commission could appoint ad hoc investigatory committees.

What started modestly has, in just over two decades, blossomed into a rich profusion of studies and recommendations. Resolution 1503 procedures have been used, as of early 1992, to investigate human rights abuses in over three dozen countries.[17] "Special" *rapporteurs*, representatives, working groups, *rapporteurs*, and experts of the Commission have reported on countries such as Afghanistan, Chile, El Salvador, Equatorial Guinea, Guatemala, Haiti, and South Africa; and on subjects such as summary or arbitrary executions, torture, use of mercenaries, religious intolerance, gross violation of human rights, enforced or involuntary disappearances, rights to development, rights of the child, rights of minorities, leaving and returning to countries, religion and beliefs, abolition of the death penalty, states of siege or emergency, independence and impartiality of the legal profession, racial discrimination, handicapped persons, administrative detention, communications, slavery, indigenous populations, mental illness, and detention. In short, numerous initiatives, based to a substantial extent on individual petitions, mark current United Nations concern with human rights. The lead has been taken by the semi-independent Sub-Commission, whose members—elected as experts in their individual capacity—have frequently pressed for stronger action than the parent Commission—whose members are named by governments—is willing to take. One result has been tension between the two groups.

Among regional human rights groups, the European Commission on Human Rights stands as a landmark institution. Its careful, extensive development contrasts markedly with all other international human rights regimes. Created primarily to protect rather than promote human rights, it was established in 1953 following the entry into force of the European Convention for the Protection of Human Rights and Fundamental Freedoms.[18] The Convention, a leading commentator has written, was drafted "not to protect States but individuals.... [Giving] the individual access to an international organ which is competent to afford him a remedy even against the government of his national State ... was a remarkable innovation in international law."[19] All twenty-three governments that had ratified the Convention by early 1992 have accepted Article 25, which permits filing of individual petitions and requires that "the High Contracting Parties who have made such a declaration [recognizing the competence of the Commission to receive petitions] undertake not to hinder in any way the effective exercise of this right."[20] The signing of the Ninth Protocol to the Convention in November 1990, permitting individuals and NGOs to address petitions directly to the European Court, will (when ratified and in force) mark another major step.

One should not assume, however, that the European Commission, which (like the European Court) includes as many members as ratifying States, readily takes on complaints for investigation and possible resolution. Comparable to the American Supreme Court in its grant of *certiorari*, the Commission does not act substantively on the overwhelming majority of communications sent to it. More than 6,800 individual communications poured into the Commission in its first nineteen years; a mere 127 were declared admissible, leading to 31 reports to the Committee of Ministers.[21] Both the number of applications (provisional files) and the number declared admissible have increased: at four-year intervals, the respective figures were: 1977, 2,181 provisional files/32 declared admissible; 1981, 2,672/21; 1985, 2,831/70; 1989, 4,900/95. In global terms, between 1955 and 1989 the European Commission opened 46,698 provisional files and took decisions on 14,241 of them, declaring 12,272 inadmissible. Some 355 were decided on their merits, of which 84 reached friendly settlement, and 33 were eliminated for lack of information.[22] However, as several commentators have remarked, the detailed, careful examination admissible complaints receive, and the willingness of governments (through recommendations made to the Council of Ministers) to accept and implement Commission and Court decisions, have resulted in a remarkable expansion of the civil and political liberties of Europeans.[23] Further, the ratification of (by early 1992) eight protocols to the European Convention steadily expanded the purview of the European system.

Different in many respects are the history and powers of the Inter-American Commission on Human Rights. It was established in 1959 by action of the Foreign Ministers of the Organization of American States (OAS). A decade later, the American Convention on Human Rights was adopted by the OAS; by 1978, this Convention had come into force, establishing the Inter-American Court of Human Rights as a companion body to the Commission. (As a result, the Commission functions as both an organ of the OAS, based on its charter and the 1948 American Declaration on the Rights and Duties of Man, and as an organ of the American Convention.) It has confronted human abuses arguably far more severe than in Western Europe.[24] Highly repressive, authoritarian governments in such States as Argentina, Chile, El Salvador, Guatemala, Haiti, and Uruguay made "disappearances" of political activists a fact of daily life. Basic freedoms were challenged to an extent unknown in North Atlantic countries—and, indeed, in the great majority of African countries. Legal niceties aside, the Inter-American Commission confronted issues far more serious than those facing the European Commission. Its formal and informal powers, outlined in the following paragraph, fell far short of what was needed; nonetheless, despite the limits of the OAS Charter and the Inter-American Convention, the Commission worked creatively to enhance its impact. For example, if a State failed to respond within six months to the Commission's request for information about a petition, the allegations made in it were deemed to be true. Needless to say, such a step increased the rapidity and detail of countries' responses!

Petitions, complaints, and other communications may be submitted to the Commission, as spelled out at some length in Articles 34–51 of the Convention.[25] Any State adhering to the American Convention agrees that its citizens have the right to file complaints directly with the Commission; under the European Convention, as already noted, ratifying governments had to grant this right specially. This ease of access contrasts sharply with the reality of the workload, however. The Commission includes a mere seven members, served by a small secretariat, who usually meet for two brief sessions annually. By contrast, the European Commission comprises one member for each High Contracting Party, each chosen for his or her personal expertise; the Court contains one member for each Council of Europe member. The Inter-American Commission cannot cope with the flood of petitions by any stretch of the imagination.[26] With respect to the Inter-American Court of Human Rights, only the Commission and the States that are parties to the Convention may file cases involving individuals with the Court. And, although the Court's judgments are final and not subject to appeal, these judgments must be enforced through the OAS General Assembly.

Of these two systems, the stronger enforcement powers obviously rest with the European Commission. The Council of Ministers, responsible for enforcement of the findings of the European Commission and the Court, can count on the prior acceptance by party States of jurisdiction in their domestic affairs. The European Commission's impact, as already noted, has been significant. The companion European Court has reached momentous decisions overriding national laws in, for example, inheritance rights of illegitimate children, requirements for trade union membership, corporal punishment, and extradition in capital punishment cases. Its mandatory jurisdiction has been accepted by all members as of early 1992.

The Inter-American Commission and Court, with briefer histories, have naturally considered fewer cases. Far fewer States have accepted mandatory jurisdiction. But these records of accomplishment must be accompanied by recognition of special circumstances. Robertson's comparison of the European and American systems merits quotation:

It is plain that they are immeasurably different. The two Commissions operate in quite different circumstances, one might almost say at quite different levels. The European Commission has, with very rare exceptions, been concerned with what might be called the finer points of human rights law.... [It] has almost always had the full co-operation of the governments concerned and the full support of its parent organisation, the Council of Europe. The Inter-American Commission, on the other hand, has had to deal with problems of a quite different order: arbitrary arrests on a massive scale, systematic use of torture, scores or hundreds of "disappeared persons," total absence of judicial remedies, and other flagrant violations of civilised standards. In dealing with such cases it has found the governments concerned more like antagonists than willing partners.[27]

In its powers and functioning—and, more important, in the challenges to human rights it must confront—the African Commission on Human and Peoples' Rights resembles the Inter-American Commission far more than the European. It faces similar issues, and confronts serious doubts from national leaders about its efficacy. Let us turn specifically to the African Commission and examine whether, given its currently shallow foundations, it can effectively promote and potentially protect human rights in signatory States.

THE ACTIVITIES OF THE AFRICAN COMMISSION

Apart from stipulating the means of election and its reporting relationship, the African Charter, which entered into force in October 1986, offers only general guidance about what the Commission should do, and how it should conduct its business. The *what* was satisfied in 1988 by adoption of a "Program of Action," the *how* by adoption of Rules of Procedure and Guidelines for Periodic National Reports.

Briefly, the African Charter sets the Commission's membership at "eleven members chosen from amongst African personalities of the highest reputation, known for their high morality, integrity, impartiality and competence in matters of human and peoples' rights." They are elected for six-year terms by the Assembly of Heads of State and Government, based on nominations by States parties; Commission members select their own Chairman and Vice-Chairman; the OAU Secretary-General provides staff and services.

According to Article 41, the Commission's functions are largely promotional:

The functions of the Commission shall be:
1. To promote Human and Peoples' Rights and in particular:
    a. To collect documents, undertake studies and researches on African problems in the field of human and peoples' rights, organize seminars, symposia and conferences, disseminate information, encourage national and local institutions concerned with human and peoples' rights, and should the case arise, give its views or make recommendations to Governments.
    b. To formulate and lay down, principles and rules aimed at solving legal problems relating to human and peoples' rights and fundamental freedoms upon which African Governments may base their legislation.
    c. To cooperate with other African and international institutions concerned with the promotion and protection of human and peoples' rights.

2. Ensure the protection of human and peoples' rights under conditions laid down by the present Charter.

3. Interpret all the provisions of the present Charter at the request of a State Party, an institution of the OAU or an African organization recognized by the OAU.

4. Perform any other tasks which may be entrusted to it by the Assembly of Heads of State and Government.

The Commission "may resort to any appropriate method of investigation," and may hear from the OAU Secretary-General "or any other person capable of enlightening it." In common with the American and European Conventions, the African Charter provides that the African Commission may deal with a matter only after local remedies have been exhausted, unless achieving these remedies "would be unduly prolonged." In instances of communications from one State party involving actions of another, the Commission shall attempt to reach an amicable solution; its report of "fact and findings" shall be sent to the Assembly, and may include recommendations. "Other" communications may be considered by vote of a majority of Commission members with several provisos: if their authors are indicated; if they are "compatible" with the OAU and African Charters; if they are "not written in disparaging or insulting language" directed against the State or the OAU; if they are not based exclusively on media reports; if local remedies have been exhausted (unless such procedure would be "unduly prolonged"); if they are submitted within a reasonable period; and if they do not deal with cases already settled by the States involved. As of late 1990, the Commission had received 105 petitions, examined them in confidential session, and had yet to make public any steps it may have taken relative to them.[28] If communications, in the Commission's judgment, "reveal the existence of a series of serious or massive violations of human and peoples' rights," the Commission shall "draw the attention of the Assembly" to these special cases; the Assembly, in turn, may request an in-depth study and factual report, accompanied by findings and recommendations. All matters considered by the Commission remain confidential until the Assembly decides otherwise, at which point its report shall be published. In short, the African Charter not only leaves to its major political arm any possible implementation of steps, but also seems to hamstring the Commission from taking significant steps on its own initiative.

The Commission approved its Program of Action at its second session (Dakar, February 1988). Three major categories exist: research and information activities, quasi-legislative activities, and cooperation activities. The following summarizes steps envisaged in each category:

A. Research and Information Activities

1. Establishment of African Library and a Documentation Centre on Human Rights;
2. Printing and dissemination of the African Charter on Human and Peoples' Rights including its Rules of Procedure;

3. Publication of an African Review on Human and Peoples' Rights;

4. Periodical radio broadcasts and television programmes on Human Rights in Africa;

5. Integration of Teaching of Human Rights in the Syllabi of secondary education;

6. Proclamation of a Human Rights Day;

7. Participation in the bicentenary activities of the declaration on the rights of man and of the citizen, 1789;

8. Institution of a prize for and a competition on Human Rights;

9. Recommendation on the Establishment of National Human Rights Committees;

10. Recommendation on the Establishment of Human Rights Institutes;

11. Symposia or Seminars on Apartheid.

B. Quasi-Legislative Activities

1. Charter ratification campaign within countries which have not yet ratified it;

2. Ratification of Human Rights Treaties prepared by international organizations (United Nations, ILO, etc.);

3. Introduction of the provisions of the Charter in the constitutions of States.

C. Co-operation Activities

1. Co-operation with international interstate or non-governmental organizations: European Commission, American Commission, United Nations Commission, International Commission of Jurists, International Academy of Human Rights, Amnesty International;

2. Co-operation with African organizations: Inter-African Union of Lawyers, Association of African Jurists, Association of African International Law;

3. Periodic Reports of States.[29]

Commission members also established means to deal with communications from one State party against another (in accordance with Article 47 of the African Charter), and communications or complaints filed by "physical and moral persons" (in accordance with Article 55 of the Charter).

At its fourth regular session (Cairo, October 1988), Commission members debated at length how periodic reports submitted by State parties should be considered and adopted formal guidelines.[30] In common with other major human rights conventions, the African Charter relies primarily upon periodic reports from State parties on "legislative or other measures taken with a view to giving effect to the rights and freedoms recognized and guaranteed by the present Charter." To provide a satisfactory long-term basis for consideration, the Commission decided that States should submit initial general reports, followed by detailed periodic reports, as a "channel of constructive dialogue" between the Commission and ratifying states. In all cases, the foundation is provided by the general legal framework; the periodic reports examine changes. Three pages of the guidelines are devoted to civil and political rights

(Articles 2–14), while nearly eighteen pages address economic and social rights (Articles 15–18).

The Commission's Rules of Procedure, adopted in February 1988, were patterned on those of comparable groups.[31] The Commission meets twice annually, for two-week sessions, with a formal agenda. Each member must attend in person. (The OAU Secretary-General or his representative may also attend, but cannot participate in deliberations or votes; States with particular interest in an item can be invited, as can national liberation movements; specialized institutions with which the OAU has reached agreements may be represented in public sessions and can participate, without voting rights, in deliberations on issues of concern to them; NGOs may send appointed authorized observers to the Commission's public sessions.) As a general principle, the Commission's meetings are private—although an increasing number are being held in public. Final summary minutes of all sessions, public or private, are "intended for general distribution unless, under exceptional circumstances, the Commission decides otherwise"; the Commission's report to the OAU Assembly on communications (Articles 47 and 49) is confidential, unless the Assembly decides otherwise; on the other hand, periodic reports submitted by State parties to the Charter are subject to general distribution, while the annual report of the Commission to the Assembly is published following its consideration by the Assembly. The eleven members (seven of whom constitute a quorum, and each of whom has one vote) elect a Chairman and Vice-Chairman for two-year terms. Committees and Working Groups may be established after consultations with the OAU Secretary-General; subcommissions of experts may be created with the prior approval of the OAU Assembly. Staff support for the Commission comes from the OAU secretariat.

The African Charter thus grants the African Commission on Human and Peoples' Rights limited powers. It can only (for cases involving the complaint of one State party against another) obtain information, attempt to reach an amicable solution, report to the States concerned and the OAU Assembly of Heads of State and Government, and "make such recommendations as it deems useful" to the Assembly. Similarly, for "special cases (based on other communications accepted by the Commission) which reveal the existence of a series of serious or massive violations of human and peoples' rights," the Commission "shall draw the attention" of the Assembly to them, with the Assembly alone being able to request the Commission "to undertake an in-depth study of these cases and make a factual report, accompanied by its findings and recommendations." The Commission formally thus confronts ambiguities, lacunae, and restrictions on its potential activities in its Charter and its Program of Action. Established as an organ to *promote* human rights, the Commission does not enjoy a clear mandate to *protect* them. Only by pressing the limits of the Charter's wording, through a significantly higher level of activity by Commissioners and the secretariat, can there be escape from the existing limits.

Prior to the establishment of its formal headquarters, the Commission met peripatetically in the national capitals of its members: in Addis Ababa, 2 November 1987 (ceremonial opening); in Dakar, 8–13 February 1988; in Libreville, 18–28 April 1988; in Cairo, 17–26 October 1988; and in Benghazi, 3–14 April 1989. It then started to meet exclusively in Banjul: first at a special session to inaugurate the headquarters, 12–14 June 1989; and thereafter on 23 October–4 November 1989; 18–28 April 1990; and 8–21 October 1990. A new pattern is now emerging, alternating meetings between Banjul and another African capital. The Commission met in Lagos, 18–25 March 1991, in Banjul 7–14 October 1991, and in Tunis 2–10 March 1992.[32] The establishment of a permanent seat removed from the OAU headquarters in Addis Ababa facilitates the Commission's quasi-independence; however, the Banjul office has limited equipment, staff, and effectiveness; meetings outside Banjul impose problems of coordination, but are attractive since the host government meets part of the costs.

Nine of the current Commission members were initially elected at the 1987 OAU summit and have been reelected as their terms expired. They represent, as should be expected, geographic balance, with Commissioners drawn (as of early 1992) from Botswana, Congo, Egypt, Gabon, Gambia, Libya, Mali, Nigeria, Senegal, and Tanzania.[33] All are males; all have legal or political backgrounds; many, in fact, are their country's Attorney General or Minister of Justice, in other words the official against whom a human rights complaint might well be lodged! Isaac Nguema (Gabon) was elected Chair in 1988, serving in that position until November 1990, when he was succeeded by U. Oji Umozurike (Nigeria); Ibrahim Badawi (Egypt) was chosen in October 1991.

Let us look in more detail at the operational problems the Commission has experienced.

The obligation to submit detailed reports has not been taken seriously by most States. The reporting obligation may appear relatively simple, yet governments appear reluctant to undertake the labor necessary to satisfy Commission mandates. The Commission itself has given the reports only limited scrutiny, at least as of early 1992. Although the African Charter entered into force in 1986, several years elapsed before the first reports, prepared in accordance with Article 62, were submitted and examined. Since the Commission wants initial reports to provide a detailed baseline for subsequent examination, documents that furnish few particulars hamstring the group's potential effectiveness. The initial reports from Libya, Rwanda, and Tunisia were considered at the ninth ordinary session (Lagos, April 1991).[34] The results were disappointing to the Commissioners and outside observers. The reports themselves were brief, referring to laws, constitutional provisions, or the like without providing precise texts; copies of the reports were not made available in advance; translations were not provided; an average of ninety minutes was devoted to examining each.[35] Even more striking was the hiatus at the tenth session (Banjul, October 1991). Although reports from four countries were scheduled for discussion, the Commission's Secretary failed to inform the States concerned; since representatives should be present to respond to Commissioners' questions, examination had to be postponed. A somewhat similar set of events transpired at the eleventh session, where representatives of Egypt and Tanzania were able to attend on short notice, but examination of Nigeria and Togo was deferred; however, the discussions were detailed and insightful.

It will no doubt take many years before the reports provide the detail Commission members require for meaningful assessment—assuming, of course, that they have sufficient time, staff resources, and NGO advice to give adequate attention to detail. The Commission must recognize that serious scrutiny can occur only if states are pressured to submit detailed, timely reports, only if the Commission's secretariat circulates them on a timely basis to NGOs as well as Commissioners, and only if the Commissioners themselves make serious efforts to "read between the lines" and utilize relevant additional information.

Second, Commission members have lacked sufficient competent staff and, until recently, adequate facilities. Headquarters have been established in Banjul, where the Gambian government provides three floors of a four-story building. An Information and Documentation Center is envisaged, but has yet (as of March 1992) to function effectively at the Banjul headquarters. Initial operations were seriously hampered by lack of basic equipment and supplies—no copy or fax machine for most of the first five years, limited files, little computing capacity—in addition to paucity of qualified professional staff. Tape recordings of sessions were not made until the tenth session, nor have final summary minutes of public and private sessions been prepared and circulated. The incumbent Secretary (appointed by the OAU) has been strongly criticized for inefficiency. The serious financial problems of the parent OAU have taken a toll on its newest body, meaning the Commission has had to seek other funding for its activities. Special assistance from the European Community and United Nations Voluntary Fund for Advisory Services, each of which has committed about $200,000, has provided the bare minimum for the secretariat's functioning. Additional resources have been promised by the Swedish government, which sent a representative to the eleventh session. Two consultants, Adama Dieng of the International Commission of Jurists and Wolfgang Benedek of the University of Graz, Austria, recommended ways of enhancing the Commission's promotional activities at its tenth session; revisions are needed in the Rules of Procedure, and more precise goals based on the Program of Action must be articulated. Unless competent staff are recruited and an increasing number of Commissioners spend significant amounts of time investigating the complaints and reports filed, the recent improvements already made and proposed will have little effect.

Confidentiality of proceedings remains a sore point. As Benedek pointedly observed, "the Rules of Procedure of the African Commission [with respect to *in camera* sittings] are unnecessarily restrictive."[36] Rule 32, with its "general principle" of private sessions, has outlived its usefulness—yet remains in force as of this writing. NGOs have been particularly critical, and continue to press for a new principle of public sittings. Such pressure has borne fruit. The ninth session, held in Lagos in March 1991, marked a turning point, as all meetings save those dealing with protection activities and the report to the OAU were opened to observers. Benedek notes three reasons for the shift in practice, if not yet in formal rules: the increased self-confidence the Commission has gained over time; the growing number of qualified observers; and the need that the work of the Commission be understood and supported by the public in order to be effective.[37] Members seem to accept these factors. Further important developments occurred at the eleventh session, held in Tunis in March 1992. Specifically,

- constructive, detailed examination of initial reports from Egypt and Tanzania were carried out in public session; anticipated discussions of Nigeria and Togo were deferred, however, apparently since these states had not been informed by the secretariat that they should attend and answer questions in open sessions;

- resolutions were adopted on the freedom of association and the right to legal recourse, both intended to clarify and in some respects expand the obligations State parties hold under the African Charter on Human and Peoples' Rights;

- constructive though by no means tension-free dialogue with NGOs (nongovernmental human rights organizations) took place, both during the formal sessions of the Commission and in a prior workshop organized by the International Commission of Jurists;

- continued willingness by the Commission to conduct much of its business in public session was evident, although all consideration of protective (as contrasted with promotional) activity and financial matters continued to take place behind closed doors; and

- greater activity by Commissioners was promised, with plans for focused seminars, strengthening of the secretariat, potential involvement as observers in the Malian presidential elections, and establishment of inter-session working groups, funding permitting.

The two resolutions resulted in part from NGO pressure, based on the narrow wording of the African Charter on Human and Peoples' Rights. Freedom of association is essential for the effective functioning of political parties, unions, interest groups, and the like. The Charter limits this right as follows: "Every individual shall have the right to free association provided that he abides by the law" (Article 10, paragraph 1). In other words, national legislation overrides broader guarantees. As noted earlier in this chapter, such "clawback" clauses are found elsewhere in the Charter, reflecting the unwillingness of African leaders in the early 1980s to restrict state powers. Unfortunately, the resolution (initially drafted by the Arab Association for Human Rights) did little to correct the inherent problems of Article 10. Although its preambular paragraphs refer to the Universal Declaration of Human Rights, the International Covenant on Civil and Political Rights, and a 1980 resolution of the Sub-Commission on the Prevention of Discrimination and Protection of Minorities, the operative paragraphs merely state that "competent authorities should not limit the exercise of this Freedom," while further indicating that "Any regulation of the exercise of this right to association should be consistent with states' obligations under the African Charter." Far more significant was the resolution (originally drafted by Interights) on the right to recourse procedure and fair trial. Its wording broadened Article 7 of the African Charter by entitling individuals to "have adequate time and facilities for the preparation of their defence . . . examine . . . witnesses against them . . . have the free assistance of an interpreter . . . [and] have a right of appeal." The resolution also urges State parties "to provide the needy with legal aid." Although this wording may seem modest, it is nonetheless an important extension of the relevant article.

Finally, among the positive results of the meeting, the Commission established its budget and moved ahead with its Program of Action. Consideration of specific activities, as well as of the Commission's finances and of petitions, took place in executive session. With respect to funding, representatives of the European Community (EC), the Swedish government, and the UN Center for Human Rights discussed staffing and equipment needs, indicating their willingness to provide additional support. Efforts will be made to hire a documentalist, translator, and administrative officer. With respect to activities, the Commission further updated the general program adopted at the second session and the consultants' report submitted to the tenth session. Steps hopefully will be taken in the near future to establish an Information and Documentation Center to serve the Commission (including translation, publication, and research). The Commission will organize a series of workshops and seminars, including implementation of the African Charter in national legal systems (to be held in Banjul late October 1992 in cooperation with the Raoul Wallenberg Institute), and African refugees and displaced persons (to be held in early 1993 in cooperation with the United Nations High Commissioner for Refugees). Other seminars may include human rights in postapartheid South Africa, popular participation, and the like.

Perhaps the greatest problem for the Commission lies outside its control. Human rights NGOs have yet to take root in much of Africa, with the result that the Commission lacks independent, Africa-based sources of information about human rights abuses and domestic advocacy groups for its activities.[38]

Effective protection of human rights within individual countries depends not only on government institutions and policies, but also on citizen awareness and participation. Human rights NGOs play a central role. Their absence or weakness provides a further ground of concern. As Scoble accurately asserted, human rights are not "given"; they are "taken."[39] The nascent (or is feeble a better adjective?) nature of African human rights NGOs emerges clearly in the directory recently compiled by Human Rights Internet.[40] In close to twenty OAU member States, no organization working openly for human rights or social justice could be identified; in another dozen or so, the editors found only one or two institutions somewhat peripheral to these aims. As the directory's editors aptly note, many factors must be taken into account: the absence of "political space" for such organizations, which are often considered subversive; limited freedom of association; and the slight international attention given human rights violations in independent Africa. Only South Africa—which accounts for over a third of the organizations described in the volume—exhibits a rich profusion of human rights groups.[41] Should NGOs become major partners with the Commission in examining annual reports, the Commission may significantly enhance its effectiveness.

Here, once again, the eleventh session provided some basis for hope. Prior to the Commission's meeting, the International Commission of Jurists convened a two-day workshop attended by three Commissioners, twenty-five African human rights NGOs, fifteen international human rights NGOs, observers from the European Community and the French and Swedish governments (among others), and other consultants.[42] In my estimation, the most important results were (1) greater communication among NGOs (whose members caucused at length about means of maintaining contact) and (2) better understanding of how NGOs can work with the Commission in protecting as well as promoting human rights in Africa. Some NGO representatives expressed impatience with what was perceived as the slow pace of Commission action, diffident attitudes of a few Commissioners, the difficulties of the secretariat, and the like. The absence of a woman member of the Commission was often noted in the workshop.[43] The main point of the workshop was enhancing awareness of the Commission, including submission of petitions, transmission of information about States' reports, promotion of the Charter, and related matters. The general report of the workshop (delivered formally to the Commission early in the eleventh session) protested the detention of human rights activists in Chad and Ivory Coast, urged Commissioners to be "imaginative and courageous," pointed to the incompatability of simultaneous service with the Commission and a government, criticized the secretariat, and "strongly regretted" the lack of opportunity for NGOs to assist the Commission in examining reports. Most of the morning of 3 March was utilized by NGOs for direct statements to the Commission, speakers coming from (among others) the International Commission of Jurists, Interights, the Arab Lawyers' Union, the Constitutional Rights Project (Nigeria), the African Centre for Democracy and Human Rights Studies, the Catholic Commission for Justice and Peace (Zimbabwe), and Amnesty International. At the conclusion of the session, Chairman Badawi emphasized the complementary roles of the NGOs and the Commission.

The experiences of the European and American Commissions show that several years may have to pass before the infrastructure and awareness necessary for major impact are established. It seems unlikely that any organization of this sort, with its inherent challenge to the "normal" way of transacting business, could rapidly transform unsatisfactory human rights situations in any OAU member State. Nonetheless, even given the restrictive nature of the African Charter, the Rules of Procedure, and the caution of the Commissioners, significantly more can be done immediately. On-site visits could be made by the Commission to countries with severe human rights problems. Even greater contacts could be made with human rights NGOs. The impact likely will be felt most in states whose leaders begrudgingly recognize human rights, but whose efforts can be encouraged by the African Charter's existence. The really difficult cases—where widespread abuses of human rights stem from civil war or ethnic conflict—will not be influenced as much, unless the Commission pursues a far more public agenda. It has yet to make an open announcement about serious situations such as Rwanda and Sudan, both of which are under review for possible reference to the OAU Assembly.

The African Commission on Human and Peoples' Rights is reformist in nature, not revolutionary. It works within and through existing systems, not against them. Many factors interact to ensure it will play a relatively quiet role in African politics in the near future. Not only the state-centric, conservative nature of the African Charter and the OAU Charter, but also the relatively legalistic outlook of the individuals selected, the limited support provided by the OAU, the nonincorporation of Charter norms into domestic law, and relative impotence of human rights NGOs[44] account for the Commission's relatively low profile in its early years. Those who expect the African Commission rapidly to ameliorate human rights conditions within ratifying States do not understand current political realities in Africa. As the former Chairman of the Commission wrote:

To live up to expectations, the Commission will have to adopt a liberal and vigorous approach in interpreting the Charter.... The Banjul Charter has cleared any doubts that may persist and African states cannot contract out of international customary law of respect for human rights. The Charter merely reaffirmed the customary law principle for the avoidance of doubt but extended the range of rights. The provisions may be, in some cases, difficult to enforce but they represent a Charter of struggle for African peoples whose expectations are now strengthened and legitimated.

The enforcement mechanism is unsatisfactory. In the absence of a court and effective measures for a breach, the Charter may well be a paper tiger except for effective public opinion that may be whipped up against the offender.... The Commission will have to develop its practice beyond the narrow confines of the express words of the Charter.[45]

Or, to quote from a 1989 workshop sponsored by the African Association of International Law and various Nordic human rights institutes, the African Commission has "lacked adequate equipment, resources and support to make it truly operational."[46]

Significant internal protection of human rights in Africa depends ultimately on the active, effective role of African governments, with pressure and assistance from outside, and far greater activity by human rights NGOs. The African Commission on Human and Peoples' Rights will find functioning as a body for the promotion of human rights difficult—unless, of course, the OAU Assembly of Heads of State and Government is dramatically transformed in its composition and outlook and awareness of human rights spreads more widely through Africa.

It would be entirely inappropriate to write off the Commission as ineffectual, however. It is benefiting from more self-critical attitudes shown by leaders at recent OAU summits. The global moves toward democratization have encouraged a positive climate for basic civil and political freedoms. External donors have placed "strings" increasingly on their assistance, demanding effective human rights records. Most important, members of the Commission and human rights NGOs have started to press (though in differing fashions) to enhance the group's effectiveness and to expand its ambit from promotional to protective activites. A communications network among NGOs, and between NGOs and the Commission itself, has emerged as a result of the International Commission of Jurists workshops. Hence, although the concept of domestic sovereignty with which this chapter started remains a paramount concern of the OAU, it is being eroded as the promotion and protection of human rights have become goals appropriately sought by transnational bodies. The African Commission, in its relatively quiet fashion, and an increasing number of NGOs in a more public manner, have taken the needs of millions of African citizens to heart.

NOTES

I am especially grateful for the incisive observations of Jack Donnelly, David Forsythe, Theodore S. Orlin, U. Oji Umozurike, and Laurie Wiseberg on earlier drafts of this chapter, and to the United States Institute of Peace for financial support. Earlier versions of parts of this chapter have been published as "The Organisation of African Unity and the Promotion of Human Rights," *Journal of Modern African Studies* 29 (4) (December 1991), pp. 535–555 and as "The African Commission on Human and Peoples' Rights: A Five-Year Report and Assessment," *Human Rights Quarterly* 14 (1) (n.d.), pp. 43–61.

    1. Claude E. Welch, Jr., "The OAU and International Recognition: Lessons from

Uganda," in Yassin El-Ayouty, ed., *The Organization of African Unity After Ten Years: Comparative Perspectives* (New York: Praeger, 1975), pp. 103–117.

2. U.O. Umozurike, "The Domestic Jurisdiction Clause in the OAU Charter," *African Affairs* 78 (April 1979), p. 202.

3. Amin was removed when Tanzanian forces, responding to an earlier Ugandan invasion, not only expelled them from Tanzanian territory, but continued all the way to the capital, Kampala, to install a new government.

4. Bokassa, too, fell as a result of external military intervention. A coup d'etat, mounted with obvious blessing from France, removed the hated ruler. Extensive documentation of Bokassa's human rights abuses incited and justified the French role.

5. A concise history of its drafting can be found in Edward Kannyo, "The Banjul Charter on Human and Peoples' Rights: Genesis and Political Background," in Claude E. Welch, Jr., and Ronald I. Meltzer, eds., *Human Rights and Development in Africa* (Albany: State University of New York Press, 1984), pp. 128–151. The text of the Banjul Charter appears on pp. 317–329. The Charter can also be found in major collections of human rights documents, such as Albert P. Blaustein, Roger S. Clark, and Jay A. Sigler, *Human Rights Sourcebook* (New York: Paragon House, 1987), pp. 632–645.

6. A convenient, article-by-article comparison of the Banjul Charter with the UDHR, the International Covenants, and the European and American Conventions appears in Welch and Meltzer, *Human Rights and Development in Africa*, pp. 331–337.

7. A.H. Robertson, *Human Rights in the World*, 3rd ed. (Manchester: Manchester University Press, 1989), p. 216.

8. Among the sharpest critics are Richard Gittleman, "The Banjul Charter on Human and Peoples' Rights: A Legal Analysis," and Harry Scoble, "Human Rights Non-Governmental Organizations in Black Africa: The Problems and Prospects in the Wake of the Banjul Charter," both in Welch and Meltzer, *Human Rights and Development in Africa*, pp. 152–176 and 177–203.

9. B. Obinna Okere, "The Protection of Human Rights in Africa and the African Charter on Human and Peoples' Rights: A Comparative Analysis with the European and American Systems," *Human Rights Quarterly* 6 (1984), p. 158.

10. *West Africa*, 11–17 March 1991, p. 337.

11. Emmanuel G. Bello, "The Mandate of the African Commission on Human and Peoples' Rights," *African Journal of International Law* 1 (1) (1988), p. 55.

12. Gittleman, "The Banjul Charter," p. 159.

13. Needless to say, numerous calls have been made for establishment of such a court, as witness the Judicial Colloquium on the Domestic Application of International Human Rights Norms, held in Banjul in November 1990. (For a summary, see *Interights Bulletin* 5 (1990), p. 39.) More significantly, the 1991 summit meeting of the OAU, held in Abuja, Nigeria, endorsed a draft treaty establishing the African Economic Community, in stages. The first three stages (respectively no more than five, eight, and ten years) would strengthen existing regional communities or create new ones, where needed, initiate removal of intraregional tariff and nontariff barriers, and create regional free trade areas and common external tariffs. The fourth stage (two years) would involve imposing a common continental external tariff; the fifth stage would result in creation of an African common market; the sixth stage would make the continent a full economic union. In terms of human rights, a Court of

Justice would come into existence upon ratification of the treaty, and a Pan-African Parliament, elected by universal continental suffrage, would be established in the final stage. Court decisions would be binding on member States of the AEC. *West Africa,* 27 May–2 June 1991, p. 846.

14. Fatsah Ouguergouz, "La Commission Africaine des droits de l'homme et des peuples: Presentation et bilan d'activités (1988–1989)," Paris: CNRS, 1990, p. 570. Author's translation.

15. In a footnote to history, some participants at the 1945 San Francisco conference that drafted the UN Charter suggested that the Charter provide directly for protection of human rights, in addition to the clauses for promotion of them. This proposal was defeated largely through American and British pressure.

16. Howard Tolley, Jr., *The UN Commission on Human Rights* (Boulder, Colo.: Westview, 1987), p. 17.

17. Convenient summaries of Commission and Sub-Commission discussions and activities appear regularly in *Human Rights Quarterly.* Historical details can be found in Tolley, *The UN Commission.*

18. Burns H. Weston, Robin Ann Lukes, and Kelly M. Hnatt, "Regional Human Rights Regimes: A Comparison and Appraisal," *Vanderbilt Journal of Transnational Law* 20 (1987), pp. 585–637.

19. Robertson, *Human Rights in the World,* p. 109.

20. Reprinted in Blaustein, Clark, and Sigler, *Human Rights Sourcebook,* p. 465.

21. European Commission of Human Rights, *Survey of Activities and Statistics* (Strasbourg: Council of Europe, 1989), p. 16.

22. Ibid.

23. The companion European Social Charter, which entered into force in 1961, lacks such elaborate enforcement procedures, as is common with "second generation" rights. Ratifying states must submit reports every two years to an independent Committee of Experts.

24. A significant exception should be noted. The Council of Europe, membership in which is limited to democratic states, confronted an obvious challenge to its basic values when the Greek military junta seized control in 1967. Faced with an authoritarian government determined to brook no challenge to its domestic policies, the Council of Europe confronted the lacuna common to regional human rights regimes: the weakness of enforcement mechanisms. Greece's decision to drop its membership as the European Court was about to act on a challenge to its participation temporarily resolved the situation, but only the collapse of the junta in 1974 brought significant change.

25. The entire Convention is reprinted in Blaustein, Clark, and Sigler, *Human Rights Sourcebook,* pp. 551–572 (Articles 34–51 on pp. 561–565); the Commission's Statute and its Regulations appear respectively on pp. 580–586 and 586–606.

26. For example, during a one-month on-site visit to Argentina in September 1979, the Commission received 4,153 new complaints! Robertson, *Human Rights in the World,* p. 194, n.10.

27. Robertson, *Human Rights in the World,* p. 173.

28. No details appear in the report about their disposition in the third and fourth activity reports of the Commission (AFR/COM/HPR/AN.RPT/3 and AHG/ 182(XXVII)). However, in the preceding report (AHG/165(XXV), p. 11), the Commission reported having received thirty-eight communications, of which fourteen had

been decided upon with respect to admissibility: three were inadmissible, six dealt with a decision taken or communication by the Commission, and five cases "will be considered at future sessions." At a conference attended by the author on 25 June 1991, Chairman Umozurike indicated that sixteen communications had been acted upon at the ninth ordinary session and that, thanks to Commission pressure, two detainees had been released. As of late 1991, the Commission seems to have acted in some fashion on thirty-five cases, a small number considering the magnitude of human rights issues in Africa, but indicative of the low profile the Commission has maintained to date. At the eleventh session (March 1992), the Commission considered complaints from Cameroon, Malawi, Nigeria, Tanzania, and Tunisia, and decided in most cases to seek further information from the governments concerned.

29. *Human Rights Law Journal* 9 (1988), p. 352; capitalization and spelling as in original.

30. "Guidelines for National Periodic Reports," Addis Ababa: OAU document AFR/COMM/HPR.5 (IV).

31. OAU document AFR/COM/HRP.1 (II); a more convenient source is *Human Rights Law Journal* 9 (1988), pp. 333–349.

32. Four reports have been published by the Commission: its first activity report, adopted by the Commission 28 April 1988, covering the Commission from its inception 2 November 1989 to the date of adoption; the second (OAU document AHG/165 (XXV)), covering the period 19 April 1988 to 14 June 1989; the third (Commission document AFR/COM/HPR/An. Rpt/3), covering the sixth and seventh ordinary sessions; and the fourth (OAU document AHG/182 (XVII)), covering the eighth and ninth ordinary sessions (since a quorum was not present at the ninth session, the Commission did not officially adopt the report before presenting it to the Assembly). Somewhat handier sources include minutes of the first four sessions, published in *Human Rights Law Journal* 9 (1988), pp. 326–358 and minutes of the fifth session in *Human Rights Law Journal* 11 (1990), pp. 361–362. To quote the third activity report, "the Commission noted with concern that the General Secretariat [of the OAU] has not published the first and second reports of activity of the Commission apparently because of lack of funds." AFR/COM/HPR/An. Rpt/3, p. 5.

33. The 1992 death of Commissioner C.L.C. Mubanga-Chipoya (Zambia) opened the second vacancy in the Commission's history, the first having been created in 1989 by the resignation of Grace Ibingira (Uganda), and his replacement by Umozurike.

34. Representatives of all three countries were present for the discussions. Reports had also been received from Egypt, Nigeria, Tanzania, and Togo; the Nigerian report, originally scheduled for discussion at the Lagos meeting, was withdrawn by the government for revision. (The report itself, a brief three pages stapled to the table of contents of the Nigerian constitution, fell far short of the desired quality.) All four were scheduled for examination at the tenth regular session but, as noted in the text, notification was not sent and only two were discussed at the eleventh session.

35. By contrast, the UN Committee on Human Rights, established by the International Covenant on Civil and Political Rights, has devoted a full day and a half to examining initial reports submitted by State parties, according to Felice Gaer, Executive Director of the International League of Human Rights. (Remarks made 26 June (n.d.) at a conference on the African Commission in New York City.) The Commission follows the practice of having one of its members serve as *rapporteur* and chief commentator on a report, meaning that an unexpected absence can cause

deferral of consideration. It should be noted that discussion of both reports at the eleventh session lasted an average of two hours.

36. Wolfgang Benedek, "The Ninth Session of the African Commission on Human and Peoples' Rights," *Human Rights Law Journal* 12(5) (31 May 1991), p. 217.

37. Ibid.

38. This observation is not intended to criticize the excellent work of transnational human rights NGOs such as Africa Watch, Amnesty International, or the International Commission of Jurists, but to underscore the political value of having a significantly larger number of groups active in obtaining information, publicizing abuses, and working within their respective national systems for better protection of human rights.

39. Scoble, "Human Rights Non-Governmental Organizations," p. 177.

40. Laurie S. Wiseberg and Laura Reiner, eds., "Africa: Human Rights Directory and Bibliography," *Human Rights Internet Reporter* 12(4) (Winter 1988–1989).

41. Ibid., p. 6.

42. The International Commission of Jurists organized a similar session for NGOs at the tenth session, with generally positive results, and has been urged to continue the practice, dependent on financing.

43. The final report of the workshop reiterated a proposal that the Commission ask the OAU Assembly to elect women to the Commission. The Commission's draft resolution directed to the State parties, which asked them to give "due consideration . . . to the election of both men and women to the African Commission," was not voted upon by the Commissioners, who felt it represented a "sort of interference to tell the [OAU] summit who or who not to elect."

44. According to Scoble, the "obvious" explanation for the lack of secular human rights organizations south of the Sahara—the region's poverty—is incorrect. He puts the blame on the disjuncture between ethnic identity and national frontiers. Scoble, "Human Rights Non-Governmental Organizations," pp. 186–188.

45. U.O. Umozurike, "The Protection of Human Rights Under The Banjul (African) Charter on Human and Peoples' Rights," *African Journal of International Law* 1(1) (Summer 1988), pp. 82–83.

46. Wolfgang Benedek, "The Judiciary and Human Rights in Africa: The Banjul Seminar and the Training Workshop for a Core of Human Rights Advocates of November 1989," *Human Rights Law Journal* 11 (1990), p. 250.

6

The OAU and African Refugees

CHRISTOPHER J. BAKWESEGHA

INTRODUCTION

As a crisis-prone continent particularly since the 1980s, Africa has remained not only a land of paradoxes but also a continent where people have little time to talk of meaningful development, of supply or abundance, of leisure or happiness. Especially for the last ten years, the language of the time has remained basically the same: civil strife or inter-State wars; erratic rainfall patterns or persistent drought; crop failures or food deficits; burgeoning foreign debts and debt servicing; galloping inflation; devastating floods, cyclones, and earthquakes; massive influxes of refugees, returnees, and displaced persons; and emergency aid and rehabilitation programs.

Tragic pictures depicting the plight of thousands of emaciated Africans fleeing from areas of actual or potential hazards within or between nations, and ghastly images of death have become a common feature on our television screens and in our national and international news media. Government appeals for, and mobilization of, national and international resources through meetings, seminars, workshops, and conferences to battle with such hazards have clearly become the order of the day. A week hardly goes by without some mention in the international news media of an unusual hazard afflicting people somewhere on the continent and making them flee their familiar environments with the belief that any life outside their own home must, perforce, be more tolerable than the one they are currently experiencing. Quite frankly, where does the future of Africa lie? And what kind of continent are we handing over to our future leaders?

That the problem of refugees in Africa has reached unmanageable proportions is no longer in doubt. In terms of magnitude and complexity African refugees are increasingly becoming a nationality: in magnitude because their number of close to 6 million, one-third of the world's total refugee population of more than 15 million, exceeds the total population of more than Africa's ten least populated States; in complexity because they cut across virtually all major African cultural groupings. Furthermore, Africa's refugee population has almost become a permanent feature on our landscape, with one successful voluntary repatriation exercise giving birth to yet another explosive and refugee-generating situation, with programs of refugee-serving organizations growing almost out of proportion, and with the causes for asylum-seeking becoming more and more compelling.

As civil and inter-State wars, political oppression, abuse of human and peoples' rights, and economic deprivation coupled with natural disasters continue to rage Africa, refugees continue to arrive in greater numbers. Indeed, exile life has become the fate of millions of human beings in Africa, with people who have been refugees since their birth giving birth to yet another generation of refugees. Thus, today Africa's Least Developed Countries are not only suffering because of poverty, but also from shouldering the burden of millions of other countries' nationals in the form of refugees. More fundamentally, while the 1980s have been aptly described as "the lost decade in development for Africa," clearly the same decade can be described as "the tragic decade for refugees in Africa."

EVOLUTION OF AFRICA'S REFUGEE PROBLEM

Admittedly, worldwide, the issue of people moving from one place to another is something that has characterized man's life from time immemorial. Biblically men, women, and children are known to have fled the wrath of tyrants in the Roman City-States and in the Empire itself. In Africa, the stream of people looking for sanctuary is traceable long before the formal legal instruments on refugees were adopted by both the United Nations and the Organization of African Unity. Ethnic wars, famine, the search for better grazing land, slave raids, and colonial occupation led to the flight of thousands of people across national frontiers in search of security or justice, food or shelter.

In traditional African societies, where regional or national frontiers were so fluid, asylum-seekers used to cross to the neighboring country into the welcoming hands of their kith and kin. The assistance then given to asylum-seekers was both informal and unpublicized. The little that the asylum-seekers found within the host communities was shared equitably between the former and the latter, and no sharp line was drawn between the asylum-seekers and the host communities. Statistics concerning asylum-seekers then were neither institutionalized nor a subject of international concern. Most important, there were no refugee camps as we see them today, sprouting on the African landscape like undergrowths in a typical tropical rain forest.

Africa's refugee problem began to gain significant momentum toward the turn of the 1950s, when Africans started fleeing from the Algerian war of independence and from the South African regime and the Portuguese colonial administration. The problem, however, became an international concern in the early 1960s, when masses of refugees also began to flee from some other African countries that were attaining independence from the colonial powers. As more countries attained independence, the refugee population on the continent increased correspondingly.

For example, in 1964, when the refugee problem was first brought to the attention of the OAU, the estimated figure was 700,000; in 1969, 900,000, with a percentage increase of 29; 1 million in 1977, with a percentage increase between 1969 and 1977 of 11; 2 million in 1978, with a percentage increase over this one-year period of 100; 4 million in 1979, with a percentage increase of 100 over the one-year period; and 5 million in 1980, with a percentage increase of 25 between 1979 and 1980. Thereafter, Africa's refugee population stabilized and subsequently assumed a downward trend: 3.6 in 1981, with a percentage decrease of 28 between 1980 and 1981; 3 million in 1983, with a percentage decrease of 17 over the period of two years; and then 5 million in 1988, with a 67 percent decrease between 1983 and 1988. It then stabilized until early 1990, when events in Liberia and Somalia pushed the figure beyond the 5 million mark.

Africa's major refugee concentrations by order of their magnitude are: Eastern Africa, Southern Africa, Central Africa and Western Africa. If illustrated in figures a disheartening picture emerges.

Refugee Populations in Africa by Region

Region	Number of Refugees
Northern Region	
Algeria	170,000
Egypt	1,600
TOTAL	171,600
Western Region	
Benin	1,200
Ivory Coast	210,000
Guinea	310,000
Nigeria	6,700
Togo	3,500
Senegal	50,000
Sierra Leone	125,000
Ghana	6,000
Mauritania	22,000
TOTAL	734,400
Central Region	
Angola	56,500
Burundi	267,500

Cameroon	51,000
Central African Republic	3,100
Congo	2,000
Rwanda	22,200
Zaire	<u>340,700</u>
TOTAL	743,000

Eastern Region

Kenya	12,500
Uganda	112,000
Tanzania	265,150
Djibouti	1,300
Ethiopia	679,500
Somalia	834,000
Sudan	<u>745,000</u>
TOTAL	2,649,450

Southern Region

Botswana	2,100
Lesotho	3,950
Malawi	850,000
Swaziland	28,800
Zambia	143,600
Zimbabwe	<u>174,500</u>
TOTAL	1,202,950

AFRICA'S GRAND TOTAL REFUGEE POPULATION   5,501,500

Source: UNHCR, 1990. Countries with fewer than 1,000 refugees are not listed.

Furthermore, if statistics are anything to go by in appreciating the dimensions of the refugee problem borne by Africa's principal host countries, then it should be noted that in 1989:

1. Somalia, with a per capita income of US$280, had a refugee/national population ratio of 1:10;

2. Malawi, with a per capita income of US$160, had a refugee/national population ratio of 1:12;

3. Burundi, with a per capita income of US$240, had a refugee/national population ratio of 1:19;

4. Sudan, with a per capita income of US$320, had a refugee/national population ratio of 1:30;

5. Zambia, with a per capita income of US$300, had a refugee/national population ratio of 1:50; and

6. Ethiopia, with a per capita income of US$120, had a refugee/national population ratio of 1:60, although in Itang (one of the shelters in Southwest Ethiopia, where Sudanese refugees have taken refuge) this ratio was 1:5, indicating that Ethiopia,

which has remained the largest refugee-generating country in Eastern Africa, has now become a haven *par excellence* for refugees emanating from the Sudan and Somalia.

The question is: What has the OAU been doing since its inception about this problem of refugees, which at the moment appears to have grown almost out of proportion?

BACKGROUND TO OAU'S CONCERN WITH THE ISSUE OF REFUGEES

In the early 1960s, when a good number of African countries were clamoring for independence, which brought in its wake more clearly defined frontiers, the greater masses of refugees that were being generated in some parts of Africa created the need for formal classification and legislation of refugee issues. At that time, in 1963, the nascent Organization of African Unity felt concerned with the rising tide of refugees; in its Charter it succinctly affirmed the will of African Heads of State and Government to work in concert for an African brotherhood and solidarity by transcending ethnic and national differences to ensure the best conditions of existence for the peoples of Africa.[1]

In February 1964, the Council of Ministers of the Organization of African Unity, in its Second Ordinary Session, decided to establish a special commission and mandated it to study the refugee problem on the continent with a view to reporting to the Council. The work of that commission culminated in identifying the guiding principles that govern OAU's actions in favor of refugees. Resolution AHG/Res. (II), adopted in October 1965 by the Heads of State and Government in Accra, Ghana, spelled out these principles, as follows:

REAFFIRMS its desire to give all possible assistance to refugees from any Member State on a humanitarian and fraternal basis;

RECALLS that Member States have pledged themselves to prevent refugees living on their territories from carrying out by any means whatsoever any act harmful to the interests of other states that are members of the Organization of African Unity; and

REQUESTS all Member States never to allow the refugee question to become a source of dispute amongst them.

These principles were further refined and elaborated by the first major International Conference on the Legal, Economic and Social Aspects of the African Refugee Problem, held in Addis Ababa in 1967, under the joint sponsorship of the OAU, the United Nations High Commission for Refugees (UNHCR), ECA, and the Dag Hammarskjold Foundation. The same principles were finally complemented and reproduced in the OAU Convention Governing the Specific Aspects of Refugee Problems in Africa, which was adopted in September 1969 by the Heads of State and Government of the OAU in Addis Ababa, Ethiopia, and subsequently entered into force on 20 June 1974.

In the early 1960s, when most African countries were racing for independence, the attitude of the general public was that the phenomenon of refugees was merely a passing cloud which, given enough time, would disappear. It was the conviction of most people that once Africa got rid of European colonial domination, naturally, the phenomenon of refugees would automatically become irrelevant. In this connection, one may recall Nkrumah's famous slogan, "Seek Ye first the Kingdom of God, and everything else will follow." With their cherished ideal of pan-Africanism, the OAU founding fathers worked tirelessly toward this political kingdom, anticipating not only a United African State that would replace the continent torn apart by the artificial state boundaries the departing colonizers had formed, but also with a conviction to find African solutions to African problems, in an African context.

Furthermore, the preoccupation of member States of the OAU relating to asylum-seeking in Africa was over the issue of refugees emanating from the dependent territories of the continent, rather than those from the then emerging independent states. But even before this independence had taken root, a new phenomenon of refugees emanating from these newly independent states began to emerge. It was also discovered that this new category of refugees was giving rise to friction within some member States unlike those refugees from the dependent territories, who were acting as a source of unity and cooperation within and among the emerging independent states. Member States, therefore, resolved to exert greater effort in tackling the problem of refugees in Africa.

Since then, African countries have been assisting refugees in many and varied ways. Chief among these have been the following:

1. Establishment of organs and instruments on refugee matters

2. Organizing meetings and conferences relating to refugee issues

3. Promoting the protection of refugees

4. Providing education and employment opportunities to refugees

5. Promoting voluntary repatriation of refugees

6. Granting citizenship to refugees

All these steps and many more have gone a long way in contributing to the solution of the problem of refugees in Africa.

OAU's Organs and Instruments for Tackling the Refugee Problem

Organs. At the inception of the OAU in 1963, the founding fathers of this organization felt that Africa's refugee problem could not be left entirely to the host countries and countries of origin.[2] It was clear that a lasting solution to the African refugee problem called for the concerted efforts of all the member States as well as the world community at large. A systematic approach was, therefore, essential to ensure coordination between the OAU member States and the organizations that would be involved in extending service and assistance to refugees in Africa. In this connection, in February 1964, the OAU Council of Ministers meeting in Lagos, Nigeria, adopted a resolution calling for the creation of a commission consisting of ten OAU member States.[3] The commission was entrusted with the responsibility of examining the refugee problem on the continent, and making pertinent recommendation to the OAU Council of Ministers on how it could be solved or, at least, halted.

Since its inception, this commission, the composition of which, due to the growing number of refugees and the complexity of the problem, was reviewed and expanded to fifteen members in June 1980, in Freetown, Sierra Leone, through Council Resolution CM/Res.814 (XXXV), has been spearheading the formulation of policies geared toward finding durable solutions to the African refugee problem. It convenes once a year in an ordinary session to consider adopting its report to the OAU Council of Ministers for consideration. At the time of writing, 1991, the Chairman of the OAU Commission of Fifteen on Refugees was H.E. Chief Segun Olusola m.n.i., Ambassador of Nigeria to Ethiopia and the OAU, with Algeria as First Vice-Chairman (Northern Region); Tanzania as Second Vice-Chairman (Eastern Region), Zaire as Third Vice-Chairman (Central Region), and Zimbabwe as *Rapporteur* (Southern Region).

A second important organ of the OAU in respect to refugee matters is known as the OAU Coordinating Committee on Assistance to Refugees in Africa. Its establishment in 1968 emerged from the recommendations of the first International Conference on Legal, Economic and Social Aspects of the African Refugee Problem that was held in Addis Ababa, Ethiopia, in 1967, under the joint sponsorship of OAU, UNHCR, the UN Economic Commission for Africa (ECA), and the Dag Hammarskjold Foundation. The Coordinating Committee, which plays the role of guiding the OAU in formulating its programs and in helping to raise the necessary funds to run them, is composed of eighteen expert organizations that have refugee programs in Africa. The committee convenes once a year in an ordinary session in one of the African capitals, to examine the activities of the OAU relating to refugees and to consider adopting its report for consideration by the OAU Commission of Fifteen on Refugees. At the time of writing, efforts were underway to review and possibly expand the composition of the OAU Co-ordinating Committee to enable it to face the new challenges of the African refugee problem. John Mpyisi, Deputy Director of the International Labor Organization/Regional Office for Africa, was the Chairman in 1991.

The other important organ of the OAU on refugee matters is the Bureau for Refugees, which constitutes a division within the Political Department. Like in the case of the OAU Coordinating Committee, the establishment of this bureau in 1968 emerged out of the 1967 refugee conference already referred to above. The bureau is the operational organ of the OAU secretariat for implementing its policies on refugee matters. It also acts as secretariat to both the OAU Commission of Fifteen and the OAU Coordinating Committee.

In collaboration and cooperation with the Office of the United Nations High Commissioner for Refugees, with which the OAU concluded an Agreement of Cooperation on refugee matters in Africa in 1969, the OAU Bureau for Refugees performs, among others, the following specific functions:

1. It promotes, through scholarship awards, the education and training of refugees in Africa, with focus on vocational training and technical education attainable within Africa with the duration varying from six months to four or five years of study. At the time of writing, the Bureau for Refugees had a total of thirty-three students pursuing various study programs, all in Africa.

2. It undertakes research on all issues relating to refugees and displaced persons on the continent, and promotes income-generating activities relating to refugees with a view to enabling these refugees to become self-reliant, and thus alleviating the burden of the OAU member States created by the presence of refugees on their economic bases. At the time of writing, twenty-nine income-generating projects in the amount of close to U.S.$500,000 were being sponsored by the OAU within some of the principal African asylum countries. From time to time, and whenever feasible, the bureau also helps to find employment for suitably qualified refugees in various member States, although in this field the bureau cannot claim much success, due to the unemployment conditions obtaining in the various member States.

3. The bureau collects, collates, and disseminates information concerning the situation of refugees in Africa with a view to drawing the attention of the general public to the plight of refugees on the continent. This it does through, among others, the publication of its newsletter entitled *African Refugees* on a regular basis and within the limits of its financial constraints.

4. From time to time, and whenever the need arises, the staff of the bureau, on the advice of the OAU Secretary-General and in consultation with the member State concerned, establishes physical contacts within member States with a view to offering the required expert advice to the appropriate authorities of the government concerned. The bureau's frequency of intervention is particularly noticeable in times of emergencies when the staff undertake needs assessment missions for the purpose of sensitizing the world community to the magnitude of the emergency

concerned and the plight of the uprooted. From time to time, the information gathered this way also enables the OAU Secretary-General to respond in a timely manner and in tangible terms, by offering the government concerned a financial contribution in favor of the victims of the emergency.

5. In collaboration with the office of the United Nations High Commissioner for Refugees, the Bureau for Refugees endeavors to promote the physical protection of refugees by establishing the necessary contacts with the government concerned as well as the refugees.

Instruments. Besides the above-mentioned organs, the OAU member States have also concluded some legal instruments in favor of African refugees. These are:

1. The 1969 OAU Convention Governing the Specific Aspects of Refugee Problems in Africa: This convention, which entered into force on 20 June 1974, and which is the regional complement of the 1951 UN Convention on Refugees, also emerged out of the 1967 Conference on African Refugees. It is, for all practical purposes, the basis of the work of the OAU on refugee matters and so far a total of forty-one member States have ratified it.

2. *The African Charter on Human and Peoples' Rights:* This Charter, which entered into force on 21 October 1986, had at the time of this writing been ratified by forty member States of the OAU. With this Charter, Africa has established a legal instrument of great political significance for upholding the fundamental human and peoples' rights and also for defending and protecting the rights and interests of the African peoples. An African Commission on Human and Peoples' Rights has also been put in place in Banjul, Gambia, to promote and protect peoples' rights performance in Africa.

These instruments embody the principles that have always inspired OAU's action in favor of refugees on the continent since the organization's inception, and whose source is no doubt the Charter of the OAU.

Meetings and Conferences. Africa's contribution to the solution of the refugee problem has also been manifested in meetings and conferences relating to refugees, organized solely or jointly by the OAU secretariat, at different levels. Such meetings and conferences have included the following:

1. The 1967 Conference on the Legal, Economic and Social Aspects of African Refugees, which was the first one of its kind, and which took place in Addis Ababa, Ethiopia

2. The 1979 Pan-African Conference on the Situation of Refugees, which was held at Ministerial level in Arusha, Tanzania, and which was attended by thirty-eight OAU member States

3. The first International Conference on Assistance to Refugees in Africa (ICARA I), held in May 1981 in Geneva, which yielded US$574 million

4. The OAU Secretariat and Voluntary Agencies Meeting, which was held in Arusha,

Tanzania, in March 1983 and which aimed at developing a coordinated strategy and mapping out new actions for solving or at least ameliorating the refugee problem in Africa

5. The Second International Conference on Assistance to Refugees in Africa (ICARA II), held in July 1984, which aimed at reviewing the results of ICARA I, mobilizing additional resources for refugees and returnees, and assessing the impact imposed on the economies of the host countries by the presence of large numbers of refugees

6. The international Conference on the Plight of Refugees, Returnees and Displaced Persons, which took place in August 1988, in Oslo, Norway, and which alerted international opinion to the magnitude and adverse effects of uprootedness on both the uprooted and the host communities caused by the apartheid system in South Africa.

Participation in Voluntary Repatriation of Refugees. One of the most durable solutions to the African refugee problem is voluntary repatriation, as mentioned in Article 5 of the OAU Convention on Refugees. But voluntary repatriation is normally preceded by a declaration of general amnesty by the government of the country concerned. Over the years, a number of African governments have endeavored to encourage their respective nationals in exile to return home by declaring general amnesty for them and enacting amnesty laws to ensure their safety on return. Such countries have, at one time or another, included Sudan, Ethiopia, Uganda, Central African Republic, Chad, Zaire, Equatorial Guinea, and Burundi, insofar as independent Africa is concerned. Besides, many OAU member States in collaboration with the office of the United Nations High Commissioner for Refugees and other international organizations have actively participated in many voluntary repatriation exercises of refugees, including refugees who have had to return home in the wake of the attainment of independence as part of the independence process of their respective countries. Such voluntary repatriation exercises have included refugees going back to Sudan (1972), Uganda (1979, 1986–1988), Equatorial Guinea (1979–1980), Central African Republic (1979–1980), Chad (1981), Ethiopia (since 1983), Zimbabwe (1980), and more recently Namibia (1989–1990). At the time of this writing, plans under the auspices of the OAU, UNHCR, and the governments of the countries concerned were underway to repatriate voluntarily the Rwandese refugees, many of whom have been in exile for thirty years now.

Emergency/Relief Assistance. Like elsewhere in the world, in Africa the majority of refugee situations that have been emerging have been of an emergency character, whereby more often than not massive numbers of people have had to suddenly cross national boundaries to seek asylum in neighboring countries. In the spirit of African traditional hospitality, the host communities have always ensured that such asylum-seekers are provided with emergency or relief assistance. This assistance has always been provided even before the international community has managed to come to the scene. In this regard,

African governments should be seen and appreciated as perhaps the most reliable donors, at least during the initial stages of a refugee situation.

Even after the intervention of the international community, African governments have continued to extend assistance to refugees in many and varied forms. These have included:

1. Physical protection, sometimes at a very high calculated political risk, as in the case of the frontline states of Southern Africa

2. Giving the refugees large tracts of land for settlement, as Uganda, Tanzania, Ethiopia, and Sudan have been doing over the years

3. Admitting refugees in various educational institutions

4. Finding refugees employment opportunities even though for obvious reasons this has always been difficult

5. Offering citizenship to refugees who are interested, as Tanzania did in 1981 when it naturalized about 36,000 Rwandese refugees

Thus, believing as they do that the grant of asylum is a peaceful and humanitarian act, which should not, in any way, be interpreted as an unfriendly act, African countries have untiringly geared their resources and energies toward redressing one of Africa's biggest challenges: the problem of millions of refugees. African nationals, in the spirit of being one's brother's keeper, especially in time of peril, have always opened their doors and hearts to their brothers and sisters seeking asylum. Unlike other situations that have occurred elsewhere in the world, under normal circumstances, African States have always refrained from turning away asylum-seekers. Even now, when most African countries are faced with serious socioeconomic difficulties, the spirit of compassion and generosity on the side of member States remains alive and encouraging.

A question could be posed at this juncture, though: Why is it that, despite all of Africa's efforts to cope with refugees, the African refugee problem continues to pose such a challenge to governments? It is because the political will of the African governments to address the root causes of refugee movements has been lagging behind the forces that have been acting and reacting against one another to generate refugees on the continent. It is to these forces that we now turn.

ROOT CAUSES OF REFUGEE MOVEMENTS IN AFRICA

Before delving into what really constitutes root causes of refugee movements in Africa, a distinction must be recognized between the different categories of refugees we have in mind.[4] For the purpose of this chapter, we shall regard the first category of such refugees as persons fleeing from apartheid South Africa. The second category are political refugees who emanate from OAU member States, fleeing from situations of civil or inter-State conflicts. A third category of refugees are people who have been forced to flee from one member State into another due to natural disasters such as famine, drought, floods, and earthquakes. The fourth category of refugees are those often referred to as "economic refugees." These are people who, compelled by poverty or disappointed hopes of getting a job at home, expatriate themselves into countries presumed to have better economic opportunities. We shall examine the different categories of African refugees and identify the reasons for their flight.

Refugees from Apartheid South Africa

One of the main causes of the refugee problem in the southern part of our continent is the infamous policy of apartheid practiced by the South African regime. With its attendant restrictions and humiliation for South African blacks, this policy of racial segregation has occasionally led to uprisings by the black community. The South African regime's response has always been brutal, resulting in the death of thousands of people or in the flight of thousands into exile. A concomitant result of the policy of racial segregation is the creation of the Bantustans or "Independent Black Homelands" by South Africa. The homeland policy was inaugurated over twenty years ago to consolidate the practice of separate development. Since then millions of people have been uprooted and/or resettled by the stroke of an administrative pen.

But while the policy of apartheid is easily identified as a cause of the refugee problem in Africa, the role of international capital finance cannot be minimized. The South African economic and military machine is largely sustained by some multinational corporations which definitely enjoy the support and blessing of some Western countries.

Since the turn of 1989, the world has witnessed unfolding events in South Africa, which have included the release of Nelson Mandela and other political prisoners, and the unbanning of the African National Congress, the Pan-Africanist Congress, and other antiapartheid organizations. In February 1991, President Willem de Klerk announced his government's intention to abolish three pillars of apartheid, namely, the Group Areas Act, the Land Act, and the Population Registration Act. All that still remains of the apartheid laws are the Bantustans, which are said to be disintegrating even before their legal abolition. Some other things are still to be done—repeal of the security laws, release of all political prisoners, granting full amnesty for all exiles, and the denial of the Africans' right to vote—although this constitutes the core issue of the present constitutional negotiations. Still, while significant steps have been taken in pulling down the pillars of apartheid in South Africa, the system cannot be said to have been totally dismantled in all its forms and manifestations.

Refugees from OAU Member States

In the rest of Africa, refugee influxes have occurred at an alarming rate, especially within the past decade, with a break between the middle of 1980 and the end of 1983. Blame has more often than not been clumped on certain individuals or insurgent movements for trying to destabilize their countries. Measures taken by governments to establish law and order have often led to the flight of such nationals across their frontiers into other countries in quest for sanctuary. Most of the refugees emanate from Eastern, Southern, and Central Africa. To a limited extent, a number of refugee influxes emanate from the Northern region. But the Western region, which has in the past been regarded as the beacon of peace and stability, has recently been punctuated by flash-points of conflict, epitomized in the Senegal/Mauritania inter-State and the Liberia intra-State conflicts, and now the Taylor faction and Sierra Leone conflict. What, then, are the root causes of the refugees emanating from OAU member States?

Inter-State Conflicts. At independence, arbitrary and artificial boundaries were inherited by African leaders on the departure of the colonial rulers. A few years after the achievement of independence, some African leaders started questioning the rationality of the colonial boundaries. In some cases, these questions have been settled within the conference halls in Africa. The OAU tried to resolve this problem in Cairo when it adopted, in July 1964, Resolution AHG/Res.16 (I) on border disputes. OAU's political decision to have these boundaries remain sacrosanct and inviolable is understandable, since any attempt at reviewing them might lead to even more serious conflicts and disintegration.

Internal Conflicts. Various internal problems and conflicts contribute to the refugee proliferation in Africa. Among these are (1) changes in governments, (2) ethnic conflicts, (3) terrorist and subversive activities, and (4) human and individual rights abuses.

The phenomena of coups and countercoups have often been cited as a cause for people to run into exile. But some African countries or regions that have had the most of such changes of government have not had so many of their nationals run into exile, and some of the countries that have generated the most refugees have not had so many coups. This implies that this phenomenon is not synonymous with refugees. It is, however, true that in certain instances the product of changes of government, often buttressed by ethnic or regional rivalries, has been people fleeing into exile, either to escape the violence that sometimes accompanies these changes, or to avoid possible subsequent recrimination.

On some occasions, ethnic conflicts have arisen, as a result of misunderstanding between people of various ethnic groups. Such misunderstanding has sometimes arisen out of simple land issues, cattle raiding, grazing land disputes, and most fundamentally, opposition of one ethnic group to the dominance of another as regards power sharing, distribution of wealth, or whatever.

Terrorist and subversive activities can also contribute to the refugee problem. While not ignoring the incidence of terrorist and subversive activities elsewhere in Africa, the types of conflict attendant on terrorism and subversion have certainly been most manifest and devastating in the Southern Africa region, particularly in Angola and Mozambique. Angola has been in a state of war since 1961: from that year until 1975, the independence struggle against the Portuguese; and from 1975 until the present, a war between the MPLA (Popular Movement for the Liberation of Angola) government and the UNITA (National Union for the Total Independence of Angola) bandit movement. Mozambique has been in a state of war since 1964: from 1964 to 1975, a war of independence; from 1975 to 1980, a resistance against acts of destabilization and aggression by the South African regime; and from 1980 the government's fight against another and clearly more ferocious war of destabilization and wanton destruction mounted by armed bandits financed, equipped, and guided by South Africa. South Africa's apartheid-generated conflict has not only driven more than a million people into exile in the countries further afield, but has also led to massive displacement of persons within national borders. Furthermore, the war and destabilization in Angola and Mozambique led to the death of 140,000 children in the course of 1986, while another 147,000 young Angolans and Mozambicans died in 1988 alone, according to UNICEF estimates.[5] The Gersony Report also reveals that over 100,000 civilians were killed by rebel forces in Mozambique in the years 1986 and 1987, alone.[6] UNICEF again estimates that since 1980, 1.3 million people have been killed, either directly or indirectly, by South Africa's destabilization activities and war in Angola and Mozambique.[7] Nor have the refugee camps themselves in the States neighboring South Africa been spared from the wrath of apartheid South Africa.

Human and individual rights abuses also contribute to the refugee situation. The question of human rights has been a subject of several debates, not only among human rights groups throughout the world but also and with great concern at the level of the OAU. That the OAU has been concerned with the issue of human rights is attested to by the existing African Charter on Human and Peoples' Rights which, as already mentioned, entered into force on 21 October 1986 as well as the establishment of an African Commission on Human and Peoples' Rights in Gambia to promote and protect peoples' rights performance in Africa. Nevertheless, much remains to be done.

It will be noticed that almost all the root causes of internal and external displacement of persons in Africa as outlined above hinge on the question of human and individual rights abuses. Lack of tolerance for opposing views or alternative opinions has, in several parts of Africa, also severely undermined the spirit of governments to respect human rights, be they civil, political, social, cultural, or economic. In some cases the rights of individuals are not fully respected even where the constitution guarantees them. In the circumstances, some nationals are forced to flee into exile for lack of respect for their rights.

Natural Disasters/Calamities. During the last decade, the African continent has been beset by grave natural disasters and calamities. Drought, famine, and poor food production have caused thousands of citizens to move from one country into another in search of the basic necessities of life. Disease and pestilence are on the increase. All these are causes, even though not necessarily natural, of the movement of people into exile. Where such disasters have occurred in poor countries that are more often than not devoid of early warning systems or where the work of such early warning systems is either sounded late or simply ignored, the results have been devastating.

All in all, the attempt to identify the root causes of refugees in Africa will not in itself lead to immediate and durable solutions. There may not be an elimination of the scourge of refugees from Africa for quite some time to come. The factors that have been acting and reacting against one another to provoke asylum-seeking in Africa have, in general terms, remained fundamentally the same. They have varied only in terms of intensity. As the causes for refugee movements in Africa have tended to become more compelling, so have human rights movements, manifested in the social protest and demonstrations currently taking place in various parts of the continent. This has introduced two fundamental and negative factors in Africa's development process: (1) governmental preoccupation with crisis management situations and lack of proper and careful planning, and (2) governments' diversion of resources from national commitments into efforts to meet the needs of other countries' nationals, the refugees, as well as to combat or engage in conflictual situations.

CONCLUSIONS AND POLICY RECOMMENDATIONS

Conclusions

It has been estimated that between the birth of the OAU in 1963, and the end of 1979, the African refugee population was rising at the average rate of 100 percent every five years. Today Africa which, at the inception of the OAU, was playing host to about half a million refugees holds the unenviable record of hosting close to 6 million refugees, or about one-third of the world's total refugee population. About 40,000 of Africa's refugee population emanate from South Africa, and the rest emanate from member States of the OAU. Moreover, Africa has had the largest number of refugees for close to two decades now, compared with other continents in the world. Thus, while Africa can justifiably boast of its success story in the field of liberation, as crowned most recently by Namibia's accession to independence, the rising tide of refugees on the continent, coupled with over 12 million internally displaced persons, casts a shadow on Africa's avowed search for unity, enshrined in the OAU Charter.

Africa's alarming refugee population is rapidly increasing at a time when the continent is faced with serious problems of economic recovery and transformation, compounded by reductions in external resources, the excruciating debt and debt-servicing burden, deteriorating terms of trade, collapse of commodity prices, as well as the vagaries of nature. Africa's deteriorating refugee situation is also taking place at a time when the attitude of many countries in the West toward refugees appears to be hardening more and more, as exemplified by the growing cases of racism and xenophobia against immigrants in Europe; at a time when momentous events are sweeping not only across Eastern Europe, but, and especially, across Africa itself; and at a time when the international community appears to be telling some of the refugee-servicing organizations in Africa to tailor their programs to fit available resources, rather than telling them to be sure that their programs meet the needs of refugees in Africa.

No doubt, Africa recognizes that the major root causes of its refugee problem are situated within Africa itself. It realizes that the total eradication of these causes is the primary responsibility of the Africans themselves. However, considering the critical economic situation confronting the continent as reflected and articulated in the Lagos Plan of Action and the Final Act of Lagos, the African Priority Program for Economic Recovery (APPER), and the United Nations Program of Action for African Economic Recovery and Development (UNPAAERD), it is obvious that Africa's capacity to handle the problem is limited, particularly when one considers that the majority of the world's Least Developed Countries are situated in Africa.

This position has been fully acknowledged on a number of occasions by the international community through the holding of such conferences as the Arusha Pan-African Conference on the Situation of Refugees of 1979; the Geneva First International Conference on Assistance to Refugees in Africa of 1981; the Arusha OAU Secretariat and Voluntary Agencies Meeting of 1983; the Geneva Second International Conference on Assistance to Refugees in Africa of 1984; and the Oslo International Conference on the Plight of Refugees, Returnees and Displaced Persons in Southern Africa of 1988. The results of all these meetings and conferences have always been shared with, and appreciated by, the United Nations system. Additionally, Africa's refugee crisis was extensively deliberated by the Twenty-sixth Summit of the African Heads of State and Government, as reflected in their Declaration on the Fundamental Changes Taking Place in the World and Their Implications for Africa: Proposals for an African Response. The OAU Commission of Fifteen on Refugees also met in September 1990, and, having exhaustively discussed the African refugee situation, adopted a Declaration on Africa's Refugee Crisis, which was taken note of by the OAU Council of Ministers meeting in its Fifty-third Ordinary Session, in Addis Ababa, in February 1991.

Indeed, while Africa has remained a target of international criticism for not doing much for its refugees, conversely one could argue that in fact Africa has remained the most reliable donor for all refugees on the continent. A great deal of sacrifice continues to be made by African countries in favor of refugees, which is not easy to codify or quantify in dollar terms. In this regard, one may wish to consider the material assistance which, within the context of Africa's traditional hospitality and especially during the early stages of any emergency, the local communities of the asylum countries extend to the asylum-seekers before the international community arrives on the scene. One also needs to take into account the large tracts of land given to refugees for settlement, and the social services in the form of education, transportation, water supply, health, and infrastructure development that have been made available for use by the refugees in the asylum countries. Nor should one forget the measures taken by the asylum countries to ensure the physical safety and protection of the refugees, let alone the level of environmental degradation suffered by the asylum countries as refugees continue to cut down trees for firewood, for house construction, and for other purposes. The reduction in population of the once vibrant wildlife as well as cases of overgrazing due to the presence of large numbers of animals brought in by the refugees, are also sacrifices often suffered by asylum countries in Africa. All these have been allowed to happen by the asylum countries at the calculated risk of dislocating further these countries' already dislocated economies.

Yet, Africa should not exonerate itself from its own continuing malady and double standards manifested in spending enormous resources in educating hundreds of thousands of its citizens who, as rejects, and therefore for no fault of their own, have had to "vote with their feet." Engineers, doctors, lawyers, and scientists have been forced to seek asylum, and to add to the development of the already developed countries in the West.

In the light of the foregoing, we submit the following recommendations.

Policy Recommendations

The epithet that prevention is better than cure is a matter of public knowledge. In other words, if it can be done before a disease strikes, it is more prudent to explore measures with which to prevent it from striking. Deeply concerned with the issue of root causes of refugee movements in Africa, and particularly inspired by the recent events in Eastern Europe that have largely resulted in the erosion of communism, the African people have been harping on the pillars of good governance, namely, accountability, transparency, openness, efficiency and efficacy, the rule of law and, of course, popular participation in the decision-making process of national life that affects the welfare of the general public. To the people of Africa who, for decades, have been suffocating under the thick cloud of communism, these pillars of good governance go a long way in helping to open up new avenues of interaction and mutual trust between the governors and the governed. This in turn helps to reduce tension that might exist between the leaders and the led, which may foster confidence-building between people of different opinions.

Overall, unless the issue of human and peoples' rights is given prominence on Africa's development agenda, Africa will remain in the throes of civil strife, wars, and armed conflicts, with all their tragic consequences of ghastly images of death, destruction of property, and human displacement. The African Charter on Human and Peoples' Rights is now the hallmark of African governments' renewed and determined effort to promote and defend human rights in Africa, thereby discouraging new influxes of refugees and creating conditions amenable for voluntary repatriation. It is, therefore, recommended that member States that have not yet done so should, as soon as possible, accede to this Charter and should also respect all the provisions laid down in the Charter.

It is the author's view that the need to include and constantly review the teaching of human rights in our school curriculums and national constitutions in Africa has never been so pressing as it is now. Governments of member States of the OAU should therefore agree to bow to the current winds of change and do everything within their power to teach our future generations the value and sanctity of life in human institutions. Indeed, the joy of living is to be certain of one's physical existence, in the first instance.

The need to tolerate racial, ethnic, religious, physiological, and ideological differences; to exercise self-restraint in respect of those with different opinions; to resist external influence; to genuinely adhere to democratic principles; and to build institutions that enjoy the confidence of the common citizen and therefore discourage people from fleeing their homes for fear of political persecution, is something worthy of immediate political attention.

The need for member States to refrain from interfering in the internal affairs of other States in accordance with the provisions of the Charter of the United Nations as well as that of the OAU, is of primordial importance, it being understood that more often than not such interference only goes to benefit, not Africa, but rather some external parties. Yet the principle of noninterference should not be misconstrued as indifference to the plight facing some of our countries. History will judge us harshly if we simply stand and stare, and fold our hands in the face of a situation involving a stronger party massacring its people and throwing the survivors across the national frontiers. There must be an end or, at least, a limit to such conduct.

On another plane, experience has revealed that once a disease has struck, it is more efficacious to seek a cure rather than prevention. Now that Africa is faced with her close to 6 million refugees and over 12 million internally displaced persons, it makes more sense also to pursue remedial measures that will promote the welfare of the victims of uprootedness, rather than confining ourselves to root causes.

That Africa is currently bedeviled by a variety of wars and armed conflicts that have driven millions of our brothers and sisters into exile cannot be disputed. But history has taught us that political negotiation is always a better solution to Africa's conflicts than military confrontation. Indeed, the past has witnessed instances where African states have successfully employed peaceful means to settle conflicts and disputes in a typical African context.

If it is perceived that peace is a *sine qua non* to development, then conflicts should be seen as a setback to, or an onslaught on, this development. People cannot develop, let alone plan for their future, if they are always compelled to run back and forth between their birth place and their potential host countries. The mental preparedness of such people for external aggression is created and kept alive and is made to replace the mental preparedness for optimum performance and increased productivity. It is for this reason that we recommend that it will not be a sign of weakness for member States that are currently beset by wars and armed conflicts and disputes, in the spirit of African brotherhood and solidarity, to come to the negotiating table in an effort to create a climate of peace and stability that will allow the return of refugees and foster development. Europe is building a common home for her people; Africa should also be seen to build a common home for her people.

Concerning voluntary repatriation of refugees, it is acknowledged that the right of a citizen to return home to his country of birth is as fundamental a human right as the right to seek asylum outside one's country of origin. It is also acknowledged that voluntary repatriation is the most durable solution to the problem of refugees. Accordingly, we recommended that, in the spirit of brotherhood and common humanity, governments concerned, especially those that fall among the world's principal sources of refugees, should from time to time review the situations within their borders that have generated refugees with a view to declaring amnesty to their fellow nationals in exile. This amnesty should be general and comprehensive in character, meaning that it should embrace the whole spectrum of those currently living in exile. It should be declared after the factors that caused people to flee into exile have been significantly reconciled. It should also be genuine, meaning that it should be buttressed by an enactment of amnesty laws to safeguard the lives of the returnees. At the same time, in countries where people who have been in exile for a decade or more are giving birth to yet another generation of refugees, governments should seriously consider offering such people opportunities for local integration or naturalization, if conditions for such an action clearly do prevail. Above all, countries of origin and asylum should, within the framework of the 1969 OAU Convention on Refugees, always ensure that refugees are not used as a source of friction between member States.

A major assumption underlies the view that economic factors play a significant role in uprooting people and aggravating their plight in the host countries. As we implement our structural adjustment programs, we should not forget that no nation can be called great or prosperous unless the basic material needs of its people, including the most vulnerable people, are met. Furthermore, if it is perceived that development is about man and that the sole purpose of development is the betterment of man, then there can be no denial that the right of citizens to participate in the development process remains the hallmark of man's existence.

Finally, provision of relief or emergency assistance to Africa's refugees to save human lives from perishing, together with the provision of inputs with which to strengthen the fragile economies of the African countries most affected by the presence of refugees and returnees, are increasingly becoming an imperative. It is true that Africa's refugees are first and foremost an African responsibility. However, as a community of nations, the international community from which emergency and development assistance are expected would be abdicating its part in this global responsibility if it chose to reduce humanitarian assistance to the refugees on the African continent. It is recommended, therefore, that the international community should again be sensitized by us Africans about the need not only for maintenance of its current level of assistance but for additional aid to host countries at this time when Africa is at the crossroads of development crises.

NOTES

1. Organization of African Unity, *OAU Charter and Rules of Procedure* (Addis Ababa: OAU Press and Information Division, 1982).

2. See also C.O.C. Amate, *Inside the OAU* (London: Macmillan, 1986).

3. OAU, *Resolution CM/Res. 19 (II)* (Addis Ababa: OAU Conference Division, February 1964).

4. See also OAU, *Secretary General's Report on the Root Causes of the Refugee Problem in Africa* (Addis Ababa: Fifty-second Ordinary Session of the OAU Council of Ministers, July 1990).

5. UNICEF, *Children on the Frontline* (New York: UNICEF, 1987).

6. Robert Gersony, *Summary of Mozambican Refugees Accounts of Principally Conflict-Related Experience in Mozambique* (Washington, DC: n.p., 1988).

7. UNICEF, *Children on the Frontline*, p. 11.

The OAU and Environmental Issues
IVOR RICHARD FUNG

INTRODUCTION

The 1960s were an especially auspicious decade for political independence in Africa—no matter the degree and nature of independence. Some of the most urgent problems for the emerging States of the time were national unity and stability, sovereignty and economic development, as well as total decolonization of the continent. That these concerns should in one way or the other consequently figure to the detriment of other vitally important issues in the Charter and in the achievements of the Organization of African Unity, is not a mistake, but rather a matter of priority in conformity with the political vision of the leaders at the time.

The general political vision of the 1960s can be said to have been blurred by the long-awaited victory over colonialism and the resulting euphoria of self-rule. Three decades have gone by and the euphoria of self-rule is gradually sinking, unrescued, into disillusionment, as African governments are increasingly faced, not only with their age-old daunting problems of political instability and economic underdevelopment, but with the serious crisis of sound and viable development and environmental policies. These policies intertwine with each other and were not given appropriate attention at the onset of nation-building upon independence.

It is now dawning on everyone that any comprehensive agenda of nation-building should have included and duly underlined the functional relationship between development and the environment. This relationship is experimentally established in Africa more than anywhere else: Here is a continent where agriculture is the lifeblood of survival in most absolute terms, a continent where the livelihood of more than 80 percent of the population depends on agriculture activity. This involves the physical or natural resource base, land in its broad sense, forests and other vegatation cover, water, and weather—the environment as a whole—which can be conceived of as the basis of development. This ultimately amounts to recognizing that the environment is more than just the place in which we live, since its judicious management can also enhance and sustain our living standards.

In view of the inextricable environment-development relationship, the wanton destruction and mismanagement of forests and other features of the entire vegetation cover, for abusive commercial purposes or otherwise, constitutes the basis of Africa's underdevelopment in all its facets. Such destruction and mismanagement are the most redoubtable threat to real security in the African context in terms of eradicating famine, malnutrition, poverty, drought, floods, and other calamities that impair the well-being and happiness of the people. Unfortunately, Africa is yet to fully perceive the harmonious relationship that should exist between development, healthy living standards, and the environment.

Even in the most modern African cities, it is hard to find lawns, flower gardens, parks, and other such places for public enjoyment and recreation that often fulfill our longing for the solace of nature. Environmental concerns, as Julius Nyerere, former Head of State of Tanzania, once pointed out, have been regarded, until the last few years, "as an American and European matter." Indeed, according to Nyerere, "there was a tendency to believe that talk of the environment was part of a conspiracy to prevent modern development on our continent. Now we have reached the stage of recognizing that environmental concern and development have to be linked together if the latter is to be real and permanent."[1]

The tardy awareness of the environmental concern by no means negates the full existence and gravity of the phenomenon both now and in the past. It must be emphasized that little has been done so far by the OAU to reverse the situation. The pace of degradation in Africa has been increasing more steadily than anywhere else on our planet earth. The seemingly uncontrollable expansiveness of the two deserts—the Kalahari in the South and the Sahara, the largest desert on earth, in the North—have combined with the entire process of desertification and various forms of deforestation from East to West to exacerbate Africa's development predicament and constitute the classical environmental evils of the continent. Other related and independent forms of such evils, including pollution in all its manifestations, natural disasters, and the dumping of toxic waste with similar or even more grievous effects, have only begun surfacing with force in Africa's long catalog of development priority action programs, especially during the past decade.

The review of the major African environmental problems, together with their development and security implications, will compose the first part of this chapter. As most of these concerns transcend national frontiers, it is but logical that they be addressed globally at the regional or continental level. It is in this vein that part two of the chapter will attempt a listing of OAU's responses and policies in the field of environment. The last part of the chapter will attempt to propose an environmental action program for the OAU.

AFRICAN ENVIRONMENTAL PROBLEMS AND THEIR DEVELOPMENT AND SECURITY IMPLICATIONS

There are multiple problems relating to the environment worldwide. This study will consider only those that are very pertinent in the case of Africa.[2] This approach should, however, not be looked upon as a means of undermining the transboundary—or for that matter the transcontinental—nature of environmental issues. The concern here is rather to bring out those problems that have had and are still likely to have immediate impact on the development and security predicament of African States. Desertification, deforestation, droughts, floods, and other natural calamities, as well as the growing imbalance between population growth and available resources, threaten and challenge Africa's development and security efforts at the national and regional levels.

Desertification

There are two deserts in Africa, the Sahara and the Kalahari. The Sahara alone has about 11 million square kilometers, making up more than one-third of Africa's total area of 30 million square kilometers. Geographically, it extends from the Atlantic Ocean on the West to the Red Sea on the East, and from the Atlas Mountains and Mediterranean Sea on the North to the savannas of the Sudan regions on the South. It stretches over twelve countries including Morocco, Algeria, Tunisia, Mauritania, Mali, Niger, Chad, Senegal, Libya, Egypt, Sudan, and the Western Sahara territory. The Sahara is one of the world's hottest areas, with mean annual temperatures reaching 38 degrees C in some places. Its very low population of only 3 million inhabitants as compared to its landspace is testimony to the hostility of life in the desert.

The Kalahari, on the other hand, is a region of Southwestern Africa extending from the Orange River to Lake Ngami, and from longitude 26 degrees E nearly to the Atlantic Ocean. It lies in Botswana, a part of the Republic of South Africa, and Eastern Namibia, and is part of the huge inner tableland of South Africa. The definition of the Kalahari as a desert is controversial.[3] However, in this study it will be conceived of and treated as a desert because it is essentially a dry, largely barren, largely treeless and sandy region. Thus, our definition of a desert stresses the generally hostile nature of such regions to the essential aspects of human life.

Desertification is the process whereby the deserts are known to be expanding. The process depends on natural factors and on human actions. It occurs through various stages, all of which present desert-related character-istics.

The erosion of soil is the main natural factor of desertification. Since 1968, rains have generally decreased in Africa. The drought that began in Sahelian countries has enclosed all semiarid and subhumid areas and has even reached the forest-endowed countries. Annual precipitation has also been fluctuating around a lower average.[4] The case of West Africa, for example, presents a great expansion of the arid zone to the detriment of the semiarid zone, which in turn is gradually shifting toward the savanna. The flow of rivers and the level of lakes have decreased noticeably. This situation has had an impact on various activities including sea-related farming and maritime transportation. One of the explanations for the decrease of precipitation in Africa as a whole holds that the situation has arisen due to the decrease of the vegetation cover. A decrease in the vegetation cover, according to this point of view, leads to a decrease in the quantity of recycled evaporated water, which represents about 20 percent of African precipitation.[5] It is this part of the precipitation that normally modifies the solar energy received by the soil and sent back to space.

In addition, the potential evapotranspiration is well above the precipitation on the greater part of the continent. Before the present drought could come, average annual precipitation for the whole continent was 740 millimeters, average evaporation was 587 millimeters, whereas the run-off was only 153 millimeters. The region of Guinea in West Africa and the Congo-Zaire basin and the Gulf of Guinea are the only two regions with excess.[6] Thus, of all the continents, Africa is one of the least water-endowed, with an average deficit of 1,100 millimeters. Worse still, the last two decades have revealed a more serious situation whereby water resources have been drastically di-minished and even the Congo-Zaire basin was seriously threatened.

Lake Chad, once known as Africa's interior sea, has been seriously affected. As a matter of fact, the area of the lake has decreased from 28,000 square kilometers to 10,000 square kilometers during the past thirty years, and the volume of water has also decreased by 60 percent during the same period. This natural phenomenon has been the result of an uninterrupted fifteen years of drought.

It has been reported that even with the return of rains to the normal levels of the early 1960s, only a small portion of the degraded soils could undergo self-regeneration.[7] The fixation of dunes, the sowing and planting of herbs, and other utilization of waterways constitute the bulk of work that should be required in order to overcome the larger part of soil degradation.

If the natural factors of desertification mainly evolve around fluctuating precipitation and precisely in the lowering of the infiltration of rainfall and increased erosion, the process is to a large extent attributable to deliberate or unconscious human activity. Overgrazing, farming of marginal zones, felling of trees, and bush fires are the most commonly practiced causes of desertification by man. The process is glaringly remarkable in the Sahelian and Sudanian regions, where human pressure on the land has resulted in overgrazing range areas, in the diminishing soil fertility, or simply in the deterioration of the structure of the soil.

A rapid transformation of ecological zones is highly noticeable and it is effected in the following fashion as the desert expands: desertification of the Sahel, Sahelization of the savanna, savannization of forests. In keeping with this process in recent years, it has been estimated that the Sahara has been moving southward at the rate of 10 kilometers per year. In sub-Saharan Africa 6.9 million square kilometers are presently threatened by desertification and 16.5 percent of Africa's existing rain-fed cropland may be lost by the end of the century if conservation measures are not intensified.[8]

It is consoling that though desertification is quite serious in Sahelian and Sudanian countries, owing to the proximity of these regions to the Sahara, the situation in the Kalahari and its immediate neighboring areas is less alarming. However, experts report that the situation could deteriorate in the near future if present farming habits of surrounding populations, such as extensive farming and overgrazing, do not change. The abnormally low level of precipitation could also consitute a major cause for concern in the near future. In this case, the northeast of Kenya, Somalia, and the south and east of Ethiopia would seriously be threatened by desertification.[9]

The degradation of soil is also proportionate to demographic pressure and the increase in population. The soil is, at present, one of Africa's most precious natural resources. A great number of African farmers are obliged by many socioeconomic factors to overexploit the soil in order to feed themselves: About 80 percent of cultivated soil bears food crops[10] and is exploited according to traditional methods of shifting cultivation, which becomes destructive when the population is above certain thresholds.

Another principally human factor of environmental degradation that does not necessarily follow the logic of the desertification process by a progressive infringement on the ecological zones (desert, Sahel, savanna, forest) as evoked earlier, is deforestation.

Deforestation

The inappropriate management of the vegetation cover—the forest—could gradually lead to a desert state in the long run. In Africa, deforestation stands out as the most alarming environmental phenomenon.

The rate of degradation of African forests has been estimated at 3.8 million hectares per year since 1975. Ivory Coast is one of those countries where deforestation has been most acute.[11] Since the beginning of the present century, about 70 percent of its forests have been destroyed. It is estimated to have cleared about 290,000 hectares per year between 1981 and 1985. The situation is also critical in Nigeria, where only about 10 percent of the rainforest is said to be remaining and that small remainder is further being depleted at an annual rate of 10 percent. According to former Head of State General Obasanjo, while at the beginning of the 1980s Nigeria was an exporter of wood, it has now changed to the position of importer "with concomitant consequences for its debt position."[12]

In Madagascar the destruction of forests and other environmental damage are estimated to be costing the economy as much as $290 million annually.[13] Other countries and regions where the extermination of the forests is an increasingly major cause for concern include the southeast of Guinea, the Fouta Djallon region, the southwest of Cameroon, lower Zambia, Kenya, and Tanzania.

A study based on the treeful woods on the savanna of western and central Africa has revealed that in the past, the forest extended northward perhaps as far as the tenth parallel and formed then an extension of the great forest belt of Cameroon and Congo, which presently constitutes about 94.5 percent of Africa's rainforest. Forty percent of Ethiopia was covered by forest, which reduced to 16 percent twenty years ago, and to 3.1 percent today.[14]

At present, about 40 hectares of tropical forests are being cleared every minute. At this speed, and if the replanting process is not accelerated, there will be no tropical forest by the next century. Indeed, replanting emerges as one of the major hopes for rehabilitating our natural vegetation cover. Today, unfortunately, worldwide only one tree is replanted against ten that are felled. The situation is even worse in Africa, where only one tree is replanted against twenty-nine felled.[15]

The natural vegetation cover as well as the animal species of the savanna—where most African populations live—are gradually been damaged by redundant traditional methods of farming and the expanding population that is constantly in search of living space. A United Nations study on these issues states that at present only 35 percent of the savanna with low production is available, since about 6,500 hectares of the savanna is destroyed daily.[16]

A few reasons or justifications can be discerned for such environmental degradation. These include farming methods, the energy crisis, and the use of ligneous resources for commercial and other ends.

The most notorious method of farming in sub-Saharan Africa in particular, where deforestation and desertification are most acute, is shifting cultivation, a method that consists of abandoning one piece of land to allow recovery of nutrients and moisture after overutilization. The method is also used in animal breeding, when pastoralists shift their herds toward new vegetation to allow used fields to recover. The recovery of nutrients is also effected in many parts of Africa through the burning of forests or the savanna grass lands. These practices have become obselete and inadequate, since available landspace is becoming very limited in view of the fast-growing population. Many people are now building their homes on the farming areas of yesterday and forest reserves of the past are being used for farming and other ends.

One of these ends is related to what can be called the energy crisis, exclusively referring in this context to the use of trees as firewood in many homes. It is a crisis because firewood, on which more than 80 percent of the African population depends for cooking, warming, and sustaining local industries such as smithing, is becoming more and more scarce. A few decades ago, firewood could be fetched within the close vicinity of most homes. Today one has to buy firewood or travel many kilometers away to the nearest forest. This situation has been exacerbated during the past few years owing to the rising prices of petroleum, which has compelled a cross-section of city dwellers to resort to charcoal for cooking, ironing, and warming. The shortage of firewood, which emerges as a greater burden to the poor and to the rural women especially to whom the tedious task of firewood fetching is often addressed, testifies to an obvious ecological fact pattern: the contraction of the forest cover, the upsetting of the environmental balance, and the reduction of potential food production.

The export of logs as a source of hard currency has been accelerated during the past decade, largely due to the economic crisis in which many if not all sub-Saharan African countries have been plunged. It is clear that, as tropical woods have become a primary export good in many countries, the deforestation process in Africa has an economic dimension closely linked to the debt problem. This situation has urged many African leaders to issue generous concessions for logging without providing any incentive or conditions to maintain or restore the productive capacity of the forests in the long-run.[17]

Woody products are, in no mean way, extensively used in what can be called the forestry-related industries such as carpentry, roofing of houses, and the production of papers and furniture for household and office purposes. Over 90 percent of the furniture found in every home in Africa is made of wood. The present trend in developed countries is to use as little wood as possible or even replace it entirely by other materials such as steel, aluminum, and plastic in the manufacturing of household and office furniture.

If the current practices of farming and consumption of woody products are not checked, the degradation of the vegetative cover in the form of desertification and deforestation in sub-Saharan Africa especially, will drastically worsen even before the year 2000 in view of the fast-rising population. The close link between the increase in population and environmental degradation is no longer a matter of scientific debate. Even the lay African in the village has become quite conscious of it. Disputes over land for farming or for housing have become the most pervasive source of disagreement among villagers across the continent, and it is almost impossible to buy a piece of land in Africa's growing cities. This serious state of affairs does more than just testify to the scarcity of land in Africa. It most importantly raises the fundamental problem of containment of the population explosion within a limited environment as well as the satisfactory allocation of precious and scarce resources of the environment among the population.

The Explosive Population Growth

Since 1954, the world population—estimated today at 5.3 billion people—has doubled, and according to recent estimates, is likely to double again by the year 2050. A degrading environment coupled with exponential population growth will inevitably lead to disaster. About 2.5 days are enough for 1 million babies to be born and for 50,000 hectares of productive land to be destroyed and sterilized by erosion or human action. Every minute, 250 children are born while 10 hectares of productive land are lost forever.[18]

As recently as 1960, Africa's population growth rates were not high as compared to those of Asia and Latin America (2.5% versus 2.5% and 2.9%).[19] It may be said that since that decade of independence for the majority of African States, the biblical command: "Be fruitful, multiply, and replenish the earth" (Gen. 1:28) is faithfully being put into practice today as it was required thousands of years ago. Paradoxically, however, the African earth is becoming sterile and is being eroded. And while the growth rates of Asia and Latin America have since fallen to 2.1 percent and 2.5 percent respectively, Africa's present growth rate stands at 3.1 percent and is expected to reach 3.13 percent by 1995.[20] In numerical terms, Africa's overall population is more than 555 million people, and is said to have risen approximately threefold since 1950. At this rate, it is projected at 877 million by the year 2000 and by 2025 at 1.617 billion,[21] more than the population projected for China that same year. Sub-Saharan Africa alone now has twice the population it had in 1965 and more than five times the population it had at the beginning of the century.

The crux of the problem with this population explosion relating to the environment is simply that, as people keep multiplying, Africa—the continent in which they have to live—does not and cannot expand. But as the people have to live, the available land space is simply overutilized and overgrazed. Meanwhile, the processes of deforestation and desertification described earlier are accelerated and are responsible, to a large extent, for the reduction of biological and economic productivity. Many African cities are growing larger and the number of slums and poor people is also being multiplied. A form of pollution relating to dirt, filth, squalor, and other aspects of poor living standards settles into the slums. And as slum dwellers cannot generally afford modern kitchen equipment such as gas or kerosene stoves they resort to charcoal and sawdust, and the demand for firewood grows. Deforestation and the entire process of environmental degradation thus accelerate. It is a vicious cycle that leads to the conclusion that population growth and man's activities in space and on water and land cannot be left out in any serious discussion on the degradation of the environment, anywhere.

Drought, Floods, and Other Calamities

Drought and floods add to the list of calamities that have persistently threatened our environment for the past three decades. Experts explain that the vegetative cover and forests in particular undergo a process of evaporation, which immensely contributes to the formation of precipitation. Following this scientific point of view, therefore, the degradation of the vegetative cover and deforestation lessen the degree of precipitation, which ultimately leads to drought. The relationship between the loss of the vegetative cover and drought has been experimentally established in recent years in the twenty-four drought-stricken and economically hard-pressed countries situated largely in the Sahelian and Sudanian regions.

In areas where trees have been cut down, the soil becomes bare, fragile, and very vulnerable to heavy rainfalls. Even though the rains may come once in a while, they easily engender floods due to the vulnerability of the soil and its limited capacity to retain water. In sub-Saharan Africa, 80 percent of the soils are fragile, and 45 percent of the land is too dry to support rainfed agriculture. Average rainfall varies from year to year by an enormous 30 to 40 percent.[22] Every year in Africa, an average of 300 people die of flood, and an inestimable quantity of property and homes are demolished. It amounts to saying that there is a permanent war waged on human beings by a deteriorating environment.

This war is then sustained by other natural calamities such as earthquakes which, though rare, are nevertheless nonnegligible especially in the northern part of the continent and the Horn region. Volcanic mountains, too, have taken their toll in human life and human displacement. Still tragically fresh in mind is the 22 August 1986 gas explosion in Nyos, a volcanic lake located in northwestern Cameroon. The Nyos incident remains controversial as a considerable cross-section of experts staunchly believe that it was not a natural but a man-made disaster resulting from a neutron bomb test on the lake. Supporters of the natural thesis argue that Nyos, a crater lake, erupted with a burst of carbon dioxide gas that formed a ground-hugging cloud that, as it moved, pushed aside breathable air. A similar thing had happened a year earlier in Lake Monoun, about fifty-nine miles to the south of Nyos. In both cases the victims were robbed of oxygen and asphyxiated.

Whatever the case, it cannot be denied that it was an environmental disaster that swept away the life of every breathing creature—insects, birds, animals, and over 4,000 human beings. It rendered Nyos and its neighboring villages a lifeless and cursed region.

Another environmental threat, though still remote, is what recent studies on the world climate call global warming. These studies have revealed that economic activities of all countries are closely related to climatic changes. Global warming is heigthened by greenhouse gases, of which carbon dioxide (CO_2) constitutes about 66 percent. In Africa, the accumulation of the CO_2 depends to a large extent on burning, bush fires, and other aspects of deforestation. An increased warming of the climate would upset world agriculture, would change and even displace forests over hundreds of kilometers, and would create new deserts. The crises in food, water, and energy would become more acute. There would be a shift in natural ecological zones that would engineer the displacement of crops and forest belts to higher latitudes; meanwhile the human tropics would become drier due to enhanced evapo-transpiration.[23]

In 1989, Delft Hydraulics carried out a study on behalf of UNEP on the vulnerability to sea level rise relating to climate change. The study indicated that of the twenty-seven vulnerable countries in the world, four African countries (Egypt, Mozambique, Senegal, and Gambia) will be seriously affected by the sea level.[24] In the case of Egypt, specifically, about 20 percent of the country's 35,000 square kilometers of arable soil will be endangered.[25] It has been estimated that the sea level rise phenomenon may fully occur about half a century from now if global warming does not abate. The UN-sponsored meeting on global warming held in April 1991 appealed for international cooperation in finding solutions to the global warming problem by the introduction of benign alternative sources of energy.

The increasing environmental degradation as indicated in the foregoing pages retards the process of development in Africa, particularly in view of the fact that any meaningful development achievement registered so far has been connected to agriculture and the exploitation of natural resources. Industrialization opportunities are very few and constitute at present less than 9 percent of the continent's overall development efforts in terms of export earnings. In this regard, the management and control of the environment should be the backbone and the basis of sustainable development. The objective of such development should be to maximize and sustain better living standards for all, including, in particular, unquantifiable indicators such as good health, education, food self-reliance, and security.

The ultimate outcome of the degradation of soils and the vegetal cover is external food dependency, which compromises national sovereignty in ways that are unaffected by even the strongest of armed forces.[26] Another result is hunger and malnutrition, which presently affect more than 100 million people in Africa. Every year, floods and other calamities take their own death toll in several hundreds. Thus, "environmental threats with the potential to erode the habitability of the planet are forcing humanity to consider national security in far broader terms than that guaranteed solely by the force of arms."[27] In the defense of their national sovereignty and territorial integrity, African States have made considerable sacrifices. For the time being, however, little determination is shown to fight against environmental threats that infringe both on badly needed development and on real security. It should be known that in Africa as elsewhere, there is no war more worth fighting than the fight against environmental degradation that continuously thwarts "nations' most fundamental aspects of security by undermining the natural support systems on which all of human activity depends."[28]

The redoubtable and all-powerful foe that the environmental degradation constitutes cannot be conquered by the most sophisticated available weapons in the world, nor can it be defeated by one nation alone. Cooperation and alliances are required at all levels. This is one of the emerging challenges that the OAU has been struggling to address in recent years.

OAU'S CONTRIBUTION TO THE RESOLUTION OF AFRICAN ENVIRONMENTAL PROBLEMS

OAU member States have begun noticing the true gravity and the specificity of problems such as desertification, deforestation, the degradation of soils, and other environment-related issues that imperil the economic development of the continent. In this connection, a number of measures aimed at protecting the environment have been taken. The content of the various arrangements adopted by the OAU to protect the environment in Africa can be broken down at the world, regional, subregional, and national levels.

At the world level, these arrangements can be appreciated in terms of cooperation policies in two areas: a North-South vertical cooperation, which is mainly political, and a horizontal cooperation with other organizations, which is mainly technical.

As far as world political cooperation on the protection of the environment is concerned, the OAU has cosponsored a number of conferences with other political institutions such as the EEC. From 31 August to 3 September 1989, for instance, the OAU joined the World Association of Social Perspectives and the Council of Europe in the organization of an important conference on the theme of "Environment and Development" in Porto Novo, Benin.

The conference fell within the framework designed by the organizers as an "Africa-Europe Encounter," where participants were called upon to focus attention not only on the inevitable nature of interdependence in this field but, most importantly on the vital necessity of solidarity between the European Community and Africa relating to environmental and development issues. The necessity of redefining the concept of environment by taking into consideration all its various meanings was emphatically underlined by participants at the conference. The OAU's involvement in the organization of the Porto Novo gathering revealed an eminently political significance that undoubtedly appealed for North-South solidarity in the preservation of the environment in Africa. On the other hand, the political role of the OAU has been superimposed on technical cooperation with other international organizations.

Indeed, OAU as an international organization has strengthened its cooperation with like organizations, in particular with those of the United Nations system. Some of the major achievements recorded in this area include the drafting of the World Charter on Nature. As a matter of fact, at the initiative of President Mobutu Sese Seko of Zaire, the OAU's Assembly of Heads of State and Government sponsored the Charter that was to be adopted by the UN General Assembly in 1982. Futhermore, in order to combat the shameful practice of dumping toxic and dangerous industrial waste on Africa, the OAU adopted in May 1988 a resolution requesting the International Atomic Energy Agency (IAEA), the UN Environment Program, and other relevant organizations to take appropriate measures to prevent such practices and to help African countries in setting up appropriate mechanisms in this field. An additional resolution adopted in June 1988 further requested the IAEA to intervene and assist in the prevention of the usage of toxic and industrial waste for commercial purposes.

It is, however, at the regional or inter-African level that OAU's contribution will be most felt. Here, distinction should be made between general and specialized measures taken by the OAU in its attempts at resolving environment problems.

The general measures taken at the level of the continent by African States under the auspices of the OAU include, among others, those taken at Algiers in 1968, at Lagos in 1980, at Addis Ababa in 1981, and at Cairo in 1985.

The first major act in the field of the environment came in 1968, five years after the creation of the OAU, when a cross-section of African leaders felt the necessity of protecting the African ecosystem. In this regard, they adopted in Algiers the African Convention on the Conservation of Nature and Natural Resources. On the other hand, in May 1984 during its tenth session held at Addis Ababa, the Conference of Ministers of the UN Economic Commission for Africa adopted the Special Memorandum of the ECA Conference of Ministers on the Economic and Social Crisis in Africa and a plan of action for the fight against the effects of drought. The objective was, on the one hand, to begin cooperation on the study of climate and drought among States in order to provide guidance to their policies and activities, and on the other hand to appeal for assistance to the international community.

In another chapter, the 1980 Lagos Plan of Action and the Lagos Final Act insisted generally on the necessity for cooperation in the field of the environment as a whole. The principle of intra-African cooperation and solidarity was reaffirmed and accentuated by the vital need for cooperation on the delicate and sensitive transborder ecological problems. The mechanism of such cooperation stipulated that it be composed of an intergovernmental committee and of a committee of experts from the UN Economic Commission for Africa. African States were requested to foster cooperation with governmental and nongovernmental international organizations. Emphasis was further laid on North-South cooperation between African countries and industrialized countries on environmental matters.

Nevertheless, the work of the OAU on resolving environmental problems has so far reached its acme with the holding in Cairo, Egypt, of the first African Ministerial Conference on the Environment in December 1985. In Cairo, major resolutions known commonly as the Cairo Plan of Action were adopted. The conference was convened in collaboration with the UN Environment Program and the UN Economic Commission for Africa, with the principal objective of establishing a program that would lead to the ending of the environmental degradation and enable food and energy self-reliance. The conference was a follow-up to important preparatory works that had resulted in the elaboration of a detailed study on the main problems of each subregion in the field of the environment.

The Cairo gathering was historically important for more than one reason: It institutionalized an African Conference on Environment through the creation of an executive committee and a permanent secretariat. In its conception it had a scientific and innovative character, which enabled the setting up of regional pilot projects of ecodevelopment. In the minds of those who assembled at Cairo, the African crisis was first an ecological crisis that became an economic crisis whose resolution could only be found through firm intra-African cooperation.

If the Cairo conference was an important landmark owing to its general approach to the overall problem of environmental degradation in Africa, due mention must also be made of a category of arrangement with a more or less specialized character that focused on a particular aspect of environmental degradation. Most measures within this category have an institutionalized aspect.

Hence, in the area of the fight against natural plagues, the Convention on Migratory Crickets signed even before the inception of the OAU in Kano, Nigeria, in 1962 became the international organization for the fight against the migratory cricket. Furthermore, the Phytosanitary Convention concluded in Kinshasa in 1967 was transformed into the inter-African Phytosanitary Council.

The inter-African Bureau of Soils is charged with the delicate problems of erosion and the degradation of soils in the continent. In the area of agriculture there exist a number of intra-African organizations that are valuable instruments for cooperation. Among these are the International Center of Animal Breeding for Africa, and the Inter-African Bureau of Animal Resources, which coordinates activities for the preservation of the animal species on the continent.

At the subregional level, the Lagos Final Act of 1980 would largely inspire the efforts of member States in addressing environmental issues in the various subregions. Subregional efforts were to be deployed within the framework of multinational centers of programming and implementation of projects set up by the UN Economic Commission for Africa with a view to rendering member States' activities more operational.

In the same manner, it is mainly the legal instruments of Lagos connected with environmental issues that would largely commit member States concerning mechanisms and coordination policies in the field of the environment. On the one hand, the Lagos Plan makes recommendations to member States concerning mechanisms and coordination policies in the field of the environment; on the other hand, it defines the priority measures that should be taken and relates them to various areas of economic activity including, in particular, food, agriculture, natural resources, science and technology, the environment and development, and finally energy. Moreover, particular emphasis is placed on sanitation, health, and a drinkable water supply. The role of the OAU is not felt significantly in the various environment action plans under implementation in more than sixteen member States. Most individual States have sought funding and expertise from international organizations including, in particular, the International Monetary Fund (IMF), the World Bank, and the UN Development Program (UNDP). Madagascar, for one, has undertaken a fifteen-year environmental project largely funded by the IMF.[29]

It cannot be gainsaid in view of the foregoing that the OAU has not acted as far as environmental issues are concerned. It recently set up within its structure an environment department that has attempted, in its own modest way, to devise mechanisms and to define policies for member States. Nevertheless, as in many other areas where the organization has been called upon to act, these mechanisms and policies have hardly produced any results. And more than ever before, there is a growing painful complicity between the degrading African environment and the continent's unprecedented level of underdevelopment. It is important at this juncture to assess critically the actions and policies of the OAU in the field of the environment with a view to highlighting their real significance and impact.

The general observation is that, as far as environmental degradation is concerned, OAU's actions and policies have not gone far enough toward meeting the expectations of the people. Either at the OAU or at the individual member States level, there are no clear-cut and well-conceived follow-up policies, even on critical matters. Most declarations do not go beyond the conference rooms and most decisions and resolutions remain on paper and are later simply relegated to archives. Besides, there is an inherent pitfall in the structure of the OAU involving information dissemination and sensitization on important issues. Because of this situation, to an extent, most African delegates participating in environment conferences lack interest in and are unaware of the subjects involved.

Many of the institutionalized mechanisms have either remained inactive or have only succeeded in producing mediocre results. This is due to many factors, including insufficient funds for projects and operation, lack of expertise and research facilities, and inadequate scientific and technological means. As most of these mechanisms are agriculture oriented, consequently, an average of 100 million Africans are threatened each year by hunger and malnutrition.

Any program or engagement should be matched with a well-defined plan of implementation. The modalities for the functioning of such a program or engagement should be unequivocal. The truth is that in the case of the OAU, most decisions are unanimous expressions that are difficult to translate into action due largely to badly defined legal provisions. In this regard, a number of complaints have been raised by experts and governments on the legal shortcomings relating to the implementation of the Lagos Plan of Action and the Lagos Final Act. While the legal shortcomings can easily be overcome, it should be underlined that the major stumbling block lies in the lack of political will on the part of member States.

It is a serious problem that has marred the realization of many projects designed by the OAU. It is unfortunate that as States become more and more aware of the gravity of the continent's environmental degradation there is a coincidental decline of their faith in the organization. It is known that in Africa most of the projects that are taken seriously are those in which the Head of State himself is involved or has shown interest. In recent years, apart from the recently concluded summit in Abuja, fewer than twenty Heads of State and Government have participated in OAU's summits, the highest and most important organ of the continental organization. Consequently, very little interest or concern has been shown in the work of the OAU in general and the important role it should play in addressing the serious and growing challenges of our environment in particular.

It is difficult to solve the problem posed by this lack of political will, as there is no coercive mechanism that binds member States regarding the enforcement of the organization's political decisions, which are often very general in character. In view of these loopholes, emphasis ought to be laid on more technical and institutionalized measures to tackle, the major environmental problems most relevant to economic development and security in the region, with little politicking.

AN ENVIRONMENTAL ACTION PLAN FOR THE OAU

It is secret to none that African economies are in shambles. The OAU has recognized that there is a vitally important relationship between the environment and development. In July 1990, the OAU Secretary-General stated that "the promotion of Science and Technology and Human Resources Development must go hand in hand with the preservation of the environment which is a source of serious concern at the international level and increasingly so in Africa."[30] In this connection, he urged African governments to "focus greater attention on this issue by incorporating the environmental component of develop in their plans, programmes and projects." Furthermore, he underlined the necessity of mapping out "a veritable strategy so as to efficiently and collectively tackle the serious dangers inherent in environmental hazards such as desertification and deforestation." In reaction to the Secretary-General's report, African Heads of State and Governement meeting in Addis Ababa in July 1990, committed themselves "to the pursuit of sound population and environmental policies conducive to economic growth and development."

The OAU has issued a number of such political commitments regarding the state of the continent's environment. Nevertheless, more action-oriented and practical measures should be sought in order to translate some of the organization's brilliant and thoroughly thought-out political statements into concrete action. The OAU should be commended for advocating a collective approach to environmental issues. As a number of member States already possess environmental action plans, the OAU should sustain and encourage these measures by establishing within its structure a regional environment center and not just a department.

1. *Objectives of the Center.* The primary objectives of the center would be:
   a. to promote economic development in the region by controlling the exploitation of the continent's ecosystems;
   b. to eradicate the main threats to Africa's security such as: famine, malnutrition, diseases, and poverty;
   c. to check Africa's population explosion.
2. *Method of Work and Responsibilities of the Center.* The center would carry out its work through coordination, research, information, and education.
   a. *Coordination*: The center would coordinate and supervise member States' efforts in the field of the environment. It would also have, as appropriate, an advisory responsibility to governments and relevant subregional organizations.
   b. *Research*: As appropriate, research would be conducted on the various environment-related issues of the continent, with a view to enhancing and deepening understanding of the phenomenon of environmental degradation. A further role of research would be to bring out the various ways and means of solving the problems under study by proposing, for instance, benign alternative uses or substitutes for the environmental resources. Research activities could be extended to include climate prevision, observation, and supervision, particularly with respect to floods, earthquakes, and other calamities. The findings of research would be put at the disposal of governments, interested institutions, and individuals.
   c. *Information*: An African Environment Campaign should be undertaken to popularize and disseminate as largely as possible the crucial environmental problems facing the continent. In this regard, the center would publish newsletters, journals, and periodicals and encourage government and private media to broadcast regularly on environmental issues in local languages. It should be borne in mind that these issues are still largely unknown to many Africans no matter the level of their education.
   d. *Education*: Efforts would be deployed to create an environment culture by (1) elaborating environmental school programs that would be inserted into the curricula of all levels of education, from preschool to university; (2) by publishing appropriate textbooks on Africa's environment. Activities relating to education could also include programs of training on the resolution of Africa's relevant environment issues such as the regeneration of the vegetal cover, water supply, irrigation, modern techniques of farming, birth control, town planning, usage of environment-related substitutes, etc.; and (3) by sensitizing rural populations on the importance and use of environmental resources with a view to creating or fostering formal environmental education and ethics.

3. *The Structure and Functioning of the Center.* The center could be divided into departments or units, each of which would focus on major environmental problems of Africa. Active cooperation would be encouraged with relevant governmental and nongovernmental organizations, research institutions, and individual countries outside Africa, in the areas of science, technology, etc.

4. *Financial Resources of the Center.* Member States would contribute regularly to the center. Project funds could include voluntary contributions from private individuals, governmental and nongovernmental organizations, or individual governments.

CONCLUSION

For the time being, Africa remains the continent that faces the greatest number of environmental threats. Here the link between development and the environment is most direct in view of the region's enormous reliance on agricultural activities and the exploitation of natural resources for the achievement of development and survival. The most dreaded features of environmental degradation in the region at present include the overall concept of desertification and its related effects as well as the inordinate population growth. Such features are indeed major factors of the continent's underdevelopment and basic insecurity in terms of hunger, malnutrition, poverty, and diseases, which more than any armed conflict threaten the life of more than 100 million Africans every year. In this light, there is an imperative need to redefine the concepts of development and security in Africa.

One of the basic characteristics of environmental problems is that they ignore the political boundaries between States. For instance, pollutants can flow from one nation to another through air or water, and cataclysmic floods unleashed by denuded watersheds can flow across many countries. Climate changes, ozone depletion, deterioration of the agricultural base, and deforestation can equally threaten the safety and well-being of an entire region. Accordingly, meaningful efforts to protect the environment have to be collective and regional.

Created in part to ensure the welfare and progress of African peoples, the OAU until very recently had not perceived this aspect of its mission from the angle of environmental protection. It has only recently begun realizing that the two processes—underdevelopment and environmental deterioration—are interactive and mutually reinforcing. It has also come to realize that real security for its poor States cannot be achieved by military build-ups and arms races when there is a worthier race, the race to save the continent's fast degrading ecosystem. Accordingly, the organization has formulated a few mechanisms and policies in this regard. Judging from their modest results, it cannot be gainsaid that in the field of environmental protection the organization's efforts are still far below the needs and expectations of the people.

Many factors, including most importantly the lack of firm political will, have hindered the realization of a great number of OAU's projects. A further shortcoming has been the fact that at the OAU issues that gain sympathy and interest are those that arouse passion, as apartheid and decolonization have done for a long time. The shameful toxic waste dumping on Africa was one of the few environmental and oddly passionate issues that brought OAU member States to act swiftly in 1988 by passing a resolution that called for international action against such dumping practices. Subsequently, OAU's efforts resulted in the adoption of the Code of Practice on the Transboundary Movement of Radioactive Waste in Vienna at the thirty-fourth regular session of the International Atomic Energy Agency in September 1990. Initiatives of this nature should be encouraged and the organization need not necessarily capitulate on passionate issues.

However, it is hoped that as African States become more and more asphyxiated by the generalized economic hardships and as the inescapable contribution of the degrading environment becomes more and more evident in the continent's gloomy development prospects, there will be enough passion not only to stir sympathy and interest, but also to incite member States to strengthen existing mechanisms and policies and to take bolder and more concrete initiatives in circumventing environmental threats. This may be feasible, particularly in view of the emerging democratic climate that is sweeping aside conservative leaders and making way not only for political openness but also for freedom to think rationally for the overall betterment of the people.

NOTES

1. Julius Nyerere, former President of Tanzania, excerpt of speech made to the Food and Agricultural Organization (FAO) in 1985. See FAO Report, "World Leaders Address the Hunger Issue," *Ceres* 18, October 16, 1985.

2. Pollution in its various aspects as well as military threats to the environment exist to a certain degree in Africa, but do not, comparatively, constitute a major cause for concern for the time being. The resolution on the denuclearization of Africa passed in 1964 following French nuclear testing on the Sahara can be conceived of as one of the major steps taken by the OAU as far as military threats to the environment are concerned. It should also be borne in mind that some of the conflict-infested areas in Liberia, Angola, Mozambique, Chad, Western Sahara, and the Horn of Africa may run the risk of becoming barren due to military actions. For further reading on the impact of military actions on the environment, see Arthur S. Westing, ed., *Cultural Norms, War and the Environment* (Stockholm: SIPRI, 1988).

3. H.J. Cooke asserts that the Kalahari is misnamed as a desert while it has vast resources of grazing free from tsetse fly infestation, and a large wildlife population. For more, see his article in *The Geographical Journal* 151(1) (March 1985), pp. 75–85.

4. The data found in this section of the chapter have been drawn largely from the Report of the Executive Director of the UN Environment Programme on the African Conference on Environment held in Cairo, Egypt, 16–18 December 1955. For this note, see page 6 of that report.

5. Ibid.

6. Ibid.

7. Ibid., p. 7.

8. Ibid., p. 6.

9. See "Special Memorandum of the Council of Ministers of the ECA on the African Economic and Social Crisis," E/ECA/CM., 10/37/Rev.1, adopted by the Conference at its tenth session in May 1984.

10. Report of the Executive Director of UNEP, p. 7.

11. Jean-Paul Lanly, *Tropical Forest Resources*, FAO Forestry Paper 30, FAO, Rome, 1982. Also see *Africa Recovery* 5 (2–3) (September 1991), p. 38.

12. Olusegun Obasanjo, Address to the Africa Leadership Forum, Lagos, Nigeria, 21 June 1990, p. 15.

13. *IMF Survey*, IMF, 2 April 1990, p. 97.

14. Obasanjo, Address to the Africa Leadership Forum.

15. *Le Plan d'Action Forestier*, FAO, WRI, Washington, D.C., 1985.

16. Report of the Executive Director of UNEP, p. 6.

17. Obasanjo, Address to the Africa Leadership Forum, p. 16.

18. Mostafa K. Tolba, *Pour un Monde Ecologiquement Equitable*, PNUE, Doc. d'Info. Ecologique No. 1, 1990, p. 6.

19. Obasanjo, Address to the Africa Leadership Forum, p. 6.

20. Ibid.

21. *CEA, Profil de la Population Africaine*, CEA, Addis Ababa, 1984.

22. Robert S. McNamara, "Africa's Development Crisis: Agricultural Stagnation, Population Explosion and Environmental Degradation," Address to the Africa Leadership Forum, Lagos, Nigeria, 21 June 1990.

23. G.O.P. Obasi, "Rechauffement Global et Développement Global," in *Afrika*, ISSN 0340/5796, January–February 1991, p. 6.

24. Delft Hydraulics, *Criteria for Assessing Vulnerability to Sea-Level Rise: A Global Inventory to High Risk Areas*. UNEP H838, 1989.

25. Ibid.

26. Michael Renner, *National Security: The Economic and Environmental Dimensions*. Worldwatch Paper 89, Washington, D.C., 1989, p. 30.

27. Ibid.

28. Ibid., p. 6.

29. *IMF Survey*.

30. Salim A. Salim. "Report of the Secretary General on the Fundamental Changes Taking Place in the World and Their Implications for Africa: Proposals for an African Response," Address made at the OAU Council of Ministers (Fifty-sixth Ordinary Session) 3–7 July 1990, Addis Ababa.

Part III

Relations with Other Organizations and Systems

8

OAU–UN Relations in a Changing World

BERHANYKUN ANDEMICAEL

INTRODUCTION

As it approaches its fourth decade, the Organization of African Unity faces seemingly insurmountable obstacles in all fields in responding to the challenges of the 1990s with the help of the international community, in particular the United Nations. In Africa, the task of recovery and reconstruction remains formidable after decades of colonial and racial struggles, conflicts within and between States, deep economic crises, and humanitarian emergencies. At this crucial time, attention is moving away from Africa as a result of the rapid changes in world politics marking the end of the Cold War and the collapse of communism in Eastern Europe. The involvement of the United Nations on behalf of Africa has, therefore, become even more important to stem the tide of marginalization.

It is the purpose of this chapter to examine the evolution of OAU–UN relations in responding to the multidimensional crisis in Africa through immediate conflict management, prompt action in disasters and humanitarian emergencies, and programs of economic recovery. It will also examine the progress made in setting broad frameworks for long-term solutions through the establishment of structures, norms, and standards for political, economic, and social development in a rapidly changing world.

COMMON OBJECTIVES AND CHANGING PRIORITIES

The raison d'etre of African regionalism as embodied in the OAU Charter is the attainment of peace and security, freedom and justice, and economic and social development through common efforts among the African States.

The OAU Charter seeks to promote within Africa the main purposes and principles enumerated in Article 1 of the United Nations Charter. The OAU Charter states in Article 2 that the purposes of the organization are:

(a) To promote the unity and solidarity of the African States;

(b) To coordinate and intensify their cooperation and efforts to achieve a better life for the peoples of Africa;

(c) To defend their sovereignty, their territorial integrity and independence;

(d) To eradicate all forms of colonialism from Africa; and

(e) To promote international cooperation, having due regard to the Charter for the United Nations and the Universal Declaration of Human Rights.

The purposes and principles of the United Nations as stated in Article 1 of the Charter are:

1. To maintain international peace and security...;

2. To develop friendly relations among nations based on respect for the principle of equal rights and self-determination of peoples...;

3. To achieve international cooperation in solving international problems of an economic, cultural, or humanitarian character, and in promoting and encouraging respect for human rights and for fundamental freedoms for all...; and

4. To be a center for harmonizing the actions of nations in the attainment of these common ends.

It is evident that the objectives of the OAU and the United Nations are compatible even though the order of priorities is not identical. The OAU goals of attaining unity, development, security, and liberation can best be achieved under conditions of universal peace and security and international cooperation in all the problem areas enumerated in the charters of both organizations.[1]

In the first decade of the OAU ending in 1973, practical ways had to be found to reconcile the priorities between the overriding purpose of the United Nations to maintain international peace and security and the OAU's uppermost preoccupation to achieve decolonization and abolition of racist policies in South Africa. Representing about one-third of the membership of the United Nations, the African States were able to persuade the vast majority in the UN General Assembly to adapt its scale of values in terms of the African priorities, namely vigorous decolonization, including moral and material support for liberation movements, prohibition of intervention in the domestic affairs of small States, and promotion of economic development. The constraints of the Cold War had blunted the role of the United Nations in the peace and security field. The OAU was, therefore, encouraged by the Security Council to seek African solutions to African conflicts. The promotion of human rights in Africa was also largely left to the discretion of the African States, ostensibly because of their overriding requirements of nation-building.

The first decade of the OAU might be considered a general success for both the OAU and the UN in their joint efforts for decolonization, development, institution-building, and the establishment of norms for nonintervention and peaceful settlement of disputes in Africa.

The second decade of the OAU marked major setbacks. By the mid–1970s, most of Africa had attained liberation except for Southern Rhodesia, Namibia, and South Africa. But the liberation of the Portuguese-administered territories in 1975 transformed the problems of Southern Africa. The breakdown of the provisional Angolan government because of rivalry among the three liberation movements prevented a peaceful transition to independence. It led to fifteen years of civil war, which was exacerbated by Cold War entanglements and military intervention by Cuba and South Africa. The South African policy of destabilization of the frontline States had also helped to devastate Mozambique, thus creating a major security and humanitarian emergency. In both Angola and Mozambique, the combination of civil war and intervention by South Africa and by the Cold War protagonists posed a complex and insurmountable challenge to both the OAU and the United Nations. Southern Rhodesia, on the other hand, was a clear-cut colonial/settler case where collaborative efforts through international economic sanctions and support of the liberation struggle did help to bring about independence in 1980.

In the economic field, the initial hopes for a New International Economic Order (NIEO), counting partly on the newly acquired clout of the OPEC oil-producing countries, induced the OAU members to place economic issues at the top of the agenda. The United Nations was skillfully used by the OAU members to mobilize support not only for the NIEO concept but also for the concept of Least Developed Countries (LDCs), which applied to most African States. But little progress was made beyond concepts, because of lack of responsiveness by the developed countries. In the absence of meaningful support from the OPEC countries, the quadrupling of oil prices in 1973–1974 so damaged the economies of African countries that their nation-building efforts were placed in jeopardy. By the end of the 1970s, aside from West Africa, most of the continent was embroiled in costly and destabilizing civil wars and ideological struggles. Due to constitutional constraints relating to national sovereignty, both the OAU and United Nations were unable to offer effective diplomatic assistance for national reconciliation.

HANDLING OF AFRICAN CRISES IN THE 1980S AND BEYOND

By the first half of the 1980s Africa had been devastated not only by civil wars, particularly in Chad, Sudan, Ethiopia, Somalia, Angola, and Mozambique, but also by drought and famine, economic stagnation, and a massive debt burden. Subsequently, the AIDS epidemic in many sub-Saharan countries added to the disruption of African countries, already devastated by the massive movement of refugees and other displaced persons.

Relationships between any entities can be defined in terms of coexistence, cooperation, competition, or conflict. Coexistence and conflict are not applicable to the relationship between the OAU and the United Nations. The relations are basically cooperative, with occasional competition in handling inter-State conflicts or disputes where both the Security Council and the OAU have overlapping jurisdictions. In such cases, the norm established in the early years of the OAU to "try the OAU first" has been observed rather consistently. In handling the various crises facing Africa today the cooperative relationship between the OAU and the United Nations has involved joint action and mutual assistance, coordination of activities and division of labor, and mutual influence in the policy-making and programming process. Let us take a closer look at the management role of the OAU and the United Nations, especially with respect to African conflicts, humanitarian emergencies in the continent, and the African economic crisis.

Management and Resolution of African Conflicts

The African conflicts of the 1980s and 1990s may be grouped into three main categories: conflicts related to the decolonization process, inter-State conflicts, and internal conflicts affecting neighboring countries.

The first category includes the case of Western Sahara and the southern African cases of Angola, Mozambique, and Namibia. These complex cases of delayed decolonization, involving ideological and ethnic rivalries and foreign intervention, gave maximum scope to a political and diplomatic role for the United Nations, while the OAU acted essentially as a pressure group for vigorous action by the international community. As a global forum and an ultimate dispenser of legitimacy, the UN was relied upon to define principles and procedures for peaceful change and to mobilize non-African diplomatic resources with leverage on the protagonists. With the onset of detente resulting from the Soviet Union's disengagement policy under Mikhail Gorbachev, the complementary diplomatic initiatives of the USSR and the United States set the stage for constructive roles by the UN and the OAU. There was no difference between the UN and the OAU with respect to the necessity to carry out an internationally supervised referendum in Western Sahara. There was also no difference about the necessity to bring about the independence of Namibia and to help preserve the sovereignty and territorial integrity of Angola and Mozambique, free of foreign troops and mercenaries. However, the OAU's admission of the Sahrawi Republic as a member of the organization was viewed by Morocco as being so partisan that the OAU's diplomatic role concerning Western Sahara was virtually eliminated. The United Nations was not so handicapped, and was able to keep alive the issue of a referendum as a means toward a solution.

In the case of Angola and Mozambique both the OAU and UN were unable to facilitate national reconciliation, as they had given unqualified support to the recognized governments and felt bound by the principles of national sovereignty and territorial integrity. They had instead chosen to condemn the insurgencies and South Africa's support of their efforts as part of a policy of destabilizing the frontline States. Once detente was underway, however, the United Nations became a convenient forum for constructive and, eventually, productive contacts among most of the external actors (the United States, the Soviet Union, and Cuba) and between them and the governments of Angola and Mozambique. It was significant that the agreed withdrawal of Cuban and South African troops from Angola was in response to the good offices of the United States and the Soviet Union in the context of the United Nations. The United Nations was responsible for monitoring the cease-fire and the troop withdrawals, while the OAU's role was limited to providing political support for that effort.

In the case of Namibia, the steadfast opposition by the UN and the OAU to South Africa's defiance and their unequivocal support for SWAPO (South West Africa People's Organization) left no room for diplomatic initiatives for the two organizations. But the United Nations served again as a forum for increasingly productive contacts between a group of concerned Western governments and South Africa. When the cooperation of the Soviet Union was secured for the resolution of the interrelated problems of Angola and Namibia, the United Nations found it necessary to shift from a policy of pressure through support for SWAPO to one of impartial implementation of the agreed plan for Namibian independence. In its largest decolonization operations, the United Nations managed in Namibia a highly successful process of peace keeping, constitution making, and election, culminating in a democratic and independent Namibia. The OAU's role was largely limited to supporting the process and maintaining solidarity with SWAPO and the forces for genuine independence.

In sum, in the foregoing cases, both the UN and the OAU resorted for many years to advocacy and pressure to complete the process of decolonization and to contain the postcolonial conflict. Because of constitutional constraints and concerns about the issue of national sovereignty, little was done to facilitate national reconciliation. However, once the superpowers shifted their policies from competitive intervention to cooperative diplomatic involvement in southern Africa, the United Nations was able to mobilize diplomatic and material resources for a resolution of the problems.

With respect to the second category, the incidence of clear-cut inter-State conflicts has been rather rare during the third decade of the OAU. The most recent inter-State conflicts of 1990–1991—Chad/Libya, Rwanda/Uganda, and Senegal/Mauritania—required no involvement by the United Nations but were handled diplomatically by the OAU.[2]

The Chad/Libya conflict was the last phase of a decade of intermittent conflict between the two countries involving a complex mix of territorial dispute and intervention in the Chad civil war. Following its abortive effort in 1981 to mobilize a six-nation African peace-keeping force in Chad, the OAU had confined its role to offering good offices to facilitate peaceful settlement between the two countries. It was partly due to the persistent efforts of the OAU that the currently more compatible governments of Chad and Libya were able to agree to refer their dispute to the International Court of Justice.

The Rwanda/Uganda tension was caused by the armed activities of Rwandese refugees against their government, operating from bases in Uganda. Retaliatory incursions by Rwanda across its borders with Uganda and clashes with Ugandan troops had caused such concern about escalation that the heads of the three neighboring countries, as well as the OAU Secretary-General, devoted considerable diplomatic effort to bring about a reduction of inter-State tension and also, significantly, a cease-fire between the Rwanda government and the refugee forces. In a precedent-setting initiative, the OAU Secretary-General was empowered by the terms of the agreement to organize a group of neutral military observers from selected member States to monitor the cease-fire under his supervision.

The Senegal/Mauritania conflict was also amenable to mediation efforts by the OAU, both in the form of initiatives by an OAU inter-African commission and by the OAU Secretary-General. Both parties remained committed to a peaceful resolution of their differences, through the OAU.

In contrast to inter-State conflicts such these, the third category of conflicts—internal conflicts affecting neighboring countries—poses the greatest challenge to both the OAU and the United Nations. The most intractable have been the civil wars in Liberia, Sudan, Ethiopia, and Somalia. All of them have involved intensive ethnic conflicts, massive outflows of refugees, and internal population displacements, and consequently, formidable humanitarian emergencies. Both the OAU and the United Nations have been inhibited by the essentially internal character of the conflicts.

In the Liberian case, the military rebellion against dictatorship had developed into a full-blown civil war in 1990, complicated by conflicts between rival factions in the insurgency movement. The resulting total disruption of the country's social, administrative, and economic infrastructure has posed a challenge and a dilemma for both the United Nations and the OAU: whether to adopt a comprehensive approach, including initiatives to facilitate a cease-fire and national reconciliation, or to limit themselves to providing emergency assistance when they could. Neither the United Nations nor the OAU were inclined to take a diplomatic or peace-keeping initiative in Liberia. They resolved their dilemma by welcoming the initiative of the fifteen-member Economic Community of West African States. With their encouragement ECOWAS provided a peace plan under the provisions of its Protocol on Non-Aggression and dispatched in August 1990 a peace-keeping force to the Liberian capital, shortly before the defeat of President Doe's forces. By November 1990, a standing mediating committee of ECOWAS was able to secure a cease-fire among the combatants while the peace-keeping force was able to serve as a cease-fire monitoring group. Furthermore, in accordance with the ECOWAS peace plan, an Interim Government of National Unity was set up in Liberia until a free and fair general election could be held within one year under the observation of international bodies, including the United Nations and the OAU.[3]

It is significant that before the ECOWAS initiative, the seige of the capital and the breakdown of order in the capital and the ensuing chaos had induced the preparation of a rescue operation by U.S. Marines to evacuate foreign citizens. Subsequently, however, unilateral action by any concerned State was obviated by the multilateral peace-keeping role of ECOWAS, whose member States were keen to protect all residents of Monrovia including their own nationals. In this context the roles of the United Nations and the OAU were confined to providing political support to the ECOWAS efforts and mobilizing emergency humanitarian assistance.[4]

In the Sudan civil war involving a North/South conflict over religious policy and the issue of autonomy, no multilateral organization was able to take a peace-keeping initiative, all having confined their contributions essentially to humanitarian assistance. Belatedly, in 1990, the Secretary-General of the OAU offered his good offices to both the Sudanese government and the leaders of the insurgency. But his contacts with both sides were no more successful than the sporadic diplomatic initiatives taken over the years by individual African governments and nongovernmental organizations, including former U.S. President Jimmy Carter's International Negotiating Network.

As in the case of the Sudanese civil war, the various conflicts within Ethiopia have run their course with virtually no diplomatic involvement by either the United Nations or the OAU. The good offices of a third party were accepted by the militaristic government of Ethiopia only after September 1989 as a result of a number of factors: a series of crucial military defeats in Eritrea and the northern provinces of Ethiopia; deterioration of army morale, accompanied by dwindling Soviet military aid; the burden of widespread famine and economic catastrophe; and pressure by both the Soviet Union and the United States to seek a peaceful solution to the Eritrean question.

The first attempt was made by former President Jimmy Carter who, in two rounds of talks that he organized between the Ethiopian Government and the Eritrean Peoples Liberation Front (EPLF), was able to secure their agreement to a process of negotiations without preconditions. However, although agreement was reached to start substantive negotiations on the future of Eritrea under the joint chairmanship of Carter and former Tanzanian President Julius Nyerere, differences over the representation of the United Nations undermined further progress. It had been agreed that, as proposed by the EPLF, the OAU and the United Nations would attend the peace negotiations as observers, along with several African States proposed by both sides. The hitch was that, while the OAU Secretary-General accepted the Carter invitation to attend as an observer, the United Nations Secretary-General was unable to accept an observer's role without an explicit invitation from Ethiopia.

In the absence of such an invitation from Ethiopia, the escalation of conflict culminated in the cut-off of most food shipments to the famine areas, thus creating such a state of emergency that the entire problem found its way into the U.S.–Soviet summit agenda. For the first time, the Reagan-Gorbachev communique of June 1990 acknowledged the seriousness of the humanitarian and political problems in Eritrea and welcomed the new clarification expressed by the Ethiopian government to have UN representatives present in the course of the negotiations between the Ethiopian government and the Eritreans.

This initiative had the effect of transferring future diplomatic efforts from the nongovernmental orbit of distinguished statesmen to that of the superpowers, culminating in the mediation efforts of the U.S. Department of State with the cooperation of the Soviet Union.[5]

The presence of representatives of the United Nations and the OAU, as well as the Soviet Union, at the U.S.–mediated roundtable between the government and the opposition forces represented a new formula of peace making. A link was established between the process of superpower peace making and the subsequent stages of constitution making and referendum supervision in which a greater role was envisaged for the UN and the OAU, particularly with respect to Eritrean self-determination. The military defeat of the unpopular government forces during the negotiation and the assumption of power in Addis Ababa by Ethiopian forces allied to the Eritrean Peoples Liberation Front made it less difficult for the United Nations and the OAU to accept the responsibility to assist in the process in the exercise of self-determination in Eritrea. In this regard, of particular importance is the legitimizing role of both the United Nations and the OAU.

In contrast to the foregoing cases where the diplomatic roles of the United Nations and the OAU were marginal, the Somali War of 1991 created such a vacuum of power in the capital that it induced abandonment of the traditional jurisdictional inhibitions by the United Nations and the OAU. Earlier, when the Somali Liberation Movement declared independence in Northern Somalia (formerly British Somaliland), the OAU Council of Ministers adopted, in June 1991, a resolution that reaffirmed the indivisibility and territorial integrity of the Somali Republic, endorsed the initiatives of certain African States to convene a national reconciliation conference, and requested the OAU Secretary-General "to undertake a good offices mission to help all parties to arrive at an agreement to safeguard unity and territorial integrity."[6]

Even before any diplomatic action could be attempted toward reunification, the situation in Mogadishu deteriorated to such an extent that the split between the victorious forces launched a more devastating civil war in the capital. The total breakdown of law and order created such a humanitarian emergency and a vacuum of central authority that the United Nations Security Council was called upon by the internationally recognized faction to consider the crisis. In an unprecedented action relating to an African civil war, the Security Council assessed the impact of the conflict on the peace and stability of the region and concluded that its continuation would constitute a threat to international peace and security. Thus, by Resolution 733 (1992) the Security Council decided, under Chapter 7 of the United Nations Charter, to impose an arms embargo on Somalia. In addition, the Security Council requested the Secretary-General of the United Nations, in cooperation with the Secretary-Generals of the OAU, the League of Arab States, and the Organization of Islamic States, to seek a cease-fire and assist in the process of political settlement of the conflict. It was clearly recognized that a cease-fire was a prerequisite for the distribution of humanitarian assistance.

It is significant that, as in the recent case of Yugoslavia, the Security Council's alarm with the uncontrolled spread of violence, the enormous loss of life, and the obstruction of humanitarian assistance had galvanized support for Security Council involvement in a situation where the involvement of regional organizations and other third parties was deemed inadequate.

To sum up, the past experience of the United Nations and the OAU in the three categories of conflicts seems to indicate that their respective roles, whenever they were exercised, were complementary and that the question of primacy was no longer an important issue. The United Nations and the OAU were among many actors in the diplomacy of peace making in Africa and the depth of their involvement depended upon the nature of the issue, their relative capacities to help, and the willingness of the governmental side in a conflict to accept third-party assistance.

Thus, in the cases of southern Africa that involved colonial, racial, and ideological issues, it was a combination of superpower diplomacy and institutionalized United Nations activities that were relied upon. The OAU's role in those cases remained one of advocacy and political support for the governments of the frontline States, with virtually no effort made toward national reconciliation. However, in the clear-cut inter-State conflicts, the OAU played a more active diplomatic role, while the United Nations remained in the background. Nothing, of course, prevented the Secretaries-General of the United Nations and the OAU from assisting the parties through quiet diplomacy. The major weakness in the roles of both organizations had to do with internal conflicts. Until the Somali crisis, most efforts at peace making in civil wars had taken place outside the framework of both organizations. Those efforts variously included statesmen, individually or in groups, occasional subregional organizations, relevant intergovernmental organizations, and the superpowers when they had leverage on the parties.

The greatest challenge for the United Nations and the OAU thus remains in the area of internal conflicts. Thanks to the post–Cold War consensus among the five permanent members of the Security Council (veto powers), it has been possible for the Council to define certain internal conflicts, including the Somali civil war, in terms of their relevance to international peace and security, and thus mobilize the peace-making capacity of the United Nations. A precedent has thus been established for African internal conflicts where major internal dislocations and a vacuum of power might have security repercussions in a wider area. The potential for expansion of this role of the United Nations to fill a vacuum will undoubtedly pose a challenge for the OAU, whose Secretary-General has already taken some diplomatic initiatives and made significant reform proposals. In the final analysis, however, the respective roles of the United Nations and the OAU might depend on their relative capacities to deliver. Given the close link between humanitarian and diplomatic involvement in civil war situations, the United Nations would undoubtedly be at an advantage, should it become necessary to follow the Somalia precedent. However, in view of the growing burden of United Nations operations in other parts of the world it would seem necessary to rely more heavily on a more active OAU role, particularly in preventive and quiet diplomacy, if the concepts could be clearly accepted by the OAU membership.

Management of African Humanitarian Emergencies

The decade of the 1980s has often been referred to as Africa's "lost decade," in which the record of development was predominantly negative. The decade was marked by repeated famines and massive displacements of people—caused by both droughts and armed conflicts. It was characterized by economic stagnation, decay of physical and social infrastructure, high debt burdens, and poor prices for Africa's key exports.

The first major African catastrophe was the 1984–1985 famine, which affected over twenty countries and several million people. The desperate need for emergency assistance from the international community required solidarity and a common approach by African States within the OAU as well as massive aid through the United Nations. In one of its most effective emergency operations, the United Nations was able to raise and deliver over $4 billion of assistance to Africa. The Office of Emergency Operations in Africa that was set up for that purpose still remains a model of effective coordination among intergovernmental and nongovernmental organizations and of efficient emergency operations.

Again in 1991, Africa was faced with a famine affecting seventeen countries and over 30 million people. The worst situations remain in those countries afflicted by civil strife—Angola, Mozambique, and Liberia, as well as Ethiopia, Somalia, and Sudan. The scope, urgency, and complexity of the humanitarian emergency in the Horn of Africa was so much greater than that of 1984–1985 that the United Nations was called upon by the donor community as well as the OAU to play an enhanced role to ensure aid delivery. The combination of drought, warfare, and refugee movements made the emergencies so much more intractable than natural disasters that the United Nations had to devise politically sensitive approaches to overcome obstacles to food delivery. The United Nations Special Emergency Program for the Horn of Africa has spared no effort to prevent food from being used as a weapon between government forces and insurgency movements; among the innovations were the delicate negotiations for food corridors, cross-border routes, airdrops, and other special arrangements with governments and with unrecognized authorities that control territories in the emergency area.

The problem of African refugees has remained in a state of emergency throughout the 1980s. By 1992, as a result of civil wars and famines, the figure for African refugees reached 6 million, while that of displaced persons within their own countries exceeded 12 million. The role of the United Nations High Commissioner for Refugees in mobilizing international assistance has been extremely significant. Its efforts to provide legal protection to refugees and to organize resettlement and rehabilitation have been equally important. Through its Commission of Fifteen on Refugees, the OAU has provided invaluable assistance and cooperation, especially in preserving solidarity among the African States in observing the requirements of existing refugee conventions. The main problem facing both the United Nations and the OAU is that, despite their intensive efforts, the magnitude of the problem has grown steadily while the flow or resources has began to dwindle. As the root causes of the refugee phenomenon have not so far been effectively addressed, both organizations have been unable to achieve large-scale voluntary repatriation of refugees.

The problem of displaced persons is even more serious, as both the United Nations and the OAU are constrained by the absence of legal instruments to facilitate access to the millions of uprooted populations in conflict areas. As mentioned above, access to the innocent victims of conflict depends on overcoming the serious political obstacles facing both the United Nations and the OAU. The role of the International Committee of the Red Cross and other nongovernmental organizations has been significant but far from sufficient.

A promising development within the United Nations is the establishment by the General Assembly in December 1991 of an Office of Emergency Relief

Coordinator. This new department of the United Nations secretariat has assumed responsibility for all emergency activities of the United Nations and will manage a $50 million central Emergency Revolving Fund. Its success will depend partly on close cooperation with regional and nongovernmental organizations as well as with relevant organizations and entities of the United Nations system, including UNHCR. Within Africa, the experience of the 1980s strongly suggests that the OAU Secretary-General requires unambiguous support from member States for low-key diplomatic initiatives in internal conflicts, at best to assist in the process of national reconciliation without prejudice to the recognition issue, and, at least, to facilitate the flow of humanitarian assistance.

Handling of the African Development Crisis

The African economies have been in a state of deepening crisis since the famine of 1984–1985. Even before that emergency the serious decline of African economies was fully recognized by the OAU Summit when it adopted in 1980 the ambitious Lagos Plan of Action for the Economic Development of Africa, 1980–2000. In 1985, the OAU Summit adopted a more realistic, carefully designed recovery strategy, known as the African Priority Program for Economic Recovery—1986–1990 (APPER).[7] In a remarkable show of support for that program, the United Nations General Assembly approved a United Nations Program of Action for African Economic Recovery and Development (UNPAAERD) for the period 1986–1990.[8] Despite the goodwill of the international community and the efforts of the African States to live up to their obligations under APPER and UNPAAERD, the record of implementation was largely negative for lack of external resources. Basically, little use was made of the program as a frame for specific action as originally intended, since most countries had to shift their focus to an agenda of structural adjustment laid down by the World Bank and the International Monetary Fund as increasingly required by donor countries.

The magnitude of African economic and social decline was marked by "severely depressed economic growth rates, stagnant agricultural production, deteriorating social services, and declines in living standards."[9] Externally, it was marked by a rising and debilitating debt burden, a sharp fall in prices for African commodities, and a decline in aid and foreign investment.[10] As a result, Africa not only continues to have the largest number of LDCs, but the number has continued to grow: by 1991, twenty of the forty-two LDCs in the world were from Africa—up from fourteen in 1979. Africa has the fastest population growth rate in the world; its population has already reached 650 million. It is indeed the only continent where per capita economic production has consistently declined during the 1980s.[11]

The major response of the OAU to the economic crisis has been to focus on the establishment of an African Economic Community, as originally recommended in 1980 in the Lagos Plan of Action. After five years of nego-tiation, under the framework of the OAU, a Treaty for the Establishment of the African Economic Community was prepared and signed at the OAU Summit in June 1991. As the continental economic community would be buttressed by the existing subcontinental communities and organizations, the OAU has requested its Secretary-General, in cooperation with the Executive Secretary of the UN Economic Commission for Africa and the President of the African Development Bank (ADB), to prepare various protocols, espe-cially one for rationalizing and harmonizing the institutions at the regional and subregional levels.

After ratification of the treaty, implementation would be carried out by a monitoring committee comprising the OAU Secretary-General and the Ex-ecutive Secretaries of subcontinental economic communities and organiza-tions, with technical support from the ADB, ECA, and the United Nations Development Program. So much importance is attached to the African Eco-nomic Community that it would eventually be made an integral part of a revised OAU Charter.[12]

The response of the United Nations to the African economic crisis has been to assess the implementation of the UNPAAERD program rigorously and to adopt a New Agenda for the Development of Africa in the 1990s, taking fully into account the OAU's commitment to achieve effective regional and subregional economic cooperation and integration.[13] The New Agenda sets as its main objectives:

1. To achieve an average real growth rate of 6 percent per annum of GNP throughout the 1990s

2. To mobilize in 1992 a minimum of $30 billion in net official development assis-tance (ODA), which should grow by 4 percent every year, and also consider establishing a commodity diversification fund

3. To find durable solutions to the African debt crisis, including cancellation of ODA debt and debt service, relief for official bilateral debt, and imaginative approaches for commercial debts

4. To pay special attention to human development goals

In this context, African countries have undertaken to persist with necessary reforms and improve their economic management, and to promote sustain-able development through the full participation of the people, for which a commitment to pursue democratization is essential. They have also agreed to redouble their efforts to implement fully the population policies, including family planning, in accordance with the 1984 United Nations Program for Action for African Population.

For the future, the most urgent task of the United Nations system is to develop specific programs for Africa that are consistent with the elements of the New Agenda. Priority would be given to resource mobilization and debt relief, two of the most controversial issues in view of the reluctance of the donor countries to make concrete commitments. On the part of the OAU, the major tasks are to maintain the momentum toward African regional and subregional economic integration and to encourage the transformation of the African economies, including policies supporting agriculture and food security, rural development, population control, and social development.

In conclusion, the responsibility for the handling of the three types of African crises has been shared by the United Nations and the OAU. As all the tasks of providing conflict management, humanitarian assistance, and economic relief are resource-intensive, heavy reliance on the United Nations seems inevitable. The role of the OAU in promoting harmonization of policies and reconciliation of differences between African States remains vital. In the current situation involving uncontrolled inter-State or internal conflicts with serious humanitarian and economic consequences, it has become necessary for both the United Nations and the OAU to go beyond their traditional diplomatic roles in seeking solutions to transnational problems involving subnational groups. In this delicate area, the potential of the OAU's assets remains yet to be developed.

IMPACT OF GLOBAL CHANGES ON OAU–UN RELATIONS

As the decade of the 1990s begins, the end of the Cold War, the collapse of communism, and the unification strides in Western Europe have transformed the international environment to such an extent that the United Nations and regional organizations are faced with new opportunities as well as new challenges. These changes in the Northern Hemisphere, combined with the widespread turmoil and instability in much of the Southern Hemisphere, have spawned new political concepts about international relations for the 1990s. As the familiar geopolitical map became obsolete with the end of the Cold War, the old ideological rivalry has given way to a new contest between forces of integration and fragmentation. As a global center for harmonizing the actions of nations for the attainment of common ends, the United Nations provides a forum for reconciling those forces. The centripetal forces include the commitment to peace and the efforts to understand and handle problems in the fields of development, the environment, human rights, and humanitarian emergencies. They also include the integrative pressures of the revolutions in communications and technology. Pitted against these are the centrifugal forces of nationalism, ethnic and religious rivalries, racial bigotry, and xenophobia that have been unleashed in transitional societies.[14]

The concept of a "new world order," advocated by the United States, is a response to this trend, both as an attempt to comprehend the dynamics of change and as a means of channelling the new forces. The term preferred within the United Nations is "better world order," a more positive term reflective of the Charter's objectives of peace, development, and multilateral cooperation.

The end of the Cold War has marked the end of an essentially bipolar world and has released energies for advancing globalism and for reform of the international society. Within the United Nations, it has meant a shift from ideological competition between the two superpowers to active co-operation in addressing global and regional issues. In the General Assembly, the traditional triangular pattern of alignments—East, West, and nonaligned—have become blurred, while consensual declarations and resolutions have become more frequent and more authoritative. In the Security Council, the superpower cooperation provides a nucleus around which the five permanent members of the Council—China, France, the Soviet Union, the United Kingdom and United States—are able to engage in consensus politics as envisaged in the UN Charter. The hitherto modest achievements of the Security Council on the basis of the nonaligned initiatives are now overshadowed by path-breaking joint initiatives by the Permanent Five in various regional conflicts. The achievements of the Security Council in regional conflicts—notably, Namibia, Central America, Cambodia, and Iraq—have so enhanced its pres-tige and authority that it can now mount major peace-keeping and peace-making operations. Given its capacity to mobilize substantial diplomatic and material resources, the Security Council is able to reclaim its predominant role in the maintenance of international peace and security in situations such as those in Africa where the competent regional organization encounters serious institutional and material constraints.

The collapse of communism and of the Soviet empire has brought about not only the removal of ideological divisiveness in the world but also the emancipation of Eastern Europe. The consequent disintegration of the Soviet Union itself and the economic and political disruption within its component republics has caused so much concern in the industrialized Western world that the future of the successor States has become the major setback for attention. Not only is the Third World deprived of external aid from the Soviet Union but it is now also faced with new competition for foreign aid from the components of the very same State. A major consequence of this shift of attention to Eastern Europe is the marginalization of the Third World, especially Africa, at a time of aid fatigue. This transformation has also di-minished the capacity of the United Nations to dispense aid to the Third World, as Eastern Europe and the former Soviet Union shift from the donor list to that of aid recipients.

The reunification of Germany and the progress made toward further in-tegration in the European Community have not shown any tendency to counter the economic marginalization of Africa, although a more unified and stronger Europe could conceivably provide greater assistance under the Lomé Convention arrangements for the African, Caribbean, and Pacific States. In the political field, as the Soviet external influence disappeared, the European

Community and the United States have assumed a parallel approach for promoting human rights and democracy as essential conditions for development in the Third World. Such political attention has had some impact on the process of democratization in Africa without, however, reversing the trend toward economic marginalization of the continent.

A redefinition of North-South relations has become necessary as a result of the foregoing transformations. The new geopolitical map represents a global security system dominated by the United States as the remaining single superpower and a tripolar economic system comprising the United States, the European Community, and Japan. The balance of power and influence, resulting from an interplay between the two systems, would shape the emerging new world order. To the extent that this new order embodies shared responsibilities for global security and an economic partnership for global economic growth and development, one can hope that the integrity of the traditional North-South cooperation may be preserved.

The interest of the OAU and its member States is to ensure that Africa is treated by the North neither as a neglected backwater nor as a permanent economic dependency. For the OAU the central issue is transfer of financial resources to Africa by fulfilling the commitments already made through the United Nations, including relief of external debt, achievement of the agreed target for official development assistance (0.7 percent of GDP), amelioration of the terms of trade, and the various measures under the UNPAAERD. If Africa is to avoid marginalization, any assistance given to Eastern Europe should have to be without prejudice to those commitments.

For the donor countries of the North, the central issues are prevention of further spread of instability in the former Soviet empire as well as cost-effectiveness in aid delivery. For these reasons, not only would they give top priority to timely assistance to Eastern Europe as a matter of security interest, but they would also insist upon new conditions for providing further aid to Africa and the Third World. The new wisdom within donor governments and international financial agencies is that without "good governance" no amount of external aid, irrespective of a wealth of natural resources, could reverse the economic deterioration in developing countries. The concept of governance comprises the restoration or implementation of the democratic process in government, the reorganization of national priorities with emphasis of human resource development, the prevention of conflicts by promoting human rights and civil liberties, and the encouragement of free enterprise and market economies.

The debate between these two approaches—the African quest for more resources and the donor countries' insistence on governance and cost-effectiveness—has been sharpened as a result of the global changes brought about by the end of the Cold War. A mutually acceptable solution can most effectively be worked out through the United Nations in accordance with established targets, strategies, and commitments. There is no longer any disagreement over the lines of reform recommended by the donor countries, as the OAU itself has acknowledged their importance as a means of conflict prevention and as a prerequisite for development. In this period of great scarcity of aid resources, this tendency toward a common approach bodes well for enhancing the capacity of the United Nations as a channel of multilateral aid. In this context, an active and continuous role of the OAU as a concerted voice of Africa is essential for preventing further marginalization of the continent.

STRENGTHENING OAU–UN COLLABORATION

In his first message to the Council of Ministers of the OAU, Secretary-General of the United Nations Boutros Boutros-Ghali stated in February 1992 that he would do his utmost to help free Africa of conflicts and disasters and to provide conditions in which its people can enjoy their right to development in freedom and peace. Stressing the common objectives of the United Nations and the OAU, he placed special emphasis on the need to build close cooperation in accordance with the provisions of Chapter 8 of the UN Charter, which govern United Nations relations with regional organizations as regards the maintenance of international peace and security. Moving away from the traditional jurisdiction-oriented perspective represented by the "try OAU first" approach, he pledged to help establish a pattern of future cooperation and the means by which the United Nations could help enhance the role of regional organizations and render practical assistance so that they may contribute to peace-keeping and peace-making efforts. The Somalia experience was cited as a precedent of joint action in Africa.[15]

For his part, Secretary-General Salim Ahmed Salim of the OAU has repeatedly called for closer OAU–UN collaboration in solving the massive problems of Africa, with little or no concern about the issue of organizational primacy.[16]

The real challenge for both organizations has been how to intervene effectively in African humanitarian emergencies caused or aggravated by internal conflicts, without unduly infringing on the domestic jurisdiction of African States. In his keynote speech at the Security Council Summit in January 1992, UN Secretary-General Boutros-Ghali resolved the dilemma by redefining State sovereignty for our times. To the well-known dimension of rights of States, he added the dimension of responsibility, both internal and external. Explaining the new meaning, he said, "Violation of State sovereignty is, and will remain, an offence against the global order. But its misuse also may undermine human rights and jeopardize a peaceful global life."[17] Within the OAU, the frequent appeals of Secretary-General Salim and his discrete diplomatic attempts in certain civil wars have reflected a similar inclination. The validity of this approach has now been acknowledged by member States as manifested in the joint UN–OAU involvement in Somalia, which is predicated on the linkage between uncontrolled civil wars and the maintenance of international peace and security.

A common perspective, followed by a joint effort, represents a significant step toward sustained collaboration, but the relative contributions of the OAU and the United Nations to that effort depend on the competence, capacity, and initiative of each organization. At present the United Nations has an advantage over the OAU in all respects. The Security Council's supranational powers and its impressive recent record of unanimous and decisive action disposes it to consider effective measures where the OAU organs may be constrained by the preoccupation with national sovereignty. The capacity of the United Nations to provide a continuous machinery and mobilize resources for large operations cannot be matched by the OAU. The statutory role of the United Nations Secretary-General in preventive diplomacy under Article 99 of the UN Charter has no counterpart in the OAU Charter. Thus, if the OAU is to make a more substantive contribution as a partner, it will need considerable institutional reform. The idea of a permanent OAU Peace Council composed of resident representatives at OAU headquarters remains valid, as does the need to strengthen the good offices of the OAU Secretary-General.[18]

Even after such reforms, equal partnership in all situations seems neither feasible nor desirable. A cost-effective, rational division of labor and mutual support could produce concrete results.

An important function of peace making and peace building is the setting of structures and norms. The OAU has brought about the adoption of various conventions, charters, declarations, and programs of action among African States, particularly with respect to an African economic community, economic recovery and development, refugees, human rights, and democratization. In some cases, these documents constituted a regional complement of existing United Nations instruments, while in others they provided a basis for broader declarations by the United Nations. The problem remains one of acceptance and full implementation by all African States, so that they may serve as an active guide for State behavior rather than merely as an expression of wishes. In the realm of action, the OAU summit should demonstrate its full commitment by implementing the operational plans of the OAU Secretary-General, including the recommended monitoring mechanisms of the secretariat.

In the peace-making area, the proposal of Secretary-General Salim for a secretariat mechanism for conflict management is urgently needed if the OAU is to engage seriously in preventive diplomacy and conflict resolution. The present ad hoc approach of the secretariat and the sporadic good offices offered by the Chairman of the OAU are simply not sufficient for a sustained role in African peace making. The OAU secretariat requires a credible peace-making capacity if the OAU expects to make a dent on the root causes of African conflicts, especially the complex internal conflicts. With such reforms, a logical division of labor between the two organizations should be arranged, with some flexibility for adjustments and mutual support in accordance with the availability of material and diplomatic resources. The OAU would be well advised to focus on conciliation efforts among its member States and to take bolder initiatives for national reconciliation within African States. In this regard, more reliance should be placed on a strengthened impartial role of the secretariat rather than on the intermittent and highly political initiatives of the Chairman of the OAU and other heads of state. The United Nations would then be able to focus on resource-intensive missions ranging from peace-keeping operations to major humanitarian activities.

In the long run, the peace-building role of the OAU, as a derivative of its unity goal, may prove to be its most important function. A good beginning has been made in facilitating African economic integration and in promoting human rights and democracy. Crucial to this process is the OAU's role of policy harmonization, which still requires reinforcement. In a world of dwindling resources for foreign aid, the United Nations' role of mobilizing resources for Africa remains vital. For both organizations, success in Africa depends on their close collaboration.

NOTES

1. Berhanykun Andemicael, *The OAU and the UN: Relations Between the Organization of African Unity and the United Nations*, UNITAR Regional Study No. 2 (New York and London: Africana Publishing, 1976), Chapter 2.

2. "Introductory Note to the Secretary-General's Activity Report," OAU Assembly of Heads of State and Government, Twenty-sixth Session (July 1990); "Introductory Note of the Secretary-General," OAU Council of Ministers, Fifty-third Ordinary Session (February 1991).

3. UN document A/45/894-S/22025 of 20 December 1990, containing the communique of the ECOWAS First Extraordinary Session of the Assembly of Heads of State and Government, Bamako, 27–28 November 1990.

4. UN General Assembly resolution 45/232 of 21 December 1990; Security Council Presidential Statement, document S/22133 of 22 January 1991.

5. "U.S.–Soviet Team Effort in Ethiopia," *Christian Science Monitor*, 15 June 1990.

6. OAU resolution CM/Res. 1340 (LIV)/Rev. 1, Forty-fourth Ordinary Session of the Council of Ministers, 27 May–1 June 1991.

7. UN document A/40/666, Annex I, Declaration AHG/Decl.1 (XXI), Annex, adopted by the OAU Assembly of Heads of State and Government at its Thirty-first Ordinary Session, 18–20 July 1985.

8. UN General Assembly resolution S–13/2 and Annex, adopted by the Thirteenth Special Session of the Assembly on 1 June 1986.

9. Society for International Development, "The Challenge of Africa in the 1990's," *Report: the North-South Roundtable*, Ottawa, Canada, 18–19 June 1991, pp. 3–7.

10. Salim A. Salim, *Development Partnership in the 1990's: The African Dimension*, Paul G. Hoffman Lecture, UNDP Development Study Programme, 1990, pp. 4–8.

11. UN Economic Commission for Africa, *African Alternative Framework to Structural Adjustment Programmes for Socio-Economic Recovery and Transformation* (Addis Ababa, April 1991), p. 1.

12. OAU resolution AHG/Res. 205 (XXVII), Abuja, Nigeria, 3–5 June 1991.

13. UN General Assembly resolution 46/151 and Annex, 18 December 1991.

14. A perceptive analysis is given in John Lewin Gaddis, "Toward the Post–Cold War World," *Foreign Affairs* 70(2) (Spring 1991).

15. Message of the Secretary-General of the United Nations to the Council of Ministers of the OAU, UN Press Release SG/SM/4703, 25 February 1992.

16. "Introductory Note to the Secretary-General's Activity Report," OAU Assembly of Heads of State and Government, presented to the Twenty-seventh Session (1991).

17. Secretary-General's statement at the Security Council Summit Meeting, UN Press Release SG/SM/4691, 31 January 1992.

18. Berhanykun Andemicael and Davidson Nicol, "The OAU: Primacy in Seeking African Solutions Within the UN Charter," in Yassin El-Ayouty and I.W. Zartman, eds., *The OAU After Twenty Years* (New York: Praeger, 1984), pp. 116–117.

9

OAU–UN Interaction over the Last Decade

EDMOND KWAM KOUASSI

Although they are derivative subjects of international law,[1] today international organizations have to all appearances become the central nervous system of international life. This is borne out by several convergent phenomena.

First, there has been a downgrading of the role of states in resolving crises, both political and economic, in favor of the regulation of international affairs through multilateral machinery. Second, for some years now, the hostility of states to international organizations[2] has been giving ground to the establishment of a dynamic process of internal change conducive to the renewal of the multilateral system. Last, and most important, the analysis of the interconnections and intertwining of the various elements of the international system highlights the role that devolves upon international organizations as the instruments best equipped for the peaceful settlement of disputes.

This international environment that is conducive to the development of international organizations will doubtless have a decisive influence on the institutional theory of international relations. In these specific conditions, an assessment of the relationship between the United Nations and the Organization of African Unity, which "identified the existence of three distinct areas oriented in three parallel ways," continues to be relevant.[3] Indeed, during the decade of the 1980s, the areas of cooperation between the two organizations were not only maintained but also strengthened.

Two major, and more or less interdependent, questions arise about the relationship between the UN and the OAU. Can one speak today of a positive trend in the relationship between the UN and the OAU? If so, what shape has this trend taken? Has it preserved the integrity, indeed the sovereignty, of the pan-African organization?

The law of international organizations assesses the relationship between the UN and the OAU in the following terms:

First, the two organizations have embarked upon and maintained a form of economic cooperation, the cornerstone of which is the United Nations Program of Action for African Economic Recovery and Development (1986–1990), adopted by the General Assembly at its thirteenth special session held in New York in May–June 1986.

Second, the maintenance of international peace and security has been enhanced by a new development. The conflict over Western Sahara and the question of Namibian independence have brought to light the phenomenon of the delegation by the OAU of its "national competence" to the UN. It is easy to observe that in the settlement of these two conflicts the world organization has outclassed the OAU and has acted in its stead without any objection being raised that it has encroached upon any autonomous or reserved areas.

Last, the relations between the OAU and the UN have in the past ten years emphasized a new area of cooperation, one that previously had only been embryonic, namely, disarmament. A case in point is the establishment of the United Nations Regional Center for Peace and Disarmament in Lomé, Togo. In short, the relationship between the OAU and the UN is bound up in a logic that embodies a twofold challenge and the code of a new multilateralism.

A TWOFOLD CHALLENGE

The challenge that has arisen has been to accommodate both the declared intentions of the policy-making bodies to organize cooperation between the UN and the OAU and at the same time the clear-cut determination of the two organizations to preserve their respective sovereignty against all comers.

These two requirements will keep the cooperation efforts of the two organizations within their original confines, with the occasional foray into areas that to date have been little explored. The commitments that the OAU and the UN have undertaken with respect to interorganization cooperation have been of two sorts: the first have been in the form of treaties, while the second have taken the form of declarations or plans. In any event, the cooperation we are witnessing has barely begun, and its basic thrust is in the economic and political spheres.

The OAU–UN Relationship in the Area of Economic Cooperation

The main themes of economic cooperation between the OAU and the UN in the decade 1980–1990 have been the persistence of economic crisis, famine, and malnutrition, and the population explosion in the African continent.

These focuses of economic cooperation between the OAU and the UN account for the participation of the United Nations Economic Commission for Africa (ECA) in the organization of the first summit conference of the Heads of State and Government of the OAU countries devoted to economic issues, which was held in Lagos in April 1980. The purpose of this meeting was to work out a plan of action for implementing the Monrovia strategy for African economic development to the year 2000.

The meeting was a prelude to intense cooperation between the OAU and the UN, which would find tangible expression in the program of action submitted to the United Nations in 1986 and the report entitled "African Framework for Structural Adjustment Programs" issued by ECA in 1989.

It has been aptly observed about the interaction between the OAU and the UN in the economic sphere that its main manifestation has been the efforts to implement the United Nations Program of Action for African Economic Recovery and Development, which was based on Africa's Priority Program for Economic Recovery, 1986–1990, adopted by the OAU Assembly of Heads of State and Government in July 1985.

At the Thirteenth Special Session of the United Nations General Assembly, the African States reaffirmed their determination to adopt the reforms and the collateral measures set out in the Priority Program in order to ensure the success of economic recovery in Africa.

In the UNPAAERD the international community undertook to support the African countries in their efforts to guarantee recovery of their economies by increasing assistance for agriculture, promoting human resources development, and fostering the expansion of their trade relations. The program's short-term objective was to halt the large-scale deterioration in living conditions in Africa by supporting "the expansion of the resources of the multinational institutions, such as the World Bank, the International Monetary Fund (IMF), the African Development Bank and the African Development Fund, to enable them to provide African countries with additional resources on concessional terms" and by taking "special measures to alleviate the external debt crisis afflicting these countries."[4]

The disenchantment of the African partners in the UNPAAERD has, however, been total and complete. Indeed, the program has had little, if any, impact on the economy of the continent. Economic performance continues to be negative. In the eyes of the OAU, "the commitment of the international community to increase official development assistance to Africa has not been honoured."[5] The very unsatisfactory results of nearly six years of cooperation in the context of the UNPAAERD invite an appraisal of the efforts that are still required and the distance that remains to be covered. Moreover, although it has not been a success in terms of what it has achieved, the UNPAAERD is still a unique example of international assistance to a whole continent.

It is in this light that we should interpret the appeal the Secretary-General of OAU made to the international community at the special session of the

General Assembly on the economic situation "to assist African countries in making Africa's economic recovery a success" and his warning that "failing to do so would not only deprive Africans of an opportunity to lay the foundation for sustainable development but would also deprive the rest of the world of the benefits that would assuredly follow for all humanity."[6] Thus, the Program of Action is an "act of faith by Africa in the ability of the international community to act together and in generosity."[7]

Although in the past a source of conflict between the OAU and the UN,[8] the relations of economic cooperation between the two organizations are today based on virtually complete agreement, even if the expected results have not been achieved. There are no longer separate spheres of influence, with cooperation based on a division of roles. Relations between the OAU and the United Nations during this decade are definitely rediscovering the virtues of interdependence and complementarity. We are experiencing the "end of ingrained habits."[9]

Does this observation also hold true for political relations between the two organizations?

A Virtually New Form of Political Cooperation

The maintenance of international peace and security, and the question of disarmament, are political issues that amply illustrate the willingness of the two organizations to cooperate.

Indeed, in these areas "cooperation is proceeding apace. At times it takes the form of one organization gearing its activities to those of the other, or often of coordination between the two organizations that may even lead to a genuine political and ideological alliance through a sharing of roles between the two organizations."[10]

During the decade, the decolonization process set in motion under the auspices of the UN leading to the satisfactory outcome of the Namibian question has highlighted an area of cooperation for peace between the OAU and the UN.

Along these same lines, the establishment in Lomé of the United Nations Center for Peace and Disarmament in Africa is proof of the peace-loving ideology of the two organizations and the fundamental principles of economic and social advancement.

The establishment of the center was a step provided for in a resolution of the United Nations General Assembly[11] calling for the establishment of regional bodies in connection with the United Nations World Disarmament Campaign.

But the most important phenomenon has been the efforts of the two organizations in the Western Sahara peace process and the Namibian independence process. The necessity of close and continuing cooperation between the United Nations and the OAU with regard to Namibia has been emphasized with regularity.

Thus, following the lead of the OAU, the world organization declared that "the installation by South Africa of an interim government in Namibia would be accorded no recognition by either the United Nations or any Member State."[12] In any event, the implementation of Security Council resolution 435 in 1978 was an irreversible process. And the United Nations is entrusted with the task of supervising and monitoring the holding of free elections for Namibia's accession to independence. We are thus witnessing the pan-African organization's yielding to the United Nations.

The principle of a division of roles has thus been thrust aside, since, in regard to regional disputes, the OAU alone had the power, according to the theory of its "national competence," to deal with this matter.

The same scenario will be played out with regard to the crisis of Western Sahara,[13] where a United Nations peace plan will be worked out for the former Spanish colony. Indeed the question of Western Sahara, having given rise to an institutional crisis within the OAU, is now beginning to be solved, thanks to the efforts of the United Nations.

"In April and May 1986, the United Nations Secretary-General and the personal representative of the current Chairman of the OAU, acting within the framework of General Assembly resolution 40/50 of 2 December 1985 and in exercise of their good offices, met separately at United Nations Headquarters with representatives of the Moroccan Government and the Frente popular para la liberación de Saguia-el-Hamra y Río de Oro."[14] This joint effort will be pursued in the coming years and will culminate in a meeting between Moroccan and Saharan representatives.

But difficulties will persist because the two parties will not interpret these meetings in the same way. No one has described the situation prevailing in the region better than United Nations Secretary-General Javier Pérez de Cuéllar: "The question is much more complex. For the Moroccans it is more a matter of a discussion than a real negotiation. As for the Saharans, they have had to tell themselves that it is more a negotiation than a mere discussion. At any rate, it is a meeting."[15] Together, the OAU and the United Nations will combine their efforts in the context of their good offices mission to settle the conflict.

Thus at the Forty-third Regular Session, the United Nations Secretary-General and the Chairman of OAU, acting

within the framework of General Assembly resolution 42/78 of 4 December 1987 ... continued their efforts for a solution to the question of Western Sahara. In this connection, the Secretary-General, in consultation with the Chairman of OAU, dispatched a technical mission to Western Sahara in November 1987 to gather certain technical information and data in order to facilitate their task of promoting a peaceful settlement of the problem.[16]

In terms of an institutional analysis, we note that the conduct of the pan-African organization marks a complete departure from the position it took during the second Congo crisis (1964–1965), for example. The African States, with the exception of Congo, succeeded in getting the members of the Security Council unanimously to adopt a resolution which provided that OAU "should be able, in the context of Article 52 of the Charter of the United Nations, to help find a peaceful solution to all the problems and disputes affecting peace and security in the continent of Africa."[17] This situation for the OAU was considered by the Secretary-General at that time to be a "privilege."

Today we are faced with the delegation of this privilege in a manner that is entirely conscious and responsible. Thus, the Council of Ministers of the Organization of African Unity at its Fifty-second Ordinary Session held at Addis Ababa from 1 to 8 July 1990 "commended the United Nations for its central role in Namibia's independence process and the international community as a whole for its firm commitment and support."[18]

The new deal of the cards that we are witnessing in the relationship between the OAU and the United Nations gives rise to some questions.

A NEW CODE OF MULTILATERALISM

As it has been implemented in practice, the system of relations between the OAU and the United Nations contains the seeds of a code of multilateralism in search of a new lease on life. This new phenomenon is being brought about through economic cooperation between the OAU and the United Nations, for which ECA continues to be the go-between, and virtual agreement in the area of peace and security on the basis of the Western Sahara conflict and the question of Namibia.

ECA: The Go-Between in Relations Between the OAU and the United Nations in the Area of Economic Cooperation

The difficulties experienced in the relations between the OAU and the United Nations[19] have certainly not disappeared, but today it can be said that the aspects of conflict in these relations have lessened to a considerable extent.

The Economic Commission for Africa has maintained close relations with the OAU throughout the decade 1980–1990. "Pursuant to various resolutions and decisions adopted by both organizations respectively, working contacts and exchanges of information between their two secretariats were established on a regular basis."[20]

More specifically, sustained cooperation has been established in the area of social development. As regards the implementation of the Lagos Plan of Action, an ECA–OAU working party entrusted with the immediate task of developing arrangements to assist member States in implementing the plan was set up shortly after the Seventeenth Ordinary Session of the OAU Assembly of Heads of State and Government held in Freetown in 1980.

In adopting the Lagos Plan of Action and the Lagos Final Act, the Conference[21] requested the Secretary-General of OAU, in cooperation with the Executive Secretary of ECA, to implement the plan and to submit progress reports to it at regular intervals.

In another sphere, the question of African debt has brought about closer cooperation between the OAU and ECA. This cooperation culminated in the publication of the African Frame of Reference for Structural Adjustment Programs in 1989. The cooperation between the OAU and ECA over the decade have resulted in a concerted policy focusing on development issues and the continent's external debt.

The thorny nature of these problems and the pertinence of the views of ECA, which, moreover, are very close to those of African leaders who oppose the solutions advocated by the World Bank, have undoubtedly paved the way for a wide-ranging economic policy on which ECA and the OAU are in agreement. A partnership between the two organizations has emerged in support of the establishment of an African Economic Community.

This strengthening of cooperation in the economic sphere has fostered coordination with regard to security issues.

New Cooperation for the Settlement of Intra-African Disputes

The relations maintained between the two organizations in the effort to settle the Western Sahara conflict and the Namibian decolonization process illustrate the new concept of cooperation between the OAU and the United Nations in the sphere of resolution of regional disputes.

The distinctive feature of this new philosophy is the eclipse of the pan-African organization. Thus, "the role of the OAU has been diminished in the settlement of regional conflicts."[22] This state of affairs accounts for the fact that in the conflict over Western Sahara and especially in the Namibian question, the OAU adopted a very low profile, yielding to the United Nations most of its prerogatives with regard to the settlement of intra-African conflicts.

This represents a fundamental turnaround in the behavior of the OAU. It is nevertheless indicative of a new division of labor that is no longer based on the criterion of geographical competence but rather takes into account the necessity for the OAU to devote its energies to the management of lesser crises.

To all appearances, while this division of roles ensures good cooperation between the OAU and the United Nations, it is not without its problems, pointedly raising the question of the ability of OAU to deal with crises arising on the African continent.

NOTES

1. D. Nguyen Quoc, *Droit International Public* (Paris: LGDJ, 1987), no. 380 et sec.

2. Etats-Unis et UNESCO ou Maroc et Zaïre à l'OUA.

3. E.K. Kouassi, *Les Rapports entre l'Organisation des Nations Unies et l'Organisation de l'Unité Africaine*, Brussels, Bruylant, 1978.

4. UN General Assembly document A/43/596, p. 4.

5. OAU, Resolution CM/Res. 1287 (LII).

6. UN General Assembly document A/41/542, p. 3.

7. Ibid.

8. Kouassi, *Les Rapports*, p. 229.

9. J. Lesourne and M. Godet, *La Fin des habitudes* (Paris: Seghers, 1985).

10. Kouassi, *Les Rapports*, p. 310.

11. UN General Assembly resolution 39/63 J.

12. UN General Assembly document A/40/536.

13. Certains commentateurs y trouveront le manque d'audace et de hardiesse du Secrétaire Général de l'OUA du moment, le Nigérien Idé OUMAROU.

14. UN General Assembly document A/41/150.

15. *Jeune Afrique*, 15 February 1989, p. 1467.

16. UN General Assembly document A/43/497, p. 3.

17. UN Security Council ONU Res. 199, 30 December 1964.

18. OAU, Resolution CM/Res. 1273 (LII)/Rev. 1.

19. Kouassi, *Les Rapports*, p. 289.

20. ONU document A/36/317/ Add. 1., p. 14.

21. Second special session held at Lagos, Nigeria, April 1980.

22. Edmond Jouve, "Ou en est l'OUA en 1985?" *Afrique Contemporaine* 134, p. 21.

The OAU and Afro-Arab Cooperation
BOUTROS BOUTROS-GHALI

Relations between Africa and the Arab world long predate the establishment of the Organization of African Unity and, for that matter, the Arab League. Moreover, African-Arab relations are multidimensional, covering multilateral, regional, as well as the bilateral planes. In this chapter, we shall deal only with the central theme of African-Arab relations, namely Afro-Arab cooperation.

In order to fully comprehend the relationship between Africa and the Arab world, it is useful to put such a relationship within a historical and political context. In fact, relations between the Arab world and the African continent can be traced back many centuries, as far as prehistoric times. However, it was the trade relations between the Arabs and the population of East Africa long before borders emerged to divide the continent and the advent of Islam that brought about the gradual fusion between Arabs and Africans. Moreover, certain geopolitical factors served to link the Arab world with Africa. Also, the fact that both Arabs and Africans shared similar experiences under colonialism and suffered from racial discrimination offered an additional reason for their cooperation in the struggle to realize liberation, development, and the establishment of a new world order. In other words, the close historical ties between African and Arab peoples, together with their geographic proximity, cultural similarities, and experiences under colonialism were instrumental in laying firm foundations for strong relations between Arab and African states.

To trace the modern historical origins and subsequent development of Afro-Arab relations and particulary Afro-Arab cooperation, we have found it useful to divide the process into three stages. We have chosen the July 1952 revolution in Egypt as the starting point, as it represents a turning point in the Arab World and in its relations with the outside world. The three stages are: (1) from the July 1952 revolution of Egypt to the June 1967 war; (2) from the June 1967 war to the first Afro-Arab Summit Conference held in Cairo in March 1977; and (3) from March 1977 to December 1990.

AFRO-ARAB COOPERATION FROM JULY 1952 TO JUNE 1967

This period constituted the heyday of Arab nationalism as well as the emergence of "Africanism." Arab nationalism, which advocated Arab unity, positive neutrality, and nonalignment and related Zionism to imperialism, was also the first Arab intellectual movement that sought to establish a formula for Afro-Arab solidarity. Africanism, on the other hand, espoused principles glorifying African identity and advocated African unity. It was the interaction between these two contemporary movements that laid the basis for modern Afro-Arab relations. The basic elements of such a relationship can be identified as follows:

1. *Pan-Africanism*, which was manifested in the Organization of African Unity created in May 1963, included eight Arab countries which were at the same time members of the League of Arab States, namely Morocco, Algeria, Tunisia, Libya, Egypt, Sudan, Mauritania, and Somalia.

2. *Africanism*, on the other hand, drew the political boundaries for Afro-Arab cooperation. Within this divide it was the Arab side that tried to win over the African side. The Arabs believed that the common stand adopted by both sides within the Organization of African Unity regarding the struggle for the decolonization of the continent helped to achieve the goals envisaged by Arab nationalism. Whereas, the Arab-Israeli conflict, which was the central concern of the Arab states, was regarded by the African governments as an issue alien to them and to their primary interests. The African countries thus preferred to maintain a neutral stand between the Arabs and the Israelis.

3. *Arab nationalism* and *Africanism*, being in essence nationalistic movements, by their very nature had to contain divergent elements. So, for example, at the Addis Ababa conference at which the Organization of African Unity was established, some African delegates demanded the disbanding of all regional African organizations in favor of the OAU. The League of Arab States was explicitly mentioned among those to be dissolved. The Arab response was that the Arab League represented a double commitment insofar as Arabism was an Afro-Asian movement reflecting the integration of both continents, besides being an indivisible part of the pan-Africanist movements.

Thus, the framework of cooperation between the Arab and African countries reflected at once the points of agreement and disagreement between the two sides.

The beginning of close ties between the Africans and the Arabs existed before the establishment of the OAU. Indeed, the League of Arab States showed a great interest in African questions immediately after it was created. One of the major problems that preoccupied the Arab League was that of Libya and the designs of Western colonialists to divide it into separate spheres of influence.[1] Subsequently, the Arab League dealt with the independence issues of both Tunisia and Morocco.[2] The Arab League was not, however, interested only in the Arab countries of Africa. Indeed, dozens of resolutions adopted by the Arab League Council confirm that its interest in Africa from the start went beyond Arab Africa to include non-Arab Africa.

As far back as 7 September 1953, to cite an example, the Arab League Council adopted a resolution[3] concerning the bases of cooperation and the consolidation of Afro-Arab solidarity which called on Arab states to increase their diplomatic representation in Asian and African countries; to encourage exchange of delegations with African and Asian countries to strengthen the ties of friendship and cooperation in the political arena, as well as cultural and economic relations; and to take all necessary measures to cement the relations between member countries in the Arab League and Afro-Asian countries, including the holding of periodic high-level meetings.

Moreover, the Arab League adopted several resolutions in the fifties calling on the Arab countries to assist African liberation movements and to support the African issues at international forums. Among the most prominent examples was the resolution adopted by the Arab League Council on 9 April 1960, which laid down the political guidelines for its member States in the international struggle against the apartheid policy of South Africa. The resolution particularly recommended the Arab League member States cooperate with the Afro-Asian group at the UN as well as with other countries in drawing up a joint plan of action within the UN system.

The Casablanca Group, created on 7 January 1961, was the first international Afro-Arab organization of its kind. The group included the African countries of Ghana, Guinea, and Mali on the one hand, and three African-Arab countries—the United Arab Republic (Egypt and Syria), the Kingdom of Morocco, and the interim government of the Algerian Republic. Its creation manifested the interdependence of African and Arab interests. Thus, as the group adopted a resolution expressing support for Algeria's struggle against French colonialism, it also adopted another denouncing the Zionist colonization of Palestine. Other resolutions supported the Zaire (Congo) and condemned the French atomic tests in the Sahara. At its second session in Cairo, 26 March–21 April 1962, the Casablanca Group set up a number of Afro-Arab bodies and agencies, including a Common African Market, an African Development Bank, an African Payments Union, and an African Civil Aviation Authority. Though these bodies never materialized, as they were superseded by the OAU in May 1963, they nonetheless indicated the extent to which some Arab and African countries were interested in consolidating relations between the Arab world and Africa. Collective Arab interest in the African continent, however, only took shape when the OAU was established.

All attempts and efforts made by the Arab side to include the Palestinian question on the agenda of the OAU, however, were met by reservations on the part of non-Arab African States. The prevalent view on the continent was that since Palestine was not an African country, the Palestinian question could not be regarded as African.

As a matter of fact, the overwhelming majority of non-Arab African States had established, immediately after their independence (beginning with Ghana in 1957), economic, political, and trade relations with Israel. Thus, on the eve of the June 1967 war, Israel had diplomatic representation in twenty-three non-Arab African countries. Israel maintained relations in the African countries in many areas—in industry, trade, and particularly in military and technical fields. Notwithstanding the efforts made by the Arab side to stem the tide of Israel's advance in the continent, the Israeli presence in Africa continued to grow throughout the sixties.

The June 1967 war brought about the first breach in the African position vis-à-vis the Middle East problem. While some countries supported the Arabs, others wanted to keep Africa away from the Middle East and its problems. Although the Israeli aggression was not formally on the agenda of the African Summit held in Kinshasa in September 1967, the African Heads of State and Government nonetheless adopted a Declaration expressing their concern about the grave situation in Egypt, being an African country part of whose territory was under foreign occupation. They expressed sympathy with Arab Egypt and resolved to endeavor within the United Nations to secure the withdrawal of the occupation forces from Egyptian territory.[4]

AFRO-ARAB COOPERATION: FROM JUNE 1967 TO MARCH 1977

A close scrutiny of developments in the period between the June 1967 war and the first Afro-Arab Summit in Cairo during March 1977 reveals a qualitative change in Afro-Arab relations. At the outbreak of the June 1967 war, eight African states—namely Guinea, Chad, Uganda, Congo (Brazzaville), Niger, Mali, Burundi, and Togo—out of thirty-one independent African States, had already severed their diplomatic relations with Israel.

Although it may be difficult to say that the Israeli aggression in June 1967 played a decisive role in changing the attitude of non-Arab African countries toward the Arab-Israeli dispute, what is clear is that the occupation of a part of the territory of an African country—a founding member of the OAU—gradually became an important issue and a matter of principle for African States. The neutral stand with regard to the Arab-Israeli conflict advocated by Africanism was gradually eroding.

Nonetheless, over the four years that followed the Israeli aggression of 1967, the Arab group within the OAU consistently failed to include the Palestinian question in the resolutions condemning colonialism and racial discrimination. These resolutions, which the OAU continued to adopt, were mostly devoted to Southern Africa, where Africans suffered from both colonialism and apartheid.

Arab states, sensing the shift in the African position, pursued a policy designed to bring about a clear African commitment to the Arab-Israeli dispute. This policy was based on the following premises:

1. The identical nature of the Israeli, South African, and Rhodesian governments was emphasized. The fact that all these governments represented settler colonial societies was underlined.

2. Interests between Israel and South Africa, which required the perpetuation of racist domination in Africa and the Arab world alike, were also emphasized.

3. A joint Afro-Arab anticolonialist and anti-imperialist front was established.

This Arab effort, however, did not come to fruition until 1971—a year that marked the beginning of real change in Africa's stand on the Arab-Israeli dispute. Certain significant signs could be detected during that year. Some of these were related to the role Israel played in Africa. A number of non-Arab African countries began to recognize how limited the amount of aid they received from Israel was, particularly in relation to the real magnitude of the problems in Africa. Furthermore, the support and assistance rendered by Israel to African secessionist movements, as happened in the case of Biafra and the South Sudan mutiny, discouraged any further progress in Israeli-African relations. Indeed, it adversely affected such relations. Lastly, the newly formed Israel–South Africa axis, which the Arab group worked hard to expose, inevitably contributed to a further shift in the position of African governments.

Meanwhile, by the middle of 1971, negotiations between OPEC and the major oil companies began to bear fruit. The share of the Arab oil-exporting countries in oil-generated revenues reached unprecedented heights. The fact that Arab countries now possessed enormous financial resources could no longer be overlooked by African States. African States were already frustrated from the inadequacy of aid from industrial countries. The shift of wealth and in financial resources from the rich industrial countries to Third World oil-exporting countries raised the hopes of African countries. It was felt that the Arab oil-exporting countries, being themselves developing countries, would be more understanding of the problems facing Africa.

It was under these circumstances that the African attitude toward Arab countries and the primary Arab concern—Palestine and the Arab territories occupied after the 1967 war—became apparent. African neutrality increasingly gave way to a deepening interest in the Middle East crisis. This development set the stage for Afro-Arab *rapprochement*.

Among the factors that also contributed to bringing about this development were:

1. A number of north African Arab countries, such as Egypt, Algeria, and Libya, played an intermediary role within the OAU to consolidate relations between non-Arab Africans and non-African Arabs.

2. The exchange of visits between the Arab and African Heads of State and Government led to the establishment of a personal rapport and relationship, which proved to be more important than the regular traditional interaction at lower levels.

3. Finally, Afro-Arab dialogue at the UN led to stronger coordination between the positions of both sides. Although slow to appear, it gradually became a reality when put to the test at voting time, particularly where the questions of South Africa and Namibia were concerned.

A parallel development took place at the Seventh African Summit held in Addis Ababa in June 1971. The summit adopted a resolution on the Arab-Israeli conflict under the heading "A resolution on the Continued Aggression Against the U.A.R."[5] This resolution differed from all previous resolutions adopted by the OAU since the Israeli 1967 aggression. It signaled the beginning of active OAU interest in the Middle East crisis by stipulating, for the first time, that the organization itself take certain definite diplomatic measures. Thus, the stand of the OAU was no longer one of sympathy vis-à-vis the plight of a member state (Egypt), but rather was an attitude of participation in the diplomatic efforts to settle the Middle East problem.

The resolution advocated the necessity of the "withdrawal of the Israeli armed forces forthwith from all Arab territories to the pre–June 67 lines." It called for the "full implementation" of Security Council resolution 242 of 22 November 1967. It expressed full support for the mission undertaken by Ambassador Gunnar Jarring, the Special Representative of the UN Secretary-General, and described the initiative contained in Ambassador Jarring's memorandum of 8 February 1971 to both Egypt and Israel as "the practical step for the establishment of a just and durable peace in the Middle East." Referring to the Israeli reply to that the initiative, the resolution spoke of "Israeli intransigence" and stressed that Israel would thus be blamed for blocking the road to peace that Jarring was attempting to open in the Middle East. More importantly, the resolution called on Africa to make an effort to secure the implementation of Security Council resolution 242 and the reactivation of Ambassador Jarring's mission. The resolution left it to the Chairman of that OAU session, the Mauritanian President, to have consultations with other African Heads of State on "using their influence to secure the full implementation of this resolution."

The Mauritanian President's consultations resulted in the setting up of two African bodies[6] charged with putting the OAU resolution into effect:

1. A committee under the chairmanship of the President of Mauritania comprising ten African Heads of State: Cameroon, Ethiopia, Ivory Coast, Kenya, Liberia, Mauritania, Nigeria, Senegal, Tanzania, and Zaire
2. A subcommittee of the ten-member committee, called the Committee of Four Presidents or the "Committee of Four Wise Men" (Cameroon, Nigeria, Senegal, and Zaire), chaired by the President of Senegal

The subcommittee was entrusted with the task of visiting both Egypt and Israel with a view to ascertaining their individual views on the implementation of Security Council resolution 242 through Ambassador Jarring. The subcommittee, however, failed to achieve its ultimate objective, that is, the reconciliation of the Arab and Israeli positions. Nonetheless, the African initiative signaled a positive African response to the Middle East, and can be regarded, therefore, as a turning point in Israeli-African relations. All OAU member countries now adopted the same position vis-à-vis the basic elements of the conflict, in spite of their differences over details. The fact that the resolution contained the strongest call by the OAU for Israel to withdraw from the occupied territories was a victory for Arab diplomacy.

It therefore can be stated that this resolution marked a further shift in the position of non-Arab African countries toward that of the Arabs. Meanwhile, Israeli influence in Africa was receding in equal proportion to the rise in the influence of OAU Arab members. This was particularly felt after the organization was chaired by Mauritania in 1971 and by Morocco in 1972, and after Somalia and Mauritania joined the League of Arab States.

As a reflection of the Arab States' increasing influence and of Israel's eroding position in Africa, Ugandan President Idi Amin expelled the Israeli technical and military mission and broke off diplomatic ties with Israel. Arab experts were soon to replace the Israelis early in 1972. During the same year the Saudi Arabian monarch made a tour of a number of African capitals. Considerable activity was immediately afoot, particularly with the conclusion of cooperation agreements between Arab and African countries. More African countries, meanwhile, were severing their diplomatic relations with Israel.

The relations between Arab and African countries had by now acquired a dynamic character. This development augured well for more effective and closer cooperation between the OAU and the League of Arab States. A further important development took place at the Eighth Extraordinary Session of the African Council of Ministers held in Mogadishu from 19 to 21 November 1973. The conference adopted a resolution[7] concerning the continued Israeli occupation of a part of Egyptian territory which, *inter alia*:

1. Considered any and all changes introduced by Israel in the occupied territories as null and void

2. Recognized for the first time that the inalienable rights of the Palestinian people should be respected

3. Declared that Israel's attitude may force the OAU member countries to adopt, on the African level, individually or collectively, certain political and economic measures against Israel in accordance with the principles of the OAU and UN Charters

4. Called on the Big Powers that continued to do so to stop providing Israel with weapons, and supported the Egyptian initiative that requested the UN Secretary-General to submit a report to the Security Council on the explosive situation in the Middle East

5. Appointed the foreign ministers of Nigeria, Chad, Tanzania, Guinea, Algeria, Kenya, and Sudan as OAU spokesmen so as to raise this question on behalf of the organization at the Security Council meeting scheduled to take place on 4–5 June 1973

6. Entrusted the OAU session chairman with presenting the organization's view on this matter at the following session of the UN General Assembly

The resolution was of special significance as it was the first ever OAU resolution to include an explicit reference to the Palestinian question and the rights of the Palestinian people. Furthermore, it called for the respect of the inalienable rights of the Palestinian people as a basic element in any fair and just solution, and as an indispensable factor for the establishment of durable peace in the region.

The African summit held on the tenth anniversary of the OAU in May 1973 thus signaled a definitive change in the OAU attitude to the Middle East crisis, particularly as compared with the position it had maintained from 1967 to 1972.

The October 1973 war accelerated the development in Afro-Arab relations, particularly as Israel continued to violate Arab territory after the Security Council had adopted its cease-fire resolutions. Contrary to what had happened following the June 1967 aggression, African countries one after the other broke off diplomatic relations with Israel. By the time the cease-fire resolution came into effect, twenty-nine non-Arab African states had severed their diplomatic relations with Israel. Apart from Malawi, Lesotho, and Swaziland, the only diplomatic relations Israel maintained in Africa were confined to South Africa and Rhodesia.

The October war was also accompanied by a number of important developments that influenced the emergence of Afro-Arab solidarity:

1. The Joint Egyptian-Syrian military initiative, designed to recover the Arab territories occupied during the June 1967 aggression and restore the rights of the Palestinian people, brought about a firm unity within the Arab ranks. This was also accompanied by the sudden financial power of a number of oil-rich Arab countries. This development revived the anticipation in Africa that financial assistance would be forthcoming from the oil-rich Arab countries.

2. African economies, having been traditionally dependent on the old colonial metropolises, suffered even more than those of the industrialized world. The Arab oil embargo, the reduction of oil production, and, finally, the oil price readjustment by OPEC, although originally directed at the industrial economies, had indirect consequences for African development.

These developments, together with the political initiative of African countries to improve relations with the Arabs, combined to accelerate the progress in Afro-Arab relations.

In the wake of the October 1973 war, the Eighth Extraordinary Session of the OAU Council of Ministers was held in Mogadishu from 19 to 21 November 1973. Following a prolonged review of the situation in the Middle East, the Council adopted two resolutions on the crisis which, *inter alia*, highlighted the relationship between Israel and South Africa, recommended that relations with Israel should continue to be broken off until Israel withdrew from all occupied Arab territories and the Palestinian people recovered their national legitimate rights, called on OAU members to impose a total economic boycott on Israel and South Africa, and finally, set up a seven-member committee to oversee Afro-Arab cooperation.[8]

The conference also sent a cable of support to President Mohamed Anwar El-Sadat of Egypt, President Hafiz Al-Assad of Syria, and Mr. Yasser Arafat, Chairman of the Palestine Liberation Organization, which read as follows:

Africa, which still suffers from Portuguese colonialism and Apartheid, cannot sit idly by vis-a-vis the plight of Egypt, a founder member of our organization—and the sister Syrian and Palestinian peoples. As the OAU has unremittingly contributed to the vindication of law and justice, in accordance with the principles of our Charter, we believe it is our duty to render you concrete and continued support. Israel will feel more isolated than ever, until it has withdrawn from all occupied Arab territories. Our action will consequently be in harmony with the national aspiration of your peoples, in full recognition of our responsibility, and with a view to the assertion of Africa's significant role in international relations, which should herald a new dawn of justice, peace and progress.[9]

The conference also adopted a resolution that reasserted the Palestinian people's claim to their inalienable national rights, their legitimate anticolonialist struggle, and their right to self-determination in accordance with the UN Charter and relevant resolutions, and took the position that the settlement of the Palestinian issue is a prerequisite for the establishment of a just and durable peace.[10]

On the other hand, the Sixth Arab Summit was held in an emergency session in Algiers (26–28 November 1973), on the initiative of Presidents Mohamed Anwar El-Sadat and Hafiz Al-Assad, to consider the post–October 1973 war developments. President Mobutu of Zaire, on behalf of the OAU, attended the conference as an observer in a gesture reflecting the solidarity of the OAU and the League of Arab States.

A statement on Afro-Arab cooperation[11] adopted by the conference stipulated, *inter alia:*

1. Appreciation for African States for their decision to sever diplomatic relations with Israel

2. Appreciation for the part played by OAU member States in bolstering Afro-Arab solidarity as manifested in the Extraordinary Session of the OAU Council of Ministers held from 19 to 21 November 1973

3. Support for African countries in their struggle for national liberation and economic progress, and against colonialism and racial discrimination

4. Welcomed the OAU Council of Ministers' decision, at its extraordinary session, to set up a seven-member committee to promote and streamline Afro-Arab cooperation

The conference also adopted a resolution[12] on Afro-Arab cooperation, calling for:

1. Consolidating Afro-Arab cooperation in the political arena and strengthening Arab diplomatic representation in Africa

2. Breaking all diplomatic, consular, economic, cultural, and other relations with South Africa, Portugal, and Rhodesia by all Arab countries that not yet done so

3. Imposing a total embargo on Arab oil exports to these three countries, with special measures to be adopted to maintain normal supplies of Arab oil to sister African countries

4. Enhancing Arab diplomatic and material backing for the struggle being waged by the African liberation movements

5. Entrusting the secretariat of the League of Arab States with the adoption of practical measures, and contacting the secretariat of the OAU, as well as the OAU seven-member committee, with the purpose of holding periodic consultations at various levels between Arab and African countries

6. Consolidating and expanding economic, financial, and cultural cooperation with sister Arab countries both bilaterally and through regional Afro-Arab institutions

The resolution also provided for the establishment of an Arab bank for the economic development of Africa, to be run on a commercial basis. The resolution also provided for urgent aid to African nations affected by natural disasters and drought.

The OAU Council of Ministers in its Twenty-third Ordinary Session held in Mogadishu from 6 to 11 June 1974 adopted a resolution on Afro-Arab cooperation[13] calling for the convening of an Afro-Arab summit. The resolution also noted with satisfaction the continued and growing cooperation between African and Arab countries, and requested the OAU Administrative Secretary-General to contact the Secretary-General of the Arab League with a view to looking into the possibility of holding a ministerial Afro-Arab conference to study the possibilities and areas of cooperation that might require joint efforts to be made, particularly regarding mutual cooperation for development and the drawing up of an Afro-Arab development strategy.

In a parallel development, the Democratic Republic of Somalia submitted a memorandum[14] to the Arab League secretariat proposing that the Arab League and the OAU convene an Afro-Arab summit.

The Seventh Arab Summit held in Rabat in October 1974 considered Afro-Arab cooperation in the light of the resolution adopted by the OAU Twenty-third Council of Ministers session and the memorandum of the Democratic Republic of Somalia. The Rabat Arab Summit approved the holding of such an Afro-Arab Summit, and entrusted the Arab League Secretary-General with conducting the necessary consultations with African States. If the consultations indicated a positive response on the part of African States, the Arab League Secretary-General could make arrangements for a meeting of African and Arab Foreign Ministers in preparation for an Afro-Arab Summit. The Council also decided that a committee of nine Arab Foreign Ministers pay visits to various African countries to promote Afro-Arab solidarity and explain the Seventh Arab Summit's resolutions.[15]

Pursuant to the contacts between the Secretary-General of the Arab League and the OAU Administrative Secretary-General, it was agreed that the latter submit the Seventh Arab Summit resolution, calling for the convening of an Afro-Arab Summit to the OAU Council of Ministers session held in February 1975. The objective of this move was to obtain a resolution empowering the OAU Administrative Secretary-General to personally undertake the necessary contacts with the Arab League for the holding of a joint Afro-Arab ministerial conference in preparation for a summit. It was also agreed that a committee be set up within the secretariats of both organizations to study all aspects of the proposed meeting and that the two committees should engage in informal consultations aimed at the formulation of a working paper, to be followed by consultations on the dates and venue of the joint foreign ministers' conference.

On 13 February 1975, the African Ministerial seven-man committee met at the headquarters of the OAU in Addis Ababa. The Chairman submitted a report on the Seventh Arab Summit, which approved the convening of an Afro-Arab summit. He informed the committee that the Arab League was making preparations for such a conference, and that it had set up a nine-member committee similar to the OAU seven-member committee, charged with coordinating work for the proposed summit. At that meeting the committee recommended that Afro-Arab cooperation required an organizational framework.[16]

The Twenty-fourth Ordinary Session of the OAU Council of Ministers held in Addis Ababa from 13 to 21 February 1975 discussed Afro-Arab cooperation and adopted the following resolution:

Noting with satisfaction the declaration adopted by the Algiers Arab Summit, and the declaration by the Rabat Arab Summit, and the Afro-Arab cooperation proposals submitted at these two conferences;

Convinced that Afro-Arab cooperation is not only a necessity but also a commitment based on the principle of solidarity dictated by unity of destiny and objectives;

Conscious of the need to bolster the conditions conducive to promoting Afro-Arab cooperation;

The Conference has decided:

1. To re-form the seven-member committee created by the eighth extraordinary session of this Council so that it would consist of twelve countries [and that was why it later came to be called the African Committee of Twelve].
2. That the new committee should work in cooperation with the Administrative Secretary General as an Afro-Arab Cooperation Coordinating Committee. Its terms of reference should be expanded to include the exploration of new horizons for mutual cooperation, the adoption of all supplementary measures required for the implementation of the resolutions and decisions of the Council of Ministers and the Assembly of the Heads of State and Government, and preparation for the Afro-Arab Summit Conference.

The OAU Council of Ministers thereby entrusted the new committee with studying all aspects of Afro-Arab cooperation and making arrangements for the proposed summit. Thus, Afro-Arab cooperation was beginning to take practical shape, and the joint efforts of the Arab League and the OAU were beginning to produce concrete results.

The African Committee of Twelve held its first meeting on 22 February 1975 to draw up its program of action. The meeting, which was attended by a representative of the Arab League, decided:

1. To empower the OAU Secretary-General to conduct more contacts with all concerned parties; he would also have wider terms of reference in connection with all subjects under consideration

2. To set up another committee comprising the ambassadors in Addis Ababa of the countries on the Committee of Twelve to prepare a report in the form of a declaration on Afro-Arab cooperation by 26 March 1975

3. That this report would be studied at a meeting in Dar-es-Salaam of the foreign ministers of the twelve countries on the committee following the Extraordinary Session of the OAU Council of Ministers in April 1975

4. That the African ambassadorial committee would subsequently hold a meeting with its Arab League counterpart to prepare for the Afro-Arab ministerial meeting

5. That the joint program would be submitted to the next session of the OAU Council of Ministers for ratification and submission to the Assembly of African Heads of State and Government

6. That the African ambassadorial committee, together with its Arab counterpart, would work out the agenda of the joint summit conference

Discussions at that meeting, which centered on the meaning of Afro-Arab cooperation, emphasized that it was not to be simply confined to continued loans and assistance by the Arab League to African countries, but rather that it should be a two-way street covering various fields of mutual interest. A meeting of the Afro-Arab cooperation coordinating committee (the Committee of Twelve) was held in April 1975 in Dar-es-Salaam, where the ambassadorial committee's report was reviewed.[17] The report contained the following proposals:

1. Principles and Objectives: Afro-Arab cooperation should be based on reciprocity, equality, cooperation, and respect for each country's permanent control of its natural resources, and should be long-term and comprehensive.

2. Methods of Cooperation: These included bilateral and multilateral consultations, joint general projects, and expansion of the activity of trade missions. Cooperation should imply definite commitments for both African and Arab countries.

3. Institutions: Similar institutions should be amalgamated, and others should be created. It was necessary to a set a later date, and machinery was agreed to by the Arab League and the OAU.

4. Fields of Cooperation: These included political and diplomatic, economic and financial, social and cultural, scientific and technical.

The ministerial Committee of Twelve expressed the hope that the Arab League would set up a ministerial committee parallel to the African twelve-member committee; set up an ambassadorial committee similar to the Addis Ababa ambassadors' committee; and prepare a working paper by the end of May 1975 corresponding to the working paper that the African ambassadors' committee had prepared pursuant to the discussion of the proposed declaration by the ministerial committee.[18]

Meanwhile the Arab League Council during its Sixty-third Session held from 24 to 27 April 1975 agreed on the following:

1. The establishment of a committee consisting of the Arab League Secretary-General and representatives of twelve Arab States to organize Afro-Arab cooperation through contacts and meetings with the OAU Committee of Twelve

2. The establishment of a committee consisting of the ambassadors of the member countries in the Committee of Twelve and the Arab League representative at the OAU, with the objective of holding meetings with the African ambassadors' committee to draw up a plan for Afro-Arab cooperation

3. An allocation of US $60,000 to cover the expenses of the preparations for the Afro-Arab Summit.

On receiving the Arab League decisions, the OAU Secretary-General sent a draft of the proposed declaration on Afro-Arab cooperation. The Arab Committee of Twelve met in Cairo at the ambassadorial level from 28 May to 2 June 1975, and discussed the draft proposed declaration.

On 9 July 1975, the first joint meeting of the African and Arab ministerial committees was held at the Arab League headquarters in Cairo. The meeting, which was also attended by the OAU Administrative Secretary-General and the Arab League Secretary-General approved the draft proposed declaration.

Agreement was reached at these meetings on a joint statement to be submitted to both organizations as an expression of effective solidarity between African and Arab countries. The statement was based on a document prepared by the African side.

The Twenty-fifth Session of the OAU Council of Ministers held in Kampala from 18 to 25 July 1975 discussed a report on the Cairo meeting. The Council subsequently decided to refer the committee's report, the draft declaration and program of action, and a report on the Council's deliberations—and the consensus of opinion thereof—to the Twelfth OAU Summit.

The OAU Summit Conference, held in Uganda from 28 July to 1 August 1975 adopted a resolution[19] on Afro-Arab cooperation which stipulated that:

1. Member States would submit their comments within two to three months on the report on Afro-Arab cooperation, the draft declaration, and the Afro-Arab program of action.

2. A joint meeting of African and Arab foreign ministers was to be held at the end of that period to agree on a final formula for the project and to prepare for the Afro-Arab Summit Conference.

3. The OAU Administrative Secretary-General would communicate with the Arab League Secretary General in order to fix a date for the Afro-Arab Summit.

Meanwhile the Arab League Council, at its Sixty-fourth Ordinary Session (18–21 October 1975),[20] requested the Secretary-General to communicate with the OAU Administrative Secretary-General in order to fix a date for a meeting of African and Arab foreign ministers. It also agreed that the secretariat should ascertain the views of Arab governments not represented on the Arab Committee of Twelve on the draft declaration and the Afro-Arab cooperation program, and that these governments should transmit their views within two months at the latest.

The consultations between the Arab League and the OAU, and the meetings held by their respective bodies, independently or jointly, reached the conclusion that the first joint conference of African and Arab foreign ministers would be held in Dakar, Senegal. The conference was held from 19 to 22 April 1976, with the objective of endorsing the draft declaration and program of action on cooperation between the Arab League and the OAU, in preparation for the holding of the Afro-Arab Summit.

Following lengthy discussions, the conference adopted a document that later came to be known as the "Dakar Document."[21] It was this document that was ultimately approved by the first Afro-Arab Summit Conference in Cairo. It was agreed at the Dakar Ministerial Conference that the OAU Secretary-General and the Arab League Secretary-General should undertake the necessary studies on the implementation of the provisions of that document. These studies would be submitted to the Committee of Twenty-four and subsequently put forward to the second session of the Afro-Arab Foreign Ministers' Council, which would precede the first Afro-Arab Summit Conference. It can, therefore, be said that the Dakar Conference afforded both African and Arab groups the opportunity to interact with one another directly and without outside interference and to better understand one another, and clarify their respective positions and properly appreciate the circumstances peculiar to the other side. At this stage Afro-Arab cooperation came to be a basic dimension of the foreign policy of both the Arab League and the OAU.

The Lomé Conference of African and Arab Foreign Ministers, consisting of members of the Committee of Twenty-four,[22] held in January 1977, was devoted to working out a final plan for the second session of the Afro-Arab Foreign Ministers' Conference. Besides the Dakar Document concerning the declaration and program of action on Afro-Arab cooperation, the Lomé Conference prepared all the other documents to be submitted to the summit, namely the political declaration, the organization and method of work for the realization of Afro-Arab cooperation, and a document entitled "The Urgent Task of Putting into Effect Afro-Arab Cooperation." It was agreed that the Foreign Ministers' Conference would be held from 3 to 6 March and be immediately followed by the summit from 7 to 9 March.

The Joint Foreign Ministers' Conference was held in Cairo, from 3 to 6 March 1977, followed by the first Afro-Arab Summit in the history of Afro-Arab relations. The documents[23] adopted by the conference were of historic importance and may be regarded as the foundation of Afro-Arab cooperation:

1. The declaration of a program of action on Afro-Arab cooperation
2. The declaration on Afro-Arab economic and financial cooperation
3. The organization of work for the realization of Afro-Arab cooperation
4. The political declaration of the First Afro-Arab Summit Conference

It is to be noted that while the political declaration outlined the political objectives of African and Arab countries, particularly the consolidation of the anticolonialist struggle, and support for the peoples of Palestine, Zimbabwe, South Africa, and Namibia, the declaration on economic and financial cooperation defined the means of establishing cooperation by closely relating the economic development of the African countries to financial assistance from Arab countries.

The summit also established an organizational structure[24] to supervise such cooperation:

1. An Afro-Arab Summit to be held every three years
2. A joint Ministerial Council to be held every eighteen months
3. A Standing Commission composed of twelve Ministers of Foreign Affairs chosen by the OAU, and a similar number chosen by the Arab League. The commission would meet twice a year alternatively at the seats of the Arab League and the OAU
4. Eight working groups in the fields of trade, mining, agriculture, energy, water resources, transportation, etc.
5. An Afro-Arab Court

AFRO-ARAB COOPERATION FROM MARCH 1977 TO DECEMBER 1990

With the holding of the First Afro-Arab Summit, the institutional set-up required for Afro-Arab cooperation was decided upon. The political will existed on both sides, as did agreement on the basic principles underlying such cooperation. Moreover, the objective conditions for Afro-Arab cooperation existed.

What was required at that stage was the initiation of practical steps to give substance to the organizational and institutional framework agreed upon at the Summit.

What emerged, however, was a different story. Afro-Arab cooperation, unfortunately, fell victim to a series of developments, both in the Middle East as well as in Africa.

First was the crisis in Arab relations caused by the Camp David Agreements (1978) and the resultant division of the Arab world into a majority rejecting peace with Israel and a minority supporting a peaceful settlement. The rejectionist majority proceeded to transfer their dispute with Egypt from the Arab to the African arena. They allied themselves with radical African States to oust Egypt from the OAU. This effort, which reached its climax at the African Summit held in Monrovia in 1979, however, failed. Nonetheless, it left a negative impact on Afro-Arab cooperation.

Second was the Iraq-Iran war that started in 1980, which caused Arabs to divert their interest and assistance from Africa to the Gulf region. Thus, the imperatives of the Iraq-Iran war superseded the imperatives of Arab-African cooperation.

Third, the problem of Western Sahara resulted in the division of African countries into two groups, the first, led by President Sekou Toure of Guinea, supported Morocco, and the second, led by President Nyerere of Tanzania, supported the Saharan Democratic Republic (SADR) and Algeria. This division almost led to the collapse of the OAU. It also led to the paralysis of the organs entrusted to oversee Afro-Arab cooperation. After the SADR was admitted to the OAU and the subsequent withdrawal of Morocco from this organization in protest, the conflict was no longer an issue for the OAU. However, it continued to be reflected in the organs of Afro-Arab cooperation.

So, for example, if a request was made to hold a meeting of the Afro-Arab Ministerial Council, the majority of African States would demand the participation of the SADR, as it is a member of the OAU. The majority of the Arab States, on the other hand, would refuse to permit its participation because Morocco threatened to leave the Arab League if such a thing occurred. There is no doubt that this dispute contributed to the paralysis of the organs of Afro-Arab cooperation, with the exception of the Committee of Twenty-four, as the SADR was not a member of that organ.

Fourth, some African countries accuse some Arab countries of interfering in their internal affairs by providing financial and military assistance to antigovernment rebel movements. African countries take the position, rightly or wrongly, that financial assistance was provided to UNITA. The fact of the matter is that the assistance received by UNITA came from the United States and South Africa. Notwithstanding, the Luanda government was convinced that Arab countries have provided assistance to UNITA. A similar accusation was made by the Mozambique government, which believes that Arab assistance has been given to the rebel movement RENAMO, which opposses the legal government in Maputo.

While it is difficult to affirm that such accusations are baseless or that indeed such assistance was provided, the general perception in Africa, particularly among the frontline States, is that some Arab countries have played a role in supporting rebel movements in their countries. Notwithstanding that such assistance seems to have ceased due to the radical changes experienced by the communist regimes in general, and particularly in Africa, the confidence gap remains. In addition, Africans continue to believe that such support remains in other fields. The statements made by President Mengistu Haile Mariam of Ethiopia at the recent OAU summit held in Addis Ababa in July 1990 indicate that African concerns persist.

Fifth, some of the crises in Africa contain an element of Afro-Arab confrontation, or what can be described as an ethnic dimension. The conflict between Mauritania and Senegal is viewed as an Arab-African dispute with ethnic overtones. The conflict between Libya and Chad is similarly viewed. Even the conflict between the group lead by John Garang and the Sudanese government, despite the fact that it is an internal conflict, is considered to be an ethnic Arab-African dispute. Also, Africans look upon the conflict between Ethiopia and Somalia as one between Africans and Arabs. Perhaps what exacerbates the problem is that African countries are convinced that non-African Arab countries support the Arab side in these conflicts. Similarly, African countries support and sympathize with African countries that are parties to such conflicts.

Sixth, African leaders are concerned over religious fundamentalism. While such a phenomenon indeed exists in some Arab-African countries, it is the Western media that has exaggerated its importance. Nevertheless, African leaders are influenced by such propaganda. Certain factors of an economic nature such as the decline of oil revenues of Arab oil-exporting countries since the mid-eighties, had their toll on the Arab world's interest in Africa.

Seventh, the declining oil prices since the mid-eighties reduced the funds available to Arab countries to invest in or lend to Africa. Thus, economic cooperation and trade were negatively affected.

Eighth and finally, recent developments in both the Middle East and Africa have diverted Arabs and Africans away from their mutual cooperation. The Gulf crisis arising from Iraq's invasion of Kuwait has become one of several priorities for the Arab States. African States, on the other hand, have had their share of problems that have shifted their attention from Afro-Arab cooperation. The latest developments in Liberia, Rwanda, Somalia, and Ethiopia are but a few examples.

If Afro-Arab cooperation witnessed some difficulties since the late seventies, it seemed to reach crisis proportion by the late eighties. Disagreements between Arabs and Africans came out in the open for the first time at the Twenty-fifth African Summit held in Addis Ababa in 1989, when President Kenneth Kaunda of Zambia openly accused some Arab countries of interfering in the internal affairs of African countries. Similar instances arose at the Eleventh Session of the Joint Commission on Afro-Arab Cooperation in New York in October 1989 and at the OAU summit in July 1990, where President Robert Mugabe of Zimbabwe expressed his anxiety over the possibility that Africa be divided along African and Arab lines as a result of the ongoing disputes with an African-Arab dimension.

Thus, since the holding of the first Afro-Arab Summit in 1977, the Standing Commission for Afro-Arab Cooperation (the Committee of Twenty-four) met twelve times, instead of twenty-four times as originally envisaged. The working groups met only during the first two years of their creation. The Joint Ministerial Council and the Arab-African Summit never met. The Arab-African Court, moreover, did not materialize. In short, the organs established in March 1977 to oversee the political and economic cooperation between Arab and African States did not perform as had been hoped for. However, this does not mean that all organs created to foster Arab-African cooperation did not fulfill their task. The Arab Fund for Technical Assistance for Arab and African Countries, an Arab League organ created at the Seventh Arab Summit in 1972, started to operate in 1976. After the Arab League moved temporarily to Tunisia, the fund continued to function under the auspices of the Egyptian Ministry of Foreign Affairs. Through the fund, hundreds of experts were dispatched to African countries, and scholarships were awarded for African students to study in Egyptian universities and institutes. In addition, the Arab Bank for Economic Development in Khartoum and the African Development Bank in Abidjan continued to work successfully. Also, various Arab funds contributed to dozens of projects in Africa. The Egyptian Technical Cooperation Fund for Africa, an organ of the Foreign Ministry created in 1980, is also very active in Africa.

In the above discussion we have tired to present the causes that have collectively given rise to the present crisis in Afro-Arab relations and stalled Afro-Arab cooperation. What is required at this stage is determining how to contain and defuse the crisis. While we do not possess a ready-made prescription to resolve the crisis, let alone a comprehensive approach to overcome it, we nevertheless can put forward the following observations that can be helpful in understanding the true nature of the crisis and thus help in devising a formula to overcome it.

First, the present crisis between Africa and the Arab world should not be exaggerated. Recent history tells us that Africa has experienced far more dangerous crises and has been able to overcome them. There are also other crises that continue to threaten the future of Africa. Therefore, this crisis should not be used as a pretext to divert attention from a far more general and pressing problem facing Africa, namely, tribal disputes. We should be conscious that disputes with an Arab-African dimension are in fact intertribal and interethnic African disputes. They do not differ from other tribal and ethnic disputes that permeate Africa. The Arab-African dimension is but another formula devised and exploited by those who do not wish well for Afro-Arab cooperation.

Second, it is necessary to present an accurate account of the assistance provided by Arab states to Africa, be it bilateral, government to government, or through Arab Funds or international arrangements funded in part by Arab capital. If such an account is made available, it would become clear that the Arab countries have provided Africa with assistance almost as much as Europe, North America, and Japan. In fact, the percentage of GDP devoted by Saudi Arabia alone as aid to African countries is many times more than what the United States provides as aid as a proportion of its GDP to the entire Third World. Unfortunately, we do not possess in the Arab world a compilation of the assistance we have provided to Africa over the past quarter of a century. Nonetheless, it would not be an exaggeration if we were to say that the total amount of assistance Arab States have provided to Africa is considerable by any standard.

Third, the political and diplomatic importance attached to African issues is no less important than financial assistance. In fact, they are complementary. Arab countries should pay more attention to Africa and more visits at the leadership level should take place to African countries. They should be receptive to African requirements. Only then will the true value of Arab moral and political support become apparent to confirm the axiom that not by bread alone does man survive.

Fourth, Egypt participated in the initiative of the Group of Five (G–5—

Egypt, India, Senegal, Yugoslavia, and Venezuela) to revive the North-South dialogue. Egypt is also a member of the Group of Fifteen (G–15—Algeria, Argentina, Brazil, Egypt, India, Indonesia, Jamaica, Malaysia, Mexico, Nigeria, Peru, Senegal, Venezuela, Yugoslavia, and Zimbabwe) for consultations and South-South cooperation. It is also a founding member of the United Nations and its specialized agencies as well as the Group of 77. Through its membership in such organizations and groups, Egypt can play a leadership role in fostering and strengthening Afro-Arab cooperation as a successful model for South-South cooperation. Moreover, such organizations and groups can be used to help Afro-Arab cooperation.

In short, the political will and the institutional framework for Afro-Arab cooperation exist. The mutuality of interests also exists. Thus, the objective conditions required for such cooperation are available. The hiatus in Afro-Arab cooperation is a result of factors that are not intrinsic to the African-Arab relationship. What is required, therefore, is to heighten the consciousness—in both Africa and the Arab world—that cooperation should be isolated from exogenous political factors. Maybe an emphasis on the micro level of the relationship is the key to overcoming the present crisis and to guaranteeing that Afro-Arab cooperation will proceed without being subject to the vagaries of the ever-shifting conditions in Africa and the Arab world.

Africans and Arabs should be made aware of their common interests and the fact that they have much to gain from cooperating in the various fields of human endeavor. Interaction between Africa and the Arab world should not be confined to the traditional framework of official and governmental contacts. Nongovernmental bodies and the business communities should be encouraged to enter into contact.

On a different plane, Africans on the official level as much as the public, should be made to realize that the solution of their development problems lies in economic integration. The experience of African countries since independence demonstrates that no country on its own can successfully tackle the problems of economic development. This is equally true for countries that have pursued a free-enterprise policy as much as those who have opted for a socialist mode of development. Past economic policies that have been highly nationalistic were not only unsuccessful but also expensive. Moreover, they have nurtured micronationalism at a time when the world was moving toward various forms of political and economic integration. In the case of Africa, much benefit can be derived from integration at the subregional and regional levels. For example, there is much potential in close cooperation between the Nile river basin countries, two of which are Arab. Some work has been done in this regard, but much remains to be done. Equally, cooperation between the Arab Maghreb and the countries of West Africa and the Sahara holds much promise.

Encouraging economic cooperation in these two directions, outside the traditional framework, would no doubt give a boost to Afro-Arab cooperation.

International organizations such as the United Nations, the various specialized agencies, and the United Nations Development Program, can play an important role to foster regional cooperation. This is so because Africa is particularly dependent on foreign aid. It is therefore the duty of foreign aid donors to encourage movement in this direction.

Ultimately, history, geography, and cultural affinity point to the fact that the destiny of Africa and the Arab World are intertwined. Arab and African States should pursue policies that give full recognition to this fact.

NOTES

1. League of Arab States, 29 May 1946, Summit Resolution 9.
2. League of Arab States, 22 February 1948, Tenth Meeting, Seventh Ordinary Session, Resolution 211.
3. League of Arab States, 21 January 1954, Sixth Meeting, Twentieth Ordinary Session, Resolution 605.
4. Ministry of Foreign Affairs of the Arab Republic of Egypt, *Resolutions, Recommendations and Statements of the Organization of African Unity 1963 1983* (1985), p. 122 (in Arabic).
5. OAU, AHG, Res. 66 (VIII).
6. Ministry of Foreign Affairs of the Arab Republic of Egypt, *White Paper on Afro-Arab Cooperation (1977 1978)*, 1980, p. 14.
7. OAU, AHG, Res. 70 (X), p. 279.
8. OAU, ECM, Res. 20, Rev. 1 (VIII) and ECM, Res.21.Rev.1 (VIII).
9. Ministry of Foreign Affairs, *White Paper*, p. 19.
10. OAU, ECM, Res. 21.Rev. 1 (VIII).
11. Secretariat of the League of Arab States, *Arab Summit Conference: Resolutions and Statements, 1946–1989* (1990), p. 63 (in Arabic).
12. League of Arab States, 28 November 1973, Sixth Session, Summit Resolution 49.
13. OAU, CM, Res. 338 (XXIII).
14. Ministry of Foreign Affairs, *White Paper*, p. 21.
15. League of Arab States, 29 October 1974, 17 /71.
16. Ministry of Foreign Affairs, *White Paper*, p. 22.
17. CM/662 (XXV).
18. Ibid.
19. AHG, Res.73 (XII).
20. Ministry of Foreign Affairs, *White Paper*, p. 25.
21. Ibid., p. 26.
22. Ibid.
23. Ibid., pp. 35–61.
24. AFRARB/Doc. 4.

11

The OAU and the Commonwealth
DEREK INGRAM

More than one-third of the membership of the Organization of African Unity—sixteen countries—are also members of the fifty-nation Commonwealth that spans all the continents. The African membership thus makes up the largest regional group in the Commonwealth.

Of these sixteen, the first African country in the Commonwealth to become independent, Ghana, played a pioneering role in the formation of the OAU. Ghana became independent on 6 March 1957. Just over a year later Kwame Nkrumah, then Prime Minister, convened on 15 April in Accra the first conference of independent States of Africa. They were only eight strong and all in the northern half of the continent. They pledged to heal "fellow Africans still subject to colonial rule," which meant, in those days, the whole of sub-Saharan Africa apart from Ghana.

In December of the same year Nkrumah called the first All-African Peoples Conference, attended by sixty-two nationalist organizations and parties from twenty-eight countries. Among those present were people who were to become some of the most important Commonwealth leaders—Julius Nyerere, Kenneth Kaunda, Tom Mboya, Joshua Nkomo, and Kamuzu Banda. These two meetings initiated by Nkrumah led to the formation of the OAU in 1963, by which time four other Commonwealth countries had become independent—Nigeria, Sierra Leone, Tanzania, and Uganda.

In 1965 Nkrumah chaired the Third OAU Summit in Accra, but by this time he was running into political problems at home and a few months later he was overthrown. Despite his fervent nationalism and pan-Africanism, Nkrumah was a firm supporter of the Commonwealth, then only beginning to emerge into its modern form, and he was a prime mover in the establishment of the Commonwealth secretariat in 1965.

Two other Commonwealth leaders in Africa were highly influential in the formation and development over many years of the OAU—President Julius Nyerere of Tanzania and President Kenneth Kaunda of Zambia. Both became its chairman for more than one term.

There has therefore been a strong input into the Commonwealth from the OAU and vice versa. The wide spread of the Commonwealth membership means that it provides windows into many international organizations. Through its meetings at many levels, its OAU members for example, are able to put over OAU views and insights before countries that belong to the Association of South East Asian States (ASEAN), the Caribbean Community (CARICOM), the South Pacific Forum, and many other such regional groupings.

Political pressures emanating from the OAU have greatly influenced Commonwealth actions in the last three decades, most notably on the issues of Rhodesia and South Africa, on which the Commonwealth was many times confronted with the threat of division and even, on occasion, breakup. Mostly the difficulties lay in the role of Britain, but in earlier years the attitudes of Australia and New Zealand confronted the Commonwealth with the possibility of a divide along racial lines, a situation avoided by the more liberal position consistently taken by successive Canadian governments.

On 11 November 1965 the white minority government of Ian Smith made its Unilateral Declaration of Independence (UDI). Rhodesia was then what was known as a self-governing colony of Britain. The British had no troops in the country, but in international eyes they were responsible for what went on there and were expected to exert their authority over what was seen as a colony in rebellion. The Labor government under Prime Minister Harold Wilson sent fighter aircraft to neighboring Zambia but took no military action, preferring instead to implement sanctions.

The OAU recommended that all African countries should break off diplomatic relations with Britain. Only Ghana and Tanzania did so, but neither country left the Commonwealth. It was a unique situation that demonstrated the changed nature of the Commonwealth; with a multinational secretariat in place (from July 1965) under a Canadian Secretary-General, Arnold Smith, it was no longer seen as a British organization. Leaders like President Nyerere did not see why they should break their Commonwealth links with all the other member countries, such as India, simply because of what they saw as the misbehavior of one of them, Britain.

But the OAU action against Britain and many subsequent stands, particularly on the issue of sanctions, made in the fifteen years between the UDI and the emergence of an independent Zimbabwe in 1980, undoubtedly helped to influence decisions in the Commonwealth. The British did not want to see the Commonwealth break up over Rhodesia—in domestic terms, it would have been highly risky electorally—and therefore the existence of the Commonwealth and the pressures exerted by its member countries helped to stay their hand. Several times during those years British governments came near to doing a deal with Smith, but on each occasion pressures from the rest of the Commonwealth were a factor in preventing them going through with it. The interplay of OAU pressures in the Commonwealth and of Commonwealth pressures on the OAU were a constant factor as the situation developed through the years.

Similarly, the OAU input into the Commonwealth through the African members has been important in the long-running struggle against apartheid. In 1970 alarm bells rang when the newly elected British government of Edward Heath announced an intention to resume the sale of arms to South Africa. Again the Commonwealth faced division and possible disintegration. President Kenneth Kaunda of Zambia, then chairman of the OAU as well as being a senior Commonwealth leader, flew to London with an OAU delegation to appeal to Heath to change his mind. It was a stormy meeting and Heath would not give ground, but this and other pressures in the months before the Commonwealth summit in Singapore in January 1971 delayed any British decision. After Britain found itself confronted with an almost totally hostile summit as well, it ended up selling only a handful of helicopters and nothing else.

In 1967 the OAU and the Commonwealth faced severe tests with the outbreak of civil war in Nigeria following its declaration of secession. Both bodies confronted the problem of how to play a mediatory role without interfering in the internal affairs of a member country. The OAU approach, as Arnold Smith relates in his account of his ten years as Commonwealth Secretary-General,[1] was to try to encourage influential African leaders to bring pressure on the government of General Yakubu Gowon and the rebel leader, Lieutenant Colonel Odumegwu Ojukwu. At the behest of General Joseph Ankrah, then head of the government of Ghana, also a member of the Commonwealth, it set up a Consultative Committee of six heads of state led by Emperor Haile Selassie of Ethiopia. But the committee held only a one-day meeting with Gowon and did not contact the Biafrans.

The OAU did nothing more for eight months and so Smith tried a different approach: simply to bring the Nigerian and Biafran leaders together. He tried to effect this in many secret meetings in London and elsewhere, often under the cover of other Commonwealth events. He finally achieved a meeting in the Uganda Parliament Buildings in Kampala, Uganda, in May 1968. Nigerian and Biafran delegations, five per side, met for nine sessions. Although in the end it was to no avail, it was the only time the parties to the war came together until Biafra surrendered. The meeting broke up without agreement and the task of promoting peace talks passed back to the OAU, but many further efforts to get the parties together by both the Commonwealth and OAU failed.

In May 1973 Arnold Smith was invited as a guest of honor to the Tenth Anniversary Summit of the OAU in Addis Ababa. In his book he tells how

Gowon startled his security guards by having his plane to Addis Ababa piloted by an Ibo who had served with the Biafran Air Force. It was one of the many ways in which he demonstrated his policy of reconciliation.

Following British admission to the membership of the European Economic Community in 1973, the Commonwealth and the EEC were often involved together in the hugely complicated negotiations that led to the signing of the Lomé Convention in 1975, bringing together the francophone and anglophone African countries in economic arrangements with the EEC. African countries had long been sensitive to ideas that they would be treated as associates of the EEC—mere appendages to be economically exploited by "the Six," as the EEC was then known.

Third World Commonwealth countries, long suspicious that the EEC would keep their exports out of Europe or at least dictate economic terms, were in danger of being divided in the negotiating process in Brussels. Arnold Smith's personal concern was to do all he could to ensure that the Commonwealth countries of Africa, the Caribbean, and the Pacific came together with the francophone countries (then already linked to the EEC under the Yaounde agreement) and thus secure a maximum bargaining position. Nigeria, in particular, had been cool toward links with the EEC, but under OAU auspices a strategy based on eight principles was worked out and adopted at the 1973 summit in Addis Ababa, chaired by Gowon.

It was agreed that further formal Commonwealth consultation would encourage separate francophone consultations, and so the OAU now took the lead. As OAU Chairman, Gowon called a meeting of all Commonwealth African, Caribbean, and Pacific (ACP) States and Yaounde States to work out a strategy to negotiate with the EEC.

In the eighties, African members of the OAU in the Commonwealth found themselves confronting Britain again over the thorny issue of sanctions against South Africa. In many ways it was a rerun of the battles that had been fought in the sixties and seventies over Rhodesia.

So often with all international organizations, divisions between members prevent joint action. On South Africa, differences of approach between Commonwealth countries were reflected at OAU summits. At the 1971 OAU summit, Ghana, Malawi, and Lesotho supported the idea of dialogue with South Africa, while Botswana, Gambia, Kenya, Nigeria, Sierra Leone, Tanzania, and Zambia opposed it.

It was not until June 1991 that the Secretary-General, now Chief Emeka Anyaoku, attended as an official guest. Although Ramphal had always the closest of relations with most African leaders, which could be traced back to the days when as Foreign Minister of Guyana he was arguing the Caribbean case in the first Lomé negotiations, Anyaoku had for obvious reasons long been intimately connected with the OAU. As the senior African in the secretariat for so many years—first as Director of the International Affairs Division and then as Deputy Secretary-General (Political), he was deputed by

Ramphal to liaise with the OAU. In 1991, now as one of Nigeria's most highly regarded sons, it was to be expected that he would be warmly welcomed at the meeting at which Nigeria took over as chair of the OAU. In addition, the OAU now had a Secretary-General in Salim Ahmed Salim, who came from a Commonwealth country and had a long experience, as Foreign Minister of Tanzania, of involvement in Commonwealth meetings.

At the 1991 OAU summit meeting in Abuja (27 May–1 June) relations between the OAU and the Commonwealth took a big step forward with Chief Anyaoku's attendance. No doubt this development had been helped by the fact that the meeting was held in his own country, that the incoming chairman of the OAU was the Nigerian President, Ibrahim Babangida, and that Salim was from a Commonwealth country. There was, however, much more to it than that. Relations with the Commonwealth had always been complicated by the fact that one of the OAU's central objectives was the complete elimination of colonialism. This has also been the aim of the Commonwealth in recent decades, but for a long time elements of colonialism remained through the British connection, most notably until 1980 in the case of Rhodesia.

As already stated, in some African countries the modern Commonwealth was not understood and therefore the role of Britain and sometimes of Australia and New Zealand made it suspect. Even in the long struggle for independence of Namibia the part played by Britain, always so firmly wedded to United States' policies—especially during the Reagan-Thatcher era—was often seen as at best ambivalent and at worst unhelpful. Its close relations with South Africa were disturbing. All this rubbed off on the Commonwealth in the eyes of some African leaders; even if most Commonwealth members were firmly opposed to the British stance, was not Britain still the central, certainly the most powerful, member of the Commonwealth?

By 1991 all this had changed. With the independence of Namibia, decolonization had finally been completed—thirty-four years after the independence of Nkrumah's Ghana had begun the process. The South African problem remained, but that had never really been seen as a colonial problem. No metropolitan power governed South Africa; the colonialists in this case, if the term had to be used, were the European population of the country itself. It was a totally different proposition from the colonial system that had been imposed on the rest of the continent.

Furthermore, there had at last been major movement in the South African situation, and optimism was high in early 1991 that real majority rule would be achieved there in the foreseeable future. Although the timetable might be stretched, the general movement in the situation was in the right direction. Britain had been opposed to sanctions, but under Secretary-General Ramphal the Commonwealth had clearly and consistently opposed apartheid. Other member countries had effectively isolated Britain without breaking the Commonwealth, forming in 1987 the Commonwealth Committee of Foreign

Ministers on Southern Africa to monitor and tighten sanctions. The Committee, whose membership included Nigeria, Tanzania, Zambia, and Zimbabwe, performed a service to the international community by studying the implications of financial sanctions and successfully lobbying Western governments when they showed any signs of weakening on sanctions. Members of the U.S. Congress were influenced by the committee's work and sometimes took their tune from its decisions.

In addition, the Commonwealth was recognized by ANC leaders as being increasingly helpful in working for a political solution in South Africa. The Eminent Persons Group sent by the Commonwealth to South Africa in 1986, while rebuffed by the Pretoria government, produced in its report a formula for a negotiating process that was largely the one used in 1990 by the South African government and the ANC to achieve a dialogue. Commonwealth programs on technical assistance and training for Namibians, Mozambicans, and South Africans were also seen as valuable contributions to the transformation of the Southern African situation. All this had helped the Commonwealth image in Africa and paved the way for closer cooperation with the OAU.

Commonwealth and OAU objectives had moved together in other ways. The Commonwealth had never been comfortable with one-party or military rule, even though several of its member countries acquired such systems. They were alien to the traditions of parliamentary democracy as practiced in the major member countries, such as Britain, India, Canada, and Australia. With the advent of multipartyism in Africa in the late eighties there was more in common.

The Commonwealth had embarked at its 1989 summit in Kuala Lumpur on programs that would enhance democracy among its member countries. To this end it began sending observer groups at the request of member countries to ensure that their elections were freely and fairly conducted. Much earlier, its observer group sent for the Zimbabwe elections of 1980 had been of huge importance in paving the path to independence. Now, with experience in such places as Malaysia (1989) and Bangladesh (1990), it stood ready to help in Africa if required.

In the early nineties Africa and the OAU are moving into a new era, as the Abuja meeting reflected. With the changes to multipartyism and the real possibility of a democratic South Africa, the Commonwealth and the OAU will have much to work on together. The roles of both bodies in the evolution of South Africa, ending up hopefully with a fully representative South Africa becoming a member of the OAU and returning to the Commonwealth, should move into closer harmony.

At the Abuja conference one of the main themes—not surprisingly in light of the many problems that have confronted African countries in the last few years—was the need to bring "good governance" to Africa. This objective is fully in line with Commonwealth policies as enunciated by Chief Anyaoku when he took over as Secretary-General and is another reason why the prospects for cooperation between the two bodies are looking brighter for the nineties.

Most urgent of all, however, is the need to bring about the economic recovery of Africa. Here again the Commonwealth, looking beyond its necessary preoccupation with South Africa, is beginning to see one of its chief roles to be giving advice and assistance to those countries trying to switch to market economies while laid low by debt and poverty. The opportunity for closer cooperation with the Commonwealth on this front came with the decision in Abuja to press ahead with plans for an African common market.

The Commonwealth can provide for Africa a unique facility: access to most of the world's major economic blocs. Its member countries all belong to one such grouping or another—among them some of those bodies already mentioned—ASEAN, the South Pacific Forum, CARICOM, the South Asian Association for Regional Cooperation (SAARC), and, of course, the most powerful of all, the European Community.

The Commonwealth has recently been giving special help and advice to CARICOM, which although it has been in existence for many years, now realizes the need for a much tighter economic community if it is to meet the challenges and dangers presented by the formation of a free trade area between Canada and the United States (and possibly Mexico) and by the elimination of all tariff barriers within the European Community after 1992. One of the great advantages of the Commonwealth is that it is a worldwide organization containing one-third of the world's countries and linking into so many regional organizations, often more informally than formally. Exchanges of experience with all these economic blocs could be of immense help to Africa in the quite massive task of forming a common market of so many countries.

The Commonwealth also has unique experience in advising on the problems of small States because it contains so many of them among its membership and has done an immense amount of research into the peculiar circumstances that render many of them vulnerable in security as well as economic terms. Some of the small States of Africa that are Commonwealth members, such as Gambia, Lesotho, and Seychelles, find themselves as vulnerable as the small island States of the Pacific and Caribbean. The Commonwealth is in a good position to advise such countries on ways in which capital resources investment might be mobilized through the newly established Commonwealth Equity Fund, which aims to help the stock exchanges now being established in several small developing countries.

The prospect of all these opportunities for closer OAU–Commonwealth cooperation led to a decision in Abuja that the Commonwealth Secretary-General and the OAU Secretary-General should sign an agreement on behalf of the two bodies. It would mark something of a watershed in their relationship.

The resolution passed in Abuja authorizing the signing talked of the "common objectives pursued by the Organisation of African Unity and the Commonwealth in their efforts to strengthen international cooperation" and said the cooperation agreement "would enable the two organisations to co-ordinate and harmonise their activities in all areas of common interest."

Before Chief Anyaoku went to the Abuja meeting he gave a lecture in Lagos to the Oxford and Cambridge Club of Nigeria entitled "Tackling the Legacy of Africa's Slavery." He concluded it with this fascinating reference to Nkrumah:

In the final analysis, African unity will surely contribute to a lasting answer to the legacy of slavery. This has now become something of a truism; but not long ago, it was restated with a special poignancy by Kwame Nkrumah almost as if he intended it to be his parting message to the African people.

On his death bed, a young Guinean, Seydou Keita, came to see him. The man was upset about allegations of corruption and sedition in the then Government of Guinea and in his frustration put it down to strong character weaknesses in black people as a whole. According to the account as set down in John Milne's compilation *Kwame Nkrumah: The Conakry Years*, Kwame Nkrumah tapped the young man's left hand and said slowly and quietly: "It is not the colour of the skin. The solution is the political unification of Africa. When Africa is a united strong power everyone will respect Africans, and Africans will respect themselves."

African unity cannot, of course, be a panacea to the problems I have spoken of; nor will it be achieved tomorrow or the day after. However, if we understand our problems and tackle the challenges they pose with due diligence, Africa as Pan-Africa, may yet prove to itself and others that she has not got feet of clay. Then her future in unity will be one of greater effectiveness and achievement. That is the great objective to which the efforts of African governments must be bent.

NOTE

1. Arnold Smith with Clyde Sanger, *Stitches in Time: The Commonwealth in World Politics* (n.p.: Andre Deutsch, 1981).

Part IV

The Future

12

An OAU for the Future: An Assessment

YASSIN EL-AYOUTY

Can the OAU handle the future? If so, how? These two questions take into account two obvious facts: The world has completely changed, since 1989; the OAU has not, since 1963. This is not to castigate the continental organization. It is to express the hope that the OAU will be truly instrumental in reversing the marginalization of Africa in the post–Cold War era.

With the end of the Cold War, Africa benefited from the absence of the superpower rivalries that made its internal political and economic problems arenas for East-West conflicts. The Cold War enhanced Africa's dependency on the two ideologically opposed camps in terms of armament, diplomatic support at the UN, and some selected economic development. In the process of playing the friendship and cooperation game with either East or West, Africa incurred the following hazards: It did not rely effectively on the OAU for conflict resolution; several of its States became pawns in the superpower chess games; the civil wars in Angola, Mozambique, Ethiopia, Sudan, Chad, and the Sahara were allowed to go on without African solutions; the motto of "African solutions for African problems" became a hollow slogan; several of the fathers of independence of Africa moved their societies into the darkness of totalitarianism; African cohesion was reflected not in deeds and programs on the continent, but in words and conference diplomacy of the African Group at the UN; and the African agenda of unity and development was invoked only in large unwieldy OAU ministerial and summit conferences, which were rocked by divisions and antagonistic national programs and priorities. Above all, the OAU became what oral political history attributes to the historic African leader, former Tanzanian President Julius Nyerere as having said: "The OAU exists only for the protection of African Heads of State."

Africa's benefit from the end of the Cold War is that it is forcing Africa toward more self-reliance as the flow of arms, aid, and interventionary advice affecting Africa's civil wars and Africa's development programs came to a halt. Consequently, Africa, as it assesses the impact of the dissolution of the Soviet empire, and the resultant ethnic and nationality explosion all over Eurasia and other parts of the world, is beginning to discover that "African solutions for African problems" is a formula that should be seriously reconsidered. There is no better place for that reconsideration and continental soul-searching than the OAU, and the African subregional organizations, such as SADDC and the Economic Community of West African States, which presently maintains a peace-keeping force in a Liberia torn by civil war. These subregional organizations have grown in power and operationalism, without substantive coordination with the OAU, because of the near paralysis of the continental organization.

During the Cold War era, it would have been unthinkable for Africa to produce through the OAU or the OAU's Secretary-General, the able Tanzanian and world statesman, Salim Ahmed Salim, credible calls for African economic integration, African democratization, and African respect for human rights and fundamental freedoms. Between 1960 and 1990, Africa was busy with three main preoccupations: liberation, confrontation with apartheid in South Africa and preindependence Namibia, and a search for continental identity on the world stage. Economic and social development were given a lower priority, as they were mainly tied to questions of foreign aid and extra-African alliances. While Africa succeeded in its first two goals, liberation and the antiapartheid struggle, thanks largely to the UN and the OAU liberation committee, it did not fare well in asserting its role in world affairs because of absence of cohesion, slowness of development, leadership betrayal such as in the cases of Idi Amin of Uganda, Mengistu of Ethiopia, and Boukassa of the Central African Republic, natural and human disasters such as drought and refugees, and absence of respect for human rights and democratic institutionalization.

It is rather encouraging to see Africa beginning what seems to be an assessment of its role in the post–Cold War period. Speaking in the name of Africa before the Third Summit of the G–15 group of developing countries that opened in Dakar, Senegal, on 21 November 1992, President Hosni Mubarak of Egypt said:

In the last few years the world has witnessed radical, profound developments that took place quickly and at unprecendented rates in our modern history. Undoubtedly, our task is to define our view of these developments, of the burdens and responsibilities they impose on us, and of the opportunities they provide for us to participate in making events and influencing developments so that we have a clear role in setting up the new world order, defining its features, and formulating the values and concepts that govern relations among nations and achieve the required balance between their rights and legitimate interests.[1]

The groping to define Africa's place and role in the new global system has begun, and the OAU could not but be affected by these changed realities. Nonetheless, it is ironic that the above-mentioned summit, which was opened by the Senegalese President Abdou Diouf, who was also the Current Chairman of the OAU, took up the question of the reorganization of the UN, apparently without reference to the OAU's need for reorganization. References to the OAU were in the past tense; those to the UN in the future tense as we read in a summit document: "The UN should be thoroughly reorganized to make its structures well-adapted to the new configuration of international relations. In this way, it can increase its capacity to promote cooperation for development, preventive diplomacy, and crisis management for the preservation of international peace and security."[2]

The change in the OAU machinery and methods of functioning should, in my view, be conceptualized within a clear frame of assumptions: that the world is economically globalizing; that such globalization will be anchored in powerful trading blocs, including the Single European Area (SEA) and the North American Free Trade Association (NAFTA); that democratization and human rights observance will reign supreme as standards of measuring national conduct; that domestic jurisdiction within national frontiers, as noted by UN Charter Article 2, paragraph 7, will gradually lose ground to the now legitimated doctrine of humanitarian intervention (as witnessed in Somalia, northern and southern Iraq, and Bosnia); that the thrust of foreign donor aid will be directed first to Europe, then to other regions including Africa; and that Africa has a very long way to go to catch up, if ever that was possible, with the world of high technology of the North and the Pacific Rim. In addition, and perhaps of crucial importance to the OAU of the future, is that the burdens of peace keeping and peace building that the UN is now shouldering in the post–Cold War era, are spreading the UN's capacity to near exhaustion. This underlies the repeated calls of UN Secretary-General Boutros Boutros-Ghali, the first post–Cold War Secretary-General of the universal organization, for burden sharing between the UN and regional organizations. It could be said that Boutros-Ghali's call for such a new global partnership was already envisaged in the UN Charter by Chapter 8, dealing with the relationship between the UN and regional organizations and arrangements.

In his report entitled *An Agenda for Peace,* the UN Secretary-General describes this new relationship as a "new era of opportunity." He goes on to say: "Under the Charter, the Security Council has and will continue to have primary responsibility for maintaining international peace and security, but regional action, as a matter of decentralization, delegation and cooperation with United Nations efforts could not only lighten the burden of the Council but also contribute to a deeper sense of participation, consensus and democratization in international affairs."[3] Unless the OAU is made ready, through meaningful restructuring of its priorities, mechanisms, and operations, the vacuum will somehow be filled by other institutional arrangements. The OAU, which was born in Addis Ababa in 1963 during the period of African quest for liberation and nonalignment (the latter goal proved largely a misnomer during the Cold War), could not be expected to be truly viable in the new global reconfiguration of power and interaction between states and regions. That would simply not work.

African leadership within the OAU itself is finding the continuation of the status quo intolerable. In his report to the Twenty-sixth Session of the OAU Assembly of Heads of State and Government (1990), Secretary-General Salim concluded as follows: "Africa today is the most economically backward region of the world." He went on to say: "The most powerful and wealthiest countries of the world, such as those in Western Europe, North America, and South-East Asia, are successfully laying the foundations of collective activity, enhanced unity, increased strength and greater prosperity. Africa, the weakest and poorest region of the world, does not appear to be making equally discernible and sustained progress in that direction." The Secretary-General's report was aptly entitled "Fundamental Changes Taking Place in the World and Their Implications for Africa: Proposals for an African Response."[4] The African summit was no less forthright in diagnosing the "real threat of marginalization of our Continent." It noted "the sharp decline in the quality of life in our countries"; the alarming rise in Africa's external debt from $50 billion in 1980 to $257 billion by 1989, a debt for the servicing of which Africa spends 50 percent of her total external earnings; and the increase in the number of African member States classified as "least developed" from twenty-one to twenty-eight. The solution envisaged by the African summit is democratization and accelerated development efforts. This they expressed in their declaration as follows: "We are fully aware that in order to facilitate this process of socio-economic transformation and integration, it is necessary to promote popular participation of our peoples in the processes of Government and development. A political environment which guarantees human rights and the observance of the rule of law, would assure high standards of probity and accountability particularly on the part of those who hold public office."[5] The trend toward democratization and development, within a framework of human rights observance on the continent, is unmistakable, as could be seen in the Ghana presidential elections in late 1992. OAU summits have been the primary vehicle for reaching some kind of African consensus at the highest political level, and the declarations cited above are clearly indicative of responsiveness to radical changes in the new international environment.

How can the OAU of the future be enabled to meet these new challenges, on the African level, subregionally and continentally, and on the global level? There are three areas that deserve consideration for change if an OAU for the future is to be fashioned. These are: the functional area, the conceptual area, and the relational area.

THE FUNCTIONAL AREA

The most important aspect of an international organization is its secretariat. In fact, the essential difference between an international organization and other forms of international contact and action, such as an international conference, is the existence of a permanent secretariat. The transformation of the OAU from what we have today to what we should have in the future must begin with revamping and strengthening the OAU secretariat. The weakness of that OAU mechanism becomes obvious in the critical areas of political and peace-keeping assignments. That weakness becomes all the more glaring when you team up UN staffers and OAU staffers in joint assignments. I have personally witnessed that variation in the level of staff efficiency in several situations, including, for example, UN–OAU intersecretariat work on the question of preparing Western Sahara for a plebiscite to decide whether the Sahrawis desired independence or integration with Morocco. The UN group soon discovered that it had to do most of the actual work, such as preparation of the plesbiscite terms of reference, work on security arrangements, and education of the populace as to the methods by which they would express their choices. The UN staff involved represented military, legal, and political expertise, as each one of us had dealt with our particular specialization several times in the field, and were the beneficiaries of extensive on-the-job and off-the-job training. Each one of us was promoted in the UN hierarchy, with field experience being one of the factors figuring in our promotion. We had been involved in the organization and implementation of many plebiscites, were attached to several peace-keeping missions as spokesmen and observers, and were trained to draft complex political assessment papers at UN Headquarters quickly and under situations of extreme stress and urgency. (I was once called upon to sum up for UN Secretary-General Kurt Waldheim the entire evolution of the concept of self-determination from 1914 to the 1970s in five pages within two hours of his departure to Europe for a meeting with the representatives of South Africa. It was done.)

The effectiveness of the UN secretariat is largely a matter of competitive selection of the junior staff and the continuous training of that staff in various tasks under continually changing circumstances. The OAU can, without too much cost, enter into cooperative arrangements with the UN, other regional organizations, and training institutions to enhance the skills of its junior staff in the complex arts of action diplomacy. Appointments, promotions, and other rewards should be contingent upon merit and achievement. The senior OAU staff is highly professional, but an international organization cannot run its daily business without trained junior personnel who are capable of assisting and learning from their superiors the effective implementation of a host of policy directives. This is the primary way of building secretarial organizations from the ground up. Conference organization, which OAU junior staff seem to be capable of handling, is only a small part of the total political performance a junior officer should be enabled to undertake on behalf of his or her organization. It should be noted here that attachment as appropriate of OAU professional staff to the Somalia relief operations or to the ECOWAS peace-keeping efforts in Liberia would provide them with invaluable experience for the future.

The position of the Secretary-General of the OAU should also be vastly strengthened. When the OAU began, the title of the bureaucracy's chief was "Administrative Secretary-General." The qualifying adjective "Administrative" has now been dropped. But the original OAU outlook on the Secretary-General, as an implementor of ministerial and summit decisions, remains largely unchanged. The present OAU Secretary-General, Dr. Salim Ahmed Salim, is a highly energetic leader. His stamp on the UN, where he served as Permanent Representative of Tanzania is indelible. His presidency of one of the General Assembly sessions and his chairmanship of one of the General Assembly's highly politicized bodies, the Committee on Decolonization, were among his several substantive contributions, attributed to Africa, to the work of the UN, over a number of years. His activism is part of his political and intellectual make-up. But there are no OAU Charter provisions that would institutionalize his political initiatives in a continent where political turmoil has characterized its modern history.

Salim and his predecessors have administered the bureaucracy in Addis Ababa, but have relied on only informal arrangements to play substantive political roles in the unending series of African crises. Here we should realize that the head of an international intergovernmental organization should in fact be two institutions in order to be effective. As an example, the UN Secretary-General, under the Charter, is both "the chief administrative officer of the Organization" (Article 97), and a political institution to which UN bodies, including the General Assembly and the Security Council, may "entrust . . . other functions" (Article 98). In addition, the UN Secretary-General "may bring to the attention of the Security Council any matter which in his opinion may threaten the maintenance of international peace and security" (Article 99).[6] It was under Article 99 that the late Dag Hammarskjold brought the crisis in the Congo (now Zaire) to the Security Council's attention. And it was that vast capacity of political initiative and judgment that held the present Secretary-General, Dr. Boutros Boutros-Ghali, in good stead, when he felt in 1992 that the Security Council, contrary to the Secretary-General's sense of priorities, was instructing him to implement action in the former Yugoslavia which he felt was not properly considered by him, at the expense of relegating Somalia to a less than first priority as he had perceived it to be. Could Salim, at the OAU, enjoy the same institutionalized and Charter-specific powers? No. The OAU Charter and OAU practice would have forced him to resort to behind-the-scenes diplomacy. In a situation similar to the dilemma faced by Boutros-Ghali vis-à-vis the Security Council, Salim would have had to exert a huge amount of quiet diplomatic activity to secure an informal consesus, first from the Current Chairman of the OAU, and then from the other States considered to be interested parties in a particular crisis.

The example advanced above indicates how crisis management by the OAU machinery lacks effectiveness and cohesion. The Current Chairman is an annually rotated post among Africa's Heads of State and Government who becomes a one-year superdiplomat. His shuttle diplomacy and other conflict resolution activities are characterized by high visibility, noncontinuity (as these last for one year), and noninstitutionalization as contrasted to the role of the OAU Secretary-General, who represents the continuity of OAU action during his tenure. Heads of State and Government are also cognizant first of the priority of their nations' interest, which may not be consistent with the continental interest.

Since the Assembly of Heads of State and Government is the highest decision-making body in the OAU, it is difficult to see such a cumbersome machinery acting on African crises with the requisite cohesiveness, the needed expedition, and the necessary submission to sanctions in case of disregard of whichever decision is taken. Simply put, the OAU Assembly could not be equated with the UN Security Council. This may explain why the OAU has no real role in the crises of Somalia, Liberia, Mozambique, Angola, the Sahara, and the like. The OAU peace-keeping role in Chad was a textbook lesson on how regional organizations should not undertake missions of such a complex nature. The disastrous mission lacked the basic elements of command and control, rules of engagement, sustained consent by the host environment, and financial and logistical stability.

There is also a broad range of OAU deficiencies in the critical areas of mediation, conciliation, and arbitration. The OAU commission charged with these functions is moribund, and Africa's dependency on informal "African solutions" cannot fill in such institutional gaps. This is especially critical for two reasons: Africa, in the post–Cold War period, cannot escape the effects of the global hurricane of ethnic and nationality strife within national borders; and the UN Secretary-General's offer of partnership between the UN and regional organizations seems to focus on peace keeping as a task for the UN, and peace making as requiring local diplomacy for regional organizations, such as the OAU.

Without OAU mechanisms in place and effectively functioning, the OAU would miss out in this global burden sharing. One could already see the absence of the OAU name from the operative parts of UN resolutions and official statements that have to do with acute conflict in Africa. Neither Security-Council resolution 788 (1992) on Liberia,[7] nor the UN Secretary-General's statement on face-to-face meetings of the parties to the Angola conflict contains any reference to the OAU.[8] With regard to Somalia, the UN Security Council resolution of 3 December 1992, which launched a massive military operation to ensure that food reached the needy, contained only a reference in its preambular part to a proposal made by the OAU Chairman for the "organization of an international conference on Somalia."[9]

No organizational action can run on principle and modality alone; proper funding is a primary ingredient of continuity, resolve, and operational stability. The OAU is perennially beset by lack of funds, and the Charter contains no sanctions against member States in arrears. By contrast, Article 19 of the UN Charter provides for a high political penalty for delinquent member States. It reads: "A Member of the United Nations which is in arrears in the payment of its financial contributions to the Organization shall have no vote in the General Assembly if the amount of its arrears equals or exceeds the amount of the contributions due from it for the preceding two full years. The General Assembly may, nevertheless, permit such a Member to vote if it is satisfied that the failure to pay is due to conditions beyond the control of the Member."

A senior OAU staff member confided recently that some OAU member States have not paid their financial contributions for twenty years. With this kind of laxity, the OAU credibility, even on the African scene, is bound to suffer, and planning is bound to be, at best, conjectural and tangential.

THE CONCEPTUAL AREA

With regard to the conceptual area, the challenges facing an OAU of the future are perhaps more intractable than those facing it in the functional area. Functionally, the OAU may be able to change its modus operandi without necessarily amending its Charter in every respect where it feels the need for strengthening. Some of those changes may be effected by a special summit of the OAU Assembly to be devoted to restructuring and reinvigorating the organization. But concepts on which the OAU is based are harder to replace by the newer concepts that have developed globally outside the context of Africa's struggle for reemergence into independence. This explains why in this chapter, the functional precedes the conceptual: The former is doable; the latter requires change that interferes with basic tenets in African politics that have acquired the lore of sacredness or sanctity.

First, there is the sanctity of domestic jurisdiction. It draws its historic roots from the long and arduous struggle for independence. But domestic jurisdiction is progressively losing ground to the exigencies of intranational ethnic strife, national calamities such as hunger, and the replacement of dictatorships by democratic institutions supervised by the UN, the European Economic Community, and human rights groups. The doctrine of humanitarian intervention has in fact become integrated into international customary law, as attested to by the use of armed force to protect human rights and save humans in Bosina Herzegovina, northern and southern Iraq, Somalia, and Macedonia. For example, no-fly zones have been established in the former Yugoslavia and Iraq by member States acting under resolutions by the UN

Security Council and/or NATO. Protective missions have been organized for Macedonia by the UN Security Council and by the Conference for Security and Cooperation in Europe (CSCE). In this context, the UN Security Council in its resolution of December 1992 on Macedonia uses the new language of humanitarian intervention as it employs these words: "Authorizes the Secretary-General to establish a presence of the United Nations Protection Force [UNPROFOR] in the former Yugosalv Republic of Macedonia."[10] It also "urges the UNPROFOR presence in the former Yugoslav Republic of Macedonia to coordinate closely with the CSCE mission there,"[11] a reflection of the new UN–regional organization partnership in peace keeping and conflict resolution.

The UN Security Council resolution of 3 December 1992 on Somalia, which was unanimously adopted, addresses itself directly to the new international humanitarian law as it states that the Council: "Further demands that all parties, movements and factions in Somalia immediately cease and desist from all breaches of international humanitarian law."[12] Such decisions accord fully with the exceptions reserved for UN action under Charter Article 2, paragraph 7, which states: "Nothing contained in the present Charter shall authorize the United Nations to intervene in matters which are essentially within the domestic jurisdiction of any state or shall require the Members to submit such matters to settlement under the present Charter; but this principle shall not prejudice the application of enforcement measures under Chapter VII."

In Africa, neither the OAU Charter nor the African political experience provides any flexibility with regard to the full application of domestic jurisdiction within sovereign frontiers. But the winds of change are blowing in a different direction, experientially and legally. After canvassing a number of International Court of Justice cases, Nigel Rodley of Amnesty International reached the following conclusion: "From this it emerges that the Court has unambiguously accepted that the obligation to respect fundamental human rights is an obligation found in general international law."[13]

Another conceptual hurdle facing the evolution of an OAU for the future is the sanctity of the inherited frontier. Member States that were admitted to the OAU with specific borders expect the organization and its members not to condone the slightest change in those borders. This is another manifestation of the African State commitment to the unchangeability of borders, of sovereignty, or of domestic jurisdiction which are bound together like a bundle of sacred rights. But with Eritrean independence, a major breach has occurred due to historic changes and a changed interpretation of legitimacy and state recognition. The Ethiopia of today is smaller (and again landlocked without Eritrean acquiescence) than the Ethiopia of the OAU founding fathers. The question here is, absent an intranational or communal agreement such as the one that led to Eritrea's independence in 1993, how would the OAU conceptually cope with secession, say, in southern Sudan or in the parts that constitute Somalia? It would be impossible for an inter-State organization like the OAU to openly plan for such contingency, but conceptual questions such as these should be at least thought about.

Would it, for example, be possible to consider functional solutions to the question of the tribal and clan division by inherited national frontiers? Such solution may lie in cosovereignty over certain areas for purposes of tribal unity or natural resources exploitation. The African national frontier is porous in many States, as the nomadic tribes in search of water and better grazing, as well as refugees and drought, have proven over the last several decades. It may be feasible to consider the possibility, indeed the attractiveness, of a functional frontier rather than a sovereign one. Such possibilities, including federal arrangements, may reduce the pressures for secession and the accentuation of inter-State conflict in Africa.

This whole cluster of sovereign rights claimed by the African States explains in part the reluctance of OAU member States to resort to the organization's mechanism for mediation, conciliation, and arbitration. Secretary-General Salim was candid when he outlined to senior African military and civilian officials in Arusha, Tanzania in March 1990 the reasons for that phenomenon. He said that the causes were: (1) divergence over the OAU's Commission mandate; (2) reluctance of member States to submit to arbitration; (3) "the sensitivity of the issue, in particular as it touches on matters of national sovereignty"; and (4) the limitation placed by the Charter on the extent of involvement in mediation.[14]

The same reasons could equally apply to the absence of an OAU Security Council, an OAU economic and social council, or an OAU court of justice. The creation of such bodies would require a change in the African political will and the creation of an African consensus responsive to changes in the world situation.

The concept of democratization in Africa is perhaps more attainable than the other conceptual concerns mentioned above. Africa's historic experience is essentially democratic, as it is based on tribal participatory practices observed in the village institution of the tribal council. But the modern African State has subverted that practice, and, as has been indicated above, dictatorships grow out of the success of the fathers of independence. Today, authoritative international law experts, such as Thomas Franck of the New York University Law School, describe democracy as a basic human right.

The interrelationship between democratization, observance of human rights, economic and social advancement, and the diminution of internal conflict in the post–Cold War era cannot be overemphasized. UN Secretary-General Boutros-Ghali describes the process of democratization as "a global phenomonon" whereby "authoritarian regimes have given way to more democratic forces and responsive Governments."[15] On the OAU level, Secretary-General Salim publicly said: "In my view, perhaps the most serious threat to Africa comes from a sometimes poor relationship between the people and their governments. . . . Whatever has been the form of the relationship between the people and the Government, the African masses have not by and large, been given adequate opportunities to find an outlet for their creative energies and apply them to development."[16]

It is noteworthy that in the presidential elections held in Ghana in late November 1992, which resulted in the victory of Jerry Rawlings, were warmly welcomed by the OAU Secretary-General. In fact, the OAU, at the invitation of Ghana, observed that free and democratic process and "the OAU election team had expressed satisfaction with the election despite minor shortcomings."[17]

Democratization and the OAU role in it promise to be the key to a revitalized OAU and a resurgent Africa. No amount of structural changes in the OAU institutional fabric can match the importance of that phenomenon, which would gradually bring about mass participation in the process of development. It would also replace the old concept of sovereignty with a "new sovereignty," which would be interactive nationally and continentally. If a fair chance is given the African (Banjul) Charter on Human and Peoples' Rights, which entered into force on 21 October 1986, for effective implementation, the chances will be brighter for the possibility of putting into effect the Abuja declaration on the African Economic Community of 1991.[18] The fate of the two documents is intertwined. While the Banjul Charter is the cornerstone for OAU involvement in humanitarian diplomacy on the Continent, the Abuja declaration may contribute to a radical change of the African economic and social scene, especially after the expected integration of a nonracial and democratic South Africa is accomplished.

THE RELATIONAL AREA

The OAU of the future ought to become known to the African student, the African laborer, the African farmer, and to other African broad masses in general. It could not hope to create or inculcate an African consensus for as long as it continues to be a diplomatic elitist organization whose flag and emblem may be known only in Addis Ababa and a few other African cities where it maintains regional offices. It needs OAU information centers, akin to the UN information centers that now exist in more than sixty capitals and cover more than that number of countries. In this connection it would be important for the OAU to make its documentation and publications available throughout the world, as it is always a struggle to secure such documentation.

The OAU of the future needs the help and support of "Friends of the OAU" to be created in various African States with the consent of these States. It needs nongovernmental organizations all over Africa to explain its mission.

On the interorganizational level, the OAU of the future needs to interact operationally, not only representationally and ceremonially, with other organizations whose membership in whole or in part is African. These include the subregional African organizations, the League of Arab States, and the Conference of the Islamic Organization. We discussed above some aspects of UN–OAU relationships that are the subject of countless UN and OAU resolutions. But these relationships are not effective as they are not symmetrical. The UN to the OAU, is, on the whole, a donor organization; the OAU is a recipient. Were the OAU to be strengthened and become effective, it could possibly someday enjoy the privileged relationship between the UN and, say, the European Economic Community. Staff of the UN Economic Commission for Africa based, like the OAU, in Addis Ababa, complain that "the OAU wants us to do the work, and they only want the credit and the flag." This may be due to bureaucratic competition, jealousy, vagueness of terms of reference, or competition for the African State's attention. Whatever the reason may be, it remains an axiom of interorganization relationship that if each of the collaborating organizations has something to give in return for what it may receive, the tension would be much less. Here one should not forget the sense of false superiority some UN staff may feel toward staff of regional organizations that they may erroneously regard as UN appendages.

UN Secretary-General Boutros Boutros-Ghali's call for a new partnership between the UN and regional organizations such as the OAU may prove to be the beginning of these relational adjustments. He says: "Today a new sense exists that they (regional organizations and arrangements) have contributions to make."[19] It is to be hoped that the OAU of the future would have many vital contributions to make for the good of Africa and the world.

NOTES

1. FBIS-AFR–92–226, p. 4.
2. Ibid.
3. UN document A/47/277, S/2411, *Report of the Secretary-General, An Agenda for Peace: Preventive Diplomacy, Peacemaking and Peace-keeping*, June 17, 1992.
4. OAU, *Report of the Secretary-General to the 26th Ordinary Session of the Assembly of Heads of State and Government* (Addis Ababa: OAU Information Service, 9 July 1990), paragraphs 88 and 91.
5. OAU, *Declaration of the Assembly of Heads of State and Government of the OAU on the Political and Socio-Economic Situation in Africa and the Fundamental Changes Taking Place in the World* (Addis Ababa: July 11, 1990), paragraphs. 2, 6, and 10.
6. *UN Charter*, Articles 97, 98, and 99.
7. UN document S/RES/788, 19 November 1992.
8. UN Press Release, SG/SM/4858, 25 November 1992.
9. UN document S/RES/794, 3 December 1992.
10. UN document S/24940, 11 December 1992, paragraph 2.
11. Ibid., paragraph 4.
12. UN document 3/RES/794, 3 December 1992.
13. Nigel S. Rodley, "Human Rights and Humanitarian Intervention: The Case

Law of the World Court," *International and Comparative Law Quarterly* 38, Part 2 (April 1989), pp. 321–333.

14. UN, *Disarmament* (New York: United Nations, 1991), p. 25.

15. UN, *Agenda for Peace*, paragraph 9.

16. UN, *Disarmament*, p. 22.

17. OAU Press Release, No. NY/OAU/BUR/17/92, "OAU Secretary General Commends the People and Government of Ghana," New York, November 24, 1992.

18. OAU, Resolution AHG/Res. 205 (XXVII), Resolution on the African Economic Community, 1991.

19. UN, *Agenda for Peace*, paragraph 65.

Appendixes

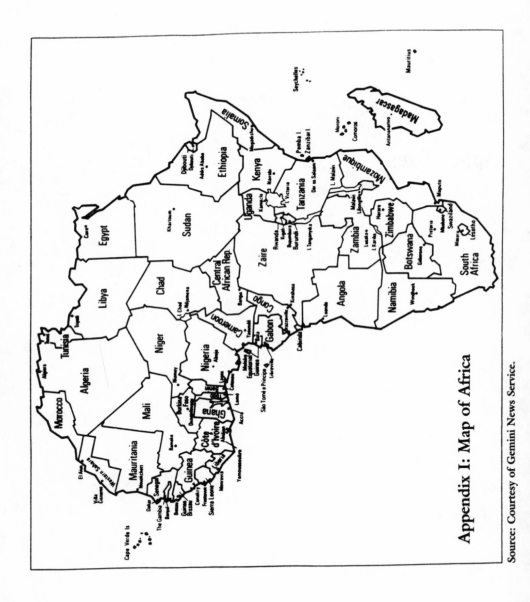

Appendix I: Map of Africa

Source: Courtesy of Gemini News Service.

Appendix II: Member States of the OAU

1. Algeria
2. Angola
3. Benin
4. Botswana
5. Burkina Faso
6. Burundi
7. Cameroon
8. Cape Verde
9. Central African Republic
10. Chad
11. Comoros
12. Congo
13. Cote d'Ivoire
14. Djibouti
15. Egypt
16. Equatorial Guinea
17. Eritrea
18. Ethiopia
19. Gabon
20. Gambia
21. Guinea
22. Guinea Bissau
23. Kenya
24. Lesotho
25. Liberia
26. Libya
27. Madagascar
28. Malawi
29. Mali
30. Mauritania
31. Mauritius
32. Mozambique
33. Namibia
34. Niger
35. Nigeria
36. Rwanda
37. SADR*
38. Sao Tome & Principe
39. Senegal
40. Seychelles
41. Sierra Leone
42. Somalia
43. Sudan
44. Swaziland
45. Tanzania
46. Togo
47. Tunisia
48. Uganda
49. Zaire
50. Zambia
51. Zimbabwe

* The OAU regards SADR (Saharan Democratic Republic) a member of the organization. The name of Morocco does not appear on the official list of membership because of Morocco's withdrawal over SADR admission to the OAU.

Selected Bibliography

Adeniran, Tunde. "Pacific Settlement Among African States: The Role of African Unity." *Conflict Quarterly* 2 (Fall 1981): 8–19.

Ait-Ahmed, H. *L'Afro-facisme: Les droits de l'homme dans la Charte et la pratique de l'OAU*. Paris: L'Harmattan, 1980.

Akinrinade, Olusola. "Africa and the Commonwealth 1960–80: Trends, Achievements and Policy Implications." *Round Table* 309 (January 1989).

Akinyemi, A. Bolaji. "Organisation of African Unity: The Practice of Recognition of Governments." *Indian Journal of Political Science* 36(1) (January–March 1975): 63–79.

———. "The Organisation of African Unity and African Identity." *African Quarterly* 20(3–4) (1981): 5–18.

Akuchu, G. E. "Peaceful Settlement of Disputes: Unsolved Problems for the OAU." *Africa Today* 24 (October 1977): 39–58.

Aluko, Olajide. "The Organisation of African Unity and Human Rights." *Round Table* 283 (July 1981): 234–243.

Amate, C.O.C. *Inside the OAU: Pan-Africanism in Practice*. New York: St. Martin's Press, 1986.

Amimour-Benderra, Meriem. *Le Peuple Sahraoui et l'Autodetermination*. Algiers, Algeria: Entreprise Algerienne de Press, 1988.

Andemicael, Berhanykun. *The OAU and the UN: Relations Between the Organization of African Unity and the United Nations*. UNITAR Regional Study No. 2. New York: Africana Publishing, 1975.

———. *Peaceful Settlement Among African States: Roles of the United Nations and the Organisation of African Unity*. UNITAR P.S. No. 5. United Nations Institute for Training and Research, 1972.

———. "Trends in OAU Quest for African Liberation with the Help of the United Nations." In Avi Shlaim, ed., *International Organizations in World Politics, Yearbook 1975*. N.p., 171–198.

————, ed. *Regionalism and the United Nations*. Dobbs Ferry, N.Y.: Oceana Publications, 1979.

Anyaoku, Emeka. *Tackling the Legacy of Africa's Slavery*. London: Commonwealth Secretariat, 1991.

Austin, Dennis. "Africa Repartitioned?" *Conflict Studies* 193 (October 1986).

Ayari, Chedly. "What Future for Cooperation?" *Africa Report* 27(3) (May–June 1982): 42–48.

Bakhshab, Omar. "The Concept of Regional Arrangements." *Revue Egyptienne de droit international* 40 (1984): 195–206.

Baynham, Simon. "Geopolitics, Glasnost and Africa's Second Liberation: Political and Security Implications for the Continent." *Africa Insight* 21(4) (1991): 263–268.

Bedjaoui, Mohamed. *Pour un nouvel ordre économique international*. Paris: UNESCO, 1979.

Bello, Emmanuel G. "The African Charter on Human and Peoples' Rights: A Legal Analysis." *Recueil des Cours de l'Académie de droit international de La Haye* 194 (5) (1985): 9–268

————. "The Mandate of the African Commission on Human and Peoples' Rights." *African Journal of International Law* 1 (1) (1988): pp. 31–64.

Beri, H.M.L. "The Monrovia OAU Summit." *African Quarterly* 19(1) (April–June 1979): 211–216.

Binaisa, Godfrey L. "Organization of African Unity and Decolonization: Present and Future Trends." *Annals of the American Academy of Political and Social Science* 432 (July 1977): 52–69. (Africa in Transition).

Bipoum-Woum, Joseph Marie. *Le droit international Africain*. Paris: L.G.D.J., 1970.

Boutros-Ghali, Boutros. *L'Organisation de l'Unité Africaine*. Paris: A. Colin, Collection U, Series Institutions Internationales, 1969.

Cervenka, Zdenek. *The Organization of African Unity and Its Charter*. New York: Praeger, 1969.

————. *The Unfinished Quest for Unity: Africa and the OAU*. New York: Africana Publishing, 1978.

Cliffe, Lionel, and David Seddon. "Africa in a New World Order." *Review of African Political Economy*. Sheffield: ROAPE Publishing, 1991.

Damis, John. "Prospects for Unity/Disunity in North Africa." *American-Arab Affairs* 6 (Fall 1983): 34–47.

————. "The Western Sahara Conflict: Myth and Reality." *Middle East Journal* 37 (2) (Spring 1983): 169–179.

————. "The Western Sahara Dispute as a Source of Regional Conflict in North Africa." In Halim Isber Barakat, *Contemporary North Africa: Issues of Development and Integration*. London: Croom Helm, 1985, 139–152.

Djiena Wembou, Michel-Cyr. *L'ONU et le Développement du Droit International*. Paris: Berger-Levrault International, 1991.

D'Sa, Rose M. "Peacekeeping and Self-Determination in the Western Sahara: The Continuing Dilemma of the United Nations and the Organisation of African Unity." *Strategic Studies* 9(3) (Spring 1986): 45–76.

Ekpo, Smart A. "Eritrea, the OAU and the Secession Issue." *Africa Report* 20(6) (November–December 1975): 33–36.

Ekue, Albert K. "L'OAU a 25 ans: L'action politique." *Rivista di studi politici internazionali* 55(4) (October–December 1988): 611–626.

El-Ayouty, Yassin, ed. *The Organization of African Unity After Ten Years: Comparative Perspectives*. New York: Praeger, 1975.

————. "The Organization of African Unity and Conflict Resolution: Looking at the Past, Aiming at the Future." *Disarmament*. New York: United Nations, 1991.

El-Ayouty, Yassin, and I. W. Zartman, eds. *The OAU After Twenty Years*. New York: Praeger, 1984.

Elias, Taslim Olamale. *Africa and the Development of International Law*. New York: Dobbs Ferry, 1972.

El-Sheikh, Ibrahim Badawi. "The African Commission on Human and Peoples' Rights: Prospects and Problems." *Netherlands Quarterly of Human Rights* 7(3) (1989): 272–283.

"Erste Afrikanisch-Arabische Gipfelkonferenz in Kairo: Politische Erklärung der Konferenz der Staats und Regierungschefs der Organisation der Afrikanischen Einheit und der ArabischenLiga aus dem Weltgeschehen." *Europa-Archiv* 32(11) (10 June 1977).

Eze, Osita C. "OAU Faces Rhodesia." *African Review* 5(1) (1975): 43–62.

Fasehun, Orobola. "Nigeria and the Issue of an African High Command: Towards a Regional and/or Continental Defence System?" *Afrika Spectrum* 15(3) (1980): 309–317. Summaries in French and German.

Fawole, W. Alade. "International Law and Territorial Acquisitions in Africa: Some Thoughts on Libya's Annexation of Chadian Territory." *Journal of Asian and African Affairs* 2(1) (July 1990): 87–107.

Fitzgerald, Mary Anne. "The OAU: A New Militancy." *Africa Report* 31(5) (September–October 1986): 66–69.

Frank, Thomas M. "The Stealing of the Sahara." *American Journal of International Law* 70 (4) (1976): 694–721.

Fund for Peace. *Conference on the African Commission on Human and People's Rights*. New York: Fund for Peace, 1991.

Gaspart, Claude. "Chronique Africaine." *Civilisation* 30 (3–4): 305.

Gifford, Prosser, and William Roger Lewis, eds. *Decolonization and African Independence: The Transfers of Power 1960–1980*. New Haven: Yale University Press, 1988.

Gittleman, Richard. "The Banjul Charter on Human and Peoples' Rights: A Legal Analysis." In Claude E. Welch, Jr., and Ronald I. Meltzer, eds., *Human Rights and Development in Africa*. Albany: State University of New York Press, 1982, 152–176.

Gruhn, Isebill. *Regionalism Reconsidered: The Economic Commission for Africa*. Boulder, Colo.: Westview, 1979.

Hallerstein, Immanuel. *Africa: The Politics of Unity*. N.p.: Pall Mall Press, 1968.

Hanning, Hugh. "Lifebelt for Africa: The OAU in the 1980's." *World Today* 37 (7–8) (July–August 1981): 311.

Hodges, Tony. *Western Sahara: The Roots of a Desert War*. Westport, Conn.: Lawrence Hill, 1983.

————. "At Odds with Self-Determination: The United States and the Western

Sahara." In Gerald G. Bender et al., eds., *African Crisis Areas and U.S. Foreign Policy*. Berkeley: University of California Press, 1985, 157–276.

Hugh, Anthony J. "President Moi's Delicate Mission." *Africa Report* 26(5) (September–October 1981): 50–54.

"Introductory Note of the Secretary-General." OAU Council of Ministers, Fifty-third Ordinary Session (February 1991).

"Introductory Note to the Secretary-General's Activity Report." OAU Assembly of Heads of State and Government, Twenty-sixth Session (July 1990).

Jouve, Edmond. *L'Organisation de l'Unité Africaine*. Paris: P.U.F., 1984.

Kamil, Leo. *Fueling the Fire: U.S. Policy Toward the Western Sahara*. Trenton, N.J.: Red Sea Press, 1987.

Kannyo, Edward. "The Banjul Charter on Human and Peoples' Rights: Genesis and Political Background," in Claude E. Welch, Jr., and Ronald I. Meltzer, eds., *Human Rights and Development in Africa*. Albany: State University of New York Press, 1984, 128–151.

Kodjo, Edem. *Et Demain l'Afrique*. Paris: Editions Stock, 1985.

Korany, Bahgat, and Dessouki H. Ali, eds. *The Foreign Policies of Arab States*. Boulder, Colo.: Westview, 1990.

Kouassi, E. Kwam. *Les Rapports entre l'Organisation des Nations Unies et L'Organisation de l'Unité Africaine*. Brussels: Establishments Emile Bruylant, 1978.

Layachi, Azzedine. *The United States and North Africa: A Cognitive Approach to Foreign Policy*. New York: Praeger, 1990.

Legum, Colin. "OAU, Success or Failure." *International Affairs* 51(2) (April 1975): 108–119.

―――. *Pan-Africanism: A Short Political Guide*. N.p.: Pall Mall Press, 1962.

―――. "The Year of Amin." *Africa Report* 20(4) (July–August 1975): 8–10.

Lewis, William H. "North Africa and the Power Balance." *Current History* 64 (377) (January 1973): 30–32, 40.

Margolis, Joseph. "OAU Summit: Dissension and Resolution." *Africa Report* 24(5) (September–October 1979): 52–55.

Mbuyinga, Elanga. *Pan Africanism or Neo-Colonialism: The Bankruptcy of the OAU*. London: Zed, 1982.

Mercer, John. "Confrontation in the Western Sahara," *World Today* 32 (6) (June 1976): 230–239.

Meyers, B. D. "Intraregional Conflict Management by the OAU." *International Organization* 28(3) (Summer 1974): 345–373.

Naldi, Gino J. *The Organization of African Unity: An Analysis of Its Role*. London and New York: Mansell, 1989.

Nkiwane, Solomon Moyo. "The OAU and the Problem of Refugees in Africa." *Africa Quarterly* 27 (3–4) (1987–1988): 25–33.

Novicki, Margaret A. "Assessing the Freetown Summit." *Africa Report* 25(5) (September–October 1980): 39–43.

Nweke, G. Aforka. "The Organization of African Unity and Intra-African Functionalism." *Annals of the American Academy of Political and Social Science* 489 (January 1987): 133–147.

Nweke, G. Aforka. *Harmonization of African Foreign Policies 1955–1975*. Boston: Boston University African Studies Center, 1980.

Nworal, Dike. "The Integration of the Commission for Technical Co-operation in

Africa with the Organization of African Unity: The Process of the Merger and the Problems of Institutional Rivalry and Complimentarity." *African Review* 6(1)(1976): 55–68.

Nyangoni, Wellington Winter. *Africa in the United Nations System*. Rutherford, N.J.: Fairleigh Dickinson University Press, 1985.

Nzo-Nguty, Bernard Tarkang. *The Arab League, United Nations, and Organization of African Unity: Contradictions and Dilemmas in Intra-Interorganizational Co-operation in Conflict Management and Development*. Ann Arbor, Mich.: University Microfilms International, 1987. Ph.D. Thesis, University of South Carolina, 1986.

OAU resolution CM/Res. 1340 (LIV) Rev. 1, Forty-fourth Ordinary Session of the Council of Ministers, 27 May–1 June 1991.

Obaseki, N. O., ed. *Africa and the Superpowers: External Involvement in Regional Disputes*. Report of the International Peace Academy, No. 14. New York, 1983.

Oyoke, F. C. *International Law and the New African States*. London: Sweet & Maxwell, 1972.

Olajid, Oluko. *The Foreign Policies of African States*. London: Hodder and Stoughton, 1977.

Onwuka, Ralph, and Amadu Sesay, eds. *The Future of Regional and Subregional Institutions in Africa*. London: Macmillan, 1983.

Organization of African Unity. Banjul Charter on Human and Peoples' Rights. *International Legal Materials* 21(1) (January 1982): 58–68.

Parker, Richard B. *North Africa: Regional Tensions and Strategic Concerns*. New York: Praeger, 1984.

Pérez de Cuéllar, Javier. *Report of the Secretary-General on the Work of the United Nations*. New York: United Nations, 1991.

Pondi, Jean-Emmanuel. "The OAU: From Political to Economic Pan-Africanism." *SAIS Review* 7(1) (Winter–Spring 1987): 199–212.

Pondi, Jean-Emmanuel, M. Kamato, and L. Zang. *L'OAU Rétrospective et Perspectives Africaines*. Paris: Economica, 1990.

Prga, Vesna. "The Organization of African Unity as an Expression of African Contradictions." *Review of International Affairs* 38(892) (5 June 1987): 20–22.

Price, David L. "Morocco in the Political Balance." *World Today* 34(12) (1978): 493–500.

Ramchandani, R. R. Africa's Debt Problem and Economic Recovery Programme: Some Related Issues. *Africa Quarterly* 27 (3–4) (1987–1988): 1–18.

Ramphul, Radha Krishna. "The Role of International and Regional Organizations in the Peaceful Settlement of Internal Disputes (With Special Emphasis on the Organization of African Unity)." *Georgia Journal of International and Comparative Law* 13 (Suppl.) (Winter 1983): 371–384.

Rifaat, Ahmed M. "Refugees and the Right of Asylum: An African Perspective." *Revue Egyptienne de droit international* 40 (1984): 71–131.

Robert, Henry J. "Politique Etrangère et Vision du Jeu International: Les Stratégies Tiers-Mondistes des Etats du Maghreb." *Annuaire de l'Afrique du Nord* (1980): 341–353.

Rodley, Nigel S. "Human Rights and Humanitarian Intervention: The Case Law of the World Court." *International and Comparative Law Quarterly* 38 (Part 2) (April 1989): 321–333.

Rossi, Gianluigi. "OAU: Un anno di activitá (guino 1980–guino 1981)." *Rivista di Studi Politici International* 480(3) (July–September 1981): 415–436.

Saenz, Paul. "The OAU in the Subordinate African Regional System." *African Studies Review* 13(2) (September 1970): 203–225.

Salim A. Salim. *Development Partnership in the 1990's: The African Dimension.* Paul G. Hoffman Lecture, UNDP Development Study Programme, 1990.

Schatzberg, Michael G. "Military Intervention and the Myth of Collective Security: The Case of Zaire." *Journal of Modern African Studies* 27(2) (June 1989): 315–340.

Schultheis, Michael J., ed. "A Symposium: Refugees in Africa: the Dynamics of Displacement and Repatriation." *African Studies Review* 32(1) (April 1989): 1–69.

Schutz, Barry M. "Peacekeeping in Africa: Breakthrough or Politics as Usual?" *Transafrica Forum* 8(3) (Fall 1991): 49–60.

Scoble, Harry. "Human Rights Non-Governmental Organizations in Black Africa: The Problems and Prospects in the Wake of the Banjul Charter." In Claude E. Welch, Jr., and Ronald I. Meltzer, eds., *Human Rights and Development in Africa.* Albany: State University of New York Press, 1984, 177–203.

Sesay, Amadu. "The Limits of Peace-Keeping by a Regional Organization: The OAU Peace-Keeping Force in Chad." *Conflict Quarterly* 11(1) (Winter 1991): 7–26.

———. "The OAU and Regime Recognition: Politics of Discord and Collaboration in Africa." *Scandinavian Journal of Development Alternatives* 4(1) (March 1985): 25–41.

Shaw, Malcolm Nathan. "Dispute-Settlement in Africa." *Yearbook of World Affairs* 37 (1983): 149–167.

———. "International Law and Intervention in Africa." *International Relations: The Journal of the David Davies Institute of International Studies* 8(4) (November 1985): 341–367.

Shaw, Timothy M. "The African Crisis: Alternative Development Strategies for the Continent." *Alternatives* 9(1) (Summer 1983): 111–127.

———. "The Future of the Great Powers in Africa: Towards a Political Economy of Intervention." *Journal of Modern African Studies* 21(4) (December 1983): 555–586.

———. "Reformism, Revisionism, and Radicalism in African Political Economy During the 1990's." *Journal of Modern African Studies* 29(2) (June 1991): 191–212.

Society for International Development. "The Challenge of Africa in the 1990's." *Report: the North-South Roundtable,* Ottawa, Canada, 18–19 June 1991.

"Sub-Saharan Africa in the 1990's: Continent in Transition." *The Fletcher Forum of World Affairs* 15 (1) (Winter 1991). Especially Millar W. Arnold's article, "Africa in the 1990's."

Swanson, Julia. "The Emergence of New Rights in the African Charter." *New York Law School Journal of International and Comparative Law* 12(1–2) (1991): 307–333.

Tandon, Yash. "The OAU, A Formula for African International Relations." *Roundtable* 246 (April 1972): 221–230.

Telli, Diallo. "The Organization of African Unity in Historical Perspectives." *African Forum* 1(2)(1965): 7–27.

Tiewul, S. Azadon. "Relations Between the United Nations Organization and the Organization of African Unity in the Settlement of Secessionist Conflicts." *Harvard International Law Journal* 16(2) (Spring 1975): 259–302.

Tokareva, Zinaida Ivanovna. *Organization of African Unity: 25 Years of Struggle.* (Translated from Russian by Clance Nsiah Jaybex.) Moscow: Progress Publishers, 1989.

Tordoff, William. *Government and Politics in Africa.* London: Macmillan, 1984.

Udofia, Offiong E. "The Organization of African Unity and Conflicts in Africa: The Chadian Crisis." *Journal of Asian and African Affairs* 1(1) (Summer 1988): 65–83.

Umozurike, U.O. "The Protection of Human Rights Under the Banjul (African) Charter on Human and Peoples' Rights." *African Journal of International Law* 1(1) (Summer 1988): 65–83.

UN document A/40/666, Annex I, Declaration AHG/Decl.1 (XXI), Annex, adopted by the OAU Assembly of Heads of State and Government at its Thirty-first Ordinary Session, 18–20 July 1985.

UN document A/45/894-S/22025 of 20 December 1990, containing the communique of the ECOWAS First Extraordinary Session of the Assembly of Heads of State and Government, Bamako, 27–28 November 1990.

UN Economic Commission for Africa. *African Alternative Framework to Structural Adjustment Programmes for Socio-Economic Recovery and Transformation.* Addis Ababa, April 1991.

UN General Assembly document A/41/542, p. 3.

UN General Assembly document A/43/596, p. 4.

UN General Assembly resolution S–13/2 and Annex, adopted by the Thirteenth Special Session of the Assembly on 1 June 1986.

UN General Assembly resolution 45/232 of 21 December 1990; Security Council Presidential Statement, document. S/22133 of 22 January 1991.

United Nations, Department of Public Information. *Africa Recovery,* Vol. 5, Nos. 1–4, 1991.

United Nations. "Report of the Visiting Mission to Spanish Sahara," in *The Report of the Special Committee on the Situation with Regard to the Implementation of the Declaration on the Granting of Independence to Colonial Countries and Peoples,* U.N. document A/10023/Add. 5, 1975.

"U.S.–Soviet Team Effort in Ethiopia." *Christian Science Monitor.* 15 June 1990.

Welch, Claude E., Jr. "The African Commission on Human and Peoples' Rights: A Five-Year Report and Assessment." *Human Rights Quarterly* 14(1) February 1992: pp. 43–61.

———. "The Organization of African Unity." In Helen Kitchen, ed. *Africa: From Maze to Mystery.* Lexington: Heath, 1976.

———. "The OAU and Human Rights: Towards a New Definition." *The Journal of Modern African Studies* 19(3) (September 1981): 401–420.

———. "The Organisation of African Unity and the Promotion of Human Rights." *Journal of Modern African Studies* 29(4) (December 1991): 535–555.

Welch, Claude E., Jr., and Ronald I. Meltzer, eds. *Human Rights and Development in Africa.* Albany: State University of New York Press, 1984.

Wild, Patricia Berko. "Radicals and Moderates in the OAU." In Paul A. Tharp, ed. *Regional International Organizations*. New York: St. Martins, 1971.

Wolfers, Michael. "The Organization of African Unity as Mediator." In Saadia Touval and I. William Zartman, *International Mediation in Theory and Practice*. Boulder, Colo.: Westview, 1985.

———. *Politics in the OAU*. London: Methuen, 1976.

Woronoff, Jon. *Organizing African Unity*. Metachen, N.J.: Scarecrow Press, 1970.

Zacher, Mark W. *International Conflicts and Collective Security, 1946–77: The United Nations, Organization of American States, Organization of African Unity, and Arab League*. New York: Praeger, 1979.

Zahran, Mounir. "The Lagos Plan of Action." *Revue Egyptienne de droit international* 1984: 187–194.

Zartman, I. William. "Africa." In James Rosenau et al., eds., *World Politics*. New York: Free Press, 1976.

———. "Africa as a Subordinate State System in International Relations." *International Organization* 21(3) (Summer 1967): 545–564.

———. "The OAU and the African State System: Interaction and Evaluation." In Yassin El-Ayouty and I. William Zartman, eds., *The OAU After Twenty Years*. New York: Praeger, 1984.

———. *Ripe for Resolution: Conflict and Intervention in Africa*. London: Oxford University Press, 1985.

Index

About the Editor and Contributors

DR. YASSIN EL-AYOUTY (Egypt; naturalized U.S.) is Professor Emeritus of Political Science, State University of New York at Stony Brook, from which he retired in 1989. Prior to joining SUNY, Stony Brook, he taught at the Institute for African Studies, Graduate School of Arts and Sciences, St. John's University, New York City (1966–1972). He has written numerous articles, as well as a series of books on Africa and international organizations. From 1954 to 1986, Dr. El-Ayouty served full time at United Nations Headquarters in various capacities, including Chief of the Africa Division, Department of Political Affairs and Decolonization, and Secretary of the UN Council for Namibia. He received his Ph.D. in international relations, international law, and international organization from New York University in 1966. His fields of academic interest are education, history, political science, and now law, which he is currently studying at the Benjamin N. Cardozo School of Law, Yeshiva University, New York City, from which a J.D. degree is expected in January 1994.

DR. BERHANYKUN ANDEMICAEL (Eritrea) is a political scientist specializing in international relations and African studies. He is presently Director of the New York Office of the International Atomic Energy Agency, one of the major UN specialized agencies. Previously, Dr. Andemicael was Assistant Director of Research and Secretary of the Board of Trustees of the United Nations Institute for Training and Research (UNITAR). He is the author of several monographs and articles on international organization and regionalism, disarmament, human rights, and racial discrimination. Dr. Andemicael was an Aggrey African Scholar and a University Research Fellow at Columbia University, New York City, from which he received his Ph.D.

DR. CHRISTOPHER J. BAKWESEGHA (Uganda) holds a Ph.D. and M.A. in urban planning and policy development from Rutgers University, New Jersey, and a B.A. in geography, religion, and sociology from Makerere University, Uganda. He was Senior Lecturer at the Faculty of Social Sciences, Makerere University, which he left in 1977. From 1977 to 1979, he was Research Officer, then Head of the Refugee Department of the All Africa Conference of Churches, Nairobi, Kenya. In 1979, Dr. Bakwesegha joined the OAU where he is currently Head of the Bureau for Refugees, in the OAU Political Department. His contributions to the study of social development in Africa have been substantial, including authorship of fifteen articles that have appeared in various books and international journals.

DR. BOUTROS BOUTROS-GHALI (Egypt) is the United Nations Secretary-General, a post to which he was appointed by the General Assembly for a five-year term beginning 1 January 1992. Prior to that, he was Egypt's Deputy Prime Minister for Foreign Affairs (May–December 1991) and Minister of State for Foreign Affairs (October 1977–May 1991). Dr. Boutros-Ghali received a Ph.D. in international law from Paris University in 1949 with a thesis on the study of regional organizations. Between 1949 and 1979, he was Professor of International Law and International Relations at Cairo University, President of the Egyptian Society of International Law, President of the Center of Political and Strategic Studies of *Al-Ahram* Establishment, Cairo, where he founded the Arabic publication *Al-Ahram Al-Iktissadi* (The Economist) and edited the Arabic quarterly *Al-Siyasa Al-Dawlyia* (International Politics). The more than one hundred publications and numerous articles that Dr. Boutros-Ghali has authored in Arabic, English, and French deal with regional and international affairs, law, and diplomacy. He was a Fulbright scholar at Columbia University (1954–1955) and Director of the Center of Research of the Hague Academy of International Law (1963–1964). Dr. Boutros-Ghali led many of Egypt's delegations to the OAU, to the Movement of Non-Aligned Countries, and to the UN General Assembly sessions.

DR. IVOR RICHARD FUNG (Cameroon) has a doctoral degree in international relations. He is currently Research Coordinator at the United Nations Regional Center for Peace and Disarmament in Africa. Prior to that, Dr. Fung served as Executive Assistant to the President of the International Peace Academy, New York City, and consultant to the United Nations Department for Disarmament Affairs in New York. His published research work include the following titles: "Redefining Security in Africa: A Quest for Disarmament and a Prerequisite for Development," "Militarism in African States: The Case of Mozambique: 1975–1990," "Africa and Prospects for Disarmament in the Next Decade," and "Militarism and African Conception of National Security." Dr. Fung is presently working on *Ethnicity, Democracy and Security in Africa*.

MR. DEREK INGRAM (United Kingdom) is the author of several books on the Commonwealth. In the early sixties he was Deputy Editor of the *London Daily Mail*. As a journalist he has reported on every Commonwealth summit since 1969. Mr. Ingram is also a regular contributor to newspapers in almost every Commonwealth country through *Gemini News Service*, of which he is founding editor. He writes the "Commonwealth Notebook" in *The Round Table*, published quarterly in London. Mr. Ingram was President of the Commonwealth Journalists Association for seven years.

DR. JAMES O. C. JONAH (Sierra Leone) is United Nations Under-Secretary-General, Department for Political Affairs. With a Ph.D. in political science from MIT, Dr. Jonah has occupied various senior UN positions at Headquarters and in the field. These included, at the Assistant Secretary-General level, the following: Office of the Secretary-General for Research and the Collection of Information (ORCI), Field Operational and External Support Activities, and Office of Personnel Services. He also served as the Secretary-General of the Second World Conference to Combat Racism and Racial Discrimination, Special Representative of the UN Secretary-General in connection with the Second Decade to Combat Racism and Racial Discrimination, and Political Advisor in various UN peace-keeping and peace-making operations. Dr. Jonah has authored several contributions to books on Africa and international organization.

DR. LEONARD T. KAPUNGU (Zimbabwe) is currently the Director of the United Nations Office of the Special Representative of the Secretary-General for Somalia, and Coordinator of Political Affairs in Somalia. At UN Headquarters, he is Chief of Research and Analysis, Department of Political Affairs. He holds a Ph.D. degree in international relations from the University of London. Dr. Kapungu is an author of a number of books and articles, including a major study on the *United Nations and Economic Sanctions against Rhodesia*. He was also Professor of Political Science at the University of Maryland.

DR. EDMOND KWAM KOUASSI (Togo) is Professor of Law and International Politics, Faculty of Law, at the University of Benin, Lomé (Togo). He is author of *Les rapports entre l'Organisation des Nations Unies et l'Organisation de l'Unité Africaine* (1978) and *Organisations Internationales Africaines* (1987). Dr. Kouassi was a Fulbright research scholar at the Johns Hopkins School of Advanced International Studies. He was also Permanent Representative of Togo to the UN (1985–1987) and Ambassador to Cuba and

Costa Rica. He received his doctorate in law and political science from the University of Paris I (Sorbonne).

DR. AZZEDINE LAYACHI (Algeria) holds an M.A. in politics and a Ph.D. in international relations from New York University. He is currently Assistant Professor at St. John's University, New York. He specializes in U.S. foreign policy; his area of concentration is the Middle East and North Africa. He is the author of *The United States and North Africa: A Cognitive Approach to Foreign Policy* (Praeger, 1990).

Dr. Layachi attended Algeria's Institute of Political Studies from 1973 to 1977. While doing his undergraduate studies there, he was also a broadcaster and reporter for Algerian television and a free-lance writer for major Algerian newspapers. While serving as a journalist, he covered extensively the war in the Western Sahara, which he visited several times.

DR. CLAUDE E. WELCH, JR. (U.S.) is SUNY Distinguished Service Professor of Political Science at the State University of New York at Buffalo. He is also cochair of the Human Rights Center, SUNY at Buffalo. A long-time specialist in human rights and civil-military relations, he edited *Human Rights and Development in Africa* (1982), and has published nine other books. He serves on the board of directors of Africa Watch, chairs the Human Rights Committee of the African Studies Association, and has been a consultant to numerous human rights groups. He has received grants from the Ford Foundation, the U.S. Institute of Peace, and the National Endowment for the Humanities for human rights activities.

DR. MICHEL-CYR DJIENA WEMBOU (Cameroon) has a *Doctorat 3e Cycle* in international relations and a *Doctorat d'Etat* in International Law. After serving as Counsellor to the Permanent Mission of the Cameroon to the UN, New York City, he was posted to his country's embassy in Ethiopia. His position in Addis Ababa is Counsellor in charge of OAU affairs. Dr. Djiena Wembou taught international law as Associate Professor at the City University of New York and at the Hague.